ROBERT BRIDGES AND GERARD HOPKINS
1863–1889
A LITERARY FRIENDSHIP

ROBERT BRIDGES, 1874

ROBERT BRIDGES

AND

GERARD HOPKINS

1863-1889

A Literary Friendship

JEAN-GEORGES RITZ

*Professor of English Literature
at the University of Lyons*

London
OXFORD UNIVERSITY PRESS
New York   Toronto
1960

Oxford University Press, Amen House, London E.C.4

GLASGOW NEW YORK TORONTO MELBOURNE WELLINGTON
BOMBAY CALCUTTA MADRAS KARACHI KUALA LUMPUR
CAPE TOWN IBADAN NAIROBI ACCRA

96682

PRINTED IN GREAT BRITAIN

To the Memory
of
Professor Floris Delattre
and of
My Friend
Professor Jean Simon

❋

FOREWORD

The years I have spent in the company of Gerard Manley Hopkins have made me aware of the importance of Robert Bridges's friendship for him. I felt attracted towards a man who obviously was almost the very opposite of Hopkins. Why did Bridges destroy his letters to him? Why did he not want strangers to know how he had reacted to his friend's letters? Was he a pedant? Was he really fair to the poet who had practically left his future literary destiny in his hands?

Such questions have puzzled the critics for years, and severe judgments have been passed on Bridges. I wanted to see whether they had been passed in all fairness. I thought that a careful reading of Hopkins's letters might help me to hear, however faintly, the true voice of Bridges. I also felt certain that in his poems, in his correspondence, in his memoirs, in his new prosody, and in some of his various literary activities, I might be able to detect the direct or indirect influence of the priest-poet who played so important a part in the first half of his life.

For this task, the letters of Bridges to the members of Hopkins's family from 1889 to 1929, which are now in the Bodleian Library, and of which the majority still remain unpublished, have helped me to come to a more balanced conclusion than most critics have been prepared to consider.

In his own way Bridges was as original and individualistic as Hopkins. His interest in innovations and experiments was as great. Their temperamental differences, their absolutely opposite views on religious matters, even Bridges's tougher moral fibre, could not destroy a fundamental kinship. They were two inquisitive minds and they both had a genius for friendship.

Outwardly Bridges, as an Anglican, a Conservative and a fine poet endowed with official prestige, felt entitled, in the first quarter of the century, to adopt a patronizing attitude towards his eccentric friend who, as a Catholic and a Jesuit, had deliberately chosen to stand outside the pale. But deep

within him Bridges knew—and letters are there to prove it—
that Hopkins was the greater poet, and that no friend had loved
him better.

By destroying his own side of the correspondence, and leaving
us to read the frank, simple, warm and humorous replies,
Bridges has willingly entrusted his fame as a faithful friend to
Hopkins. The two poets, the grumpish and the saintly, would
not be what they now are in the eyes of a more serene literary
criticism, had they not been constantly encouraging and discouraging each other by turns. The more we know them and
their works, the less is it possible to separate them. My intention has been to prove this, and I think that the facts, even if
some of the evidence will always be lacking, bear witness to my
explanation.

Lyon. J.-G. R.

NOTE: This book is my 'thèse secondaire' submitted to a Sorbonne
jury in May, 1958, for the 'doctorat d'Etat'.

Mr. Simon Nowell-Smith has been kind enough to read my
typescript before it was sent to the press and I want to thank him
for the labour of revising it and making a number of valuable suggestions.

CONTENTS

ILLUSTRATIONS

ABBREVIATIONS

The following abbreviations are used in the footnotes for works frequently cited:

GMH to RB	*The Letters of Gerard Manley Hopkins to Robert Bridges*, edited by C. C. Abbott, 1935.
GMH & RWD	*The Correspondence of Gerard Manley Hopkins and Richard Watson Dixon*, edited by C. C. Abbott, 1935.
Further Letters	*Further Letters of Gerard Manley Hopkins*, edited by C. C. Abbott, second edition, 1956.
GMH Journals	*The Journals and Papers of Gerard Manley Hopkins*, edited by Humphry House, completed by Graham Storey, 1958.
[GMH] Poems	*Poems of Gerard Manley Hopkins*, third edition, edited by W. H. Gardner, 1948 (first edition, edited by R. Bridges, 1918; second edition, edited by C. Williams, 1930).
[RB] Poet. Works	*Poetical Works of Robert Bridges*, second edition, reissued with *The Testament of Beauty*, 1953.

INTRODUCTION

Robert Bridges and Gerard Manley Hopkins became friends when they were at the University of Oxford. They met in the last term of 1863. Hopkins had gone from Highgate School to Balliol in April and Bridges to Corpus Christi from Eton in October. Their friendship lasted twenty-six years, till Hopkins's death in Dublin on June 8, 1889. Since they were living far from each other most of the time, they had to rely on letters for the expression of thoughts and feelings, and these they exchanged at shorter or longer intervals.

Hopkins's letters were carefully kept by Bridges and ultimately published in 1935. But those that Bridges had written were sent back to him after his friend's death, and he destroyed them. The consequence is that we have a one-sided view of the friendship, and it is most difficult to assess Bridges's personal reactions to the views expressed so frankly and so abundantly on the greatest variety of topics by his correspondent.

Such is the problem that faces the critic who wants to know more about Bridges and his friendship with the Jesuit poet. Many facts remain obscure and many questions unanswerable, which the letters of Bridges, had they not been destroyed, would have explained and answered. Without his side of the correspondence, the gap is hard to bridge. Unless one gives the most careful attention to the letters written by Hopkins, guess-work is the only method left to the critic; but Bridges's decision looks so strange, or so rash, that it is easy to feel biased against him. Somewhat crudely, but clearly and tersely, Herbert Read has expressed a view which it is difficult not to accept, at least when taking the facts at their face value. He writes:

What Bridges thought we do not know, but he had no sympathy for the religious life of his friend, even a definite antipathy. One wonders on what the friendship subsisted, so little were Hopkins's

profoundest feelings appreciated by Bridges. But friendship is perhaps never solidly grounded on intellectual interests. Hopkins had
known Bridges for ten years before he discovered (and then from a
review!) that his friend wrote poetry. We can assume, therefore,
that the attraction was instinctive, even physical. How otherwise
could Hopkins have tolerated the conceit, the pedantry, the complete lack of perception that were the return for all his frankness,
humility and grace? Bridges has cautiously destroyed his side of the
correspondence, but that very caution is significant. A man has not
such a care for his reputation but from what we call a good conceit
of himself, which is a fault even Hopkins found in Bridges.[1]

This is a terrible indictment. What truth there is in it we shall
try to discover in the course of this study. But clearly the critic
is voicing his feelings in terms too violent to be strictly fair.

Some years after Herbert Read had spoken so strongly
against Bridges's baffling decision, another critic, who had the
advantage of having known the Poet Laureate intimately, put
forward a wealth of arguments in his favour.

Was the destruction of Bridges's letters to Hopkins necessarily due,
as Mr. Read asserts, to 'conceit'? Has there ever lived a good poet
who would not be glad if he could destroy his own letters, at any
rate those written in his younger days? What have other people to
do with our personal affairs—unless they come on them by acci-
dent, which is something that cannot be helped? Bridges . . . was
not pompous enough, and he was far too devoted to poetry, to want
whatever fame was ultimately his to be cluttered up with correspondence, much of it inevitably ephemeral, so that the temple he
had raised with care was flanked by a rubble pile . . . Is it only
'conceit' that is at pains to leave nothing except the carefully written
verse into which a man has put his best? Few effective professional
writers have been good letter-writers, and Bridges' letters were not
usually very interesting ones, they were mostly practical. He could
easily have printed excerpts from his letters to Hopkins, which would
have showed him up as wise and all that was good, but—regarding
his letters as his own concern—he saw them as like his suppressed
imperfect early poems, and he did not choose to cumber his best
writing with superfluous and largely irrelevant matter.[2]

[1] H. Read, 'Gerard Manley Hopkins', in *In Defence of Shelley and Other Essays*,
1936, pp. 111–44.
[2] E. Thompson, *Robert Bridges*, 1944, pp. 87–88.

Now not all Thompson's arguments carry the same weight. If we remember that the correspondence between the two poets, which began in 1865, was most active from 1877 to 1889, when Bridges was in his thirty-third to forty-fifth years, we can hardly let Thompson speak of 'letters written in his younger days'. We can understand that an artist like Bridges, who cared so much for his good name and his own privacy, might not want to leave behind him any writing that was not in his opinion fully satisfactory or that revealed more than he wished his fellow-countrymen to know. But Thompson seems to suggest that Bridges destroyed his letters because he considered them too superficial: his were 'not usually very interesting letters, they were mostly practical'. If such was the case, no doubt the comparison with Hopkins's letters would have been unfavourable; for everyone agrees about both the topical and the lasting interest of the letters written to Bridges by his friend. Thus a well-meaning excuse becomes a damning criticism.

But we doubt that Bridges's letters to Hopkins were uninteresting.[1] Would Hopkins have continued writing for so many years, and have shewn openly the great value he set upon this correspondence, if he had not found in his friend a man ready to discuss his views, to share or to oppose his own conceptions and original ideas? We cannot admit that what Bridges had to say on literature, on prosody, or on music was of little or no importance. Even if, set against those of Hopkins, his letters had appeared less brilliant or too humble a foil to the fine criticism of the Jesuit, they could never be deemed valueless or purposeless. But does their destruction either imply that Bridges passed such a harsh judgment on them, or that out of vanity and conceit he refused any literary or artistic comparison with his correspondent? If we had to accept either of these explanations, or both, we should be led to detect in the poet's character a moral flaw for which his life and his work offer not the slightest hint. We refuse to portray Bridges with such dark strokes of the

---

[1] In a letter to A. W. M. Baillie (*Further Letters*, Letter CXXVII, September 15, 1867, pp. 229–30), Hopkins writes: 'I will end as Bridges always does to me with saying I am well aware what a stupid letter this is.' Among young men this only suggests a little self-conscious vanity.

brush as Herbert Read has seen fit to use. It is not necessary because Hopkins had 'frankness, humility and grace' to deny virtues to Bridges simply because he destroyed his side of their correspondence. The best and simplest explanation is to be found in a revealing fact disclosed by Thompson. He tells us that Bridges 'asked friends who were within reach to return, if they had kept them, letters he had written to them; he destroyed all that was really not relevant to the work for which he had lived'.[1] Such a determination to remain, as far as possible, the master of his own writings and the sole judge of their worth is in perfect conformity with the avowed ideals of beauty and excellence to which Bridges as a conscious artist had dedicated himself from the outset of his poetical career. Much as we may regret it, we understand the better his character with its reserve, its aristocratic aloofness from the general public, and his firm desire to tell about his friends nothing more than was strictly necessary or sufficient or helpful.

It is true that about three of his best friends Bridges said much more than he ever said about Hopkins.[2] Digby Mackworth Dolben, Richard Watson Dixon and Henry Bradley received at his hands the fairest gift friendship can bestow, that of a loving memory set in quiet, pellucid prose style. Why is there no memoir of Gerard Manley Hopkins, written in the same vein? Perhaps the answer is that in the eyes of one who had been entrusted with the 'lov'd legacy' of his friend's poems, no better monument could be erected to his memory than the volume of his *Poems* which Bridges prepared and edited with the most scrupulous attention; a fine, moving sonnet introduced it, and careful, if slightly over-critical, notes completed it. The *Poems*, as they were published in 1918, testify to the loving care of the Poet Laureate for his friend's poetical work. When Charles Williams introduced the second edition in July, 1930, soon after Bridges's death, he mentioned having consulted the aged poet, and having obtained his 'general approval'. Bridges 'being then preoccupied with *The Testament of Beauty* and feeling also that his own duty to his friend had been satisfyingly

---

[1] E. Thompson, *op. cit.*, p. 119.

[2] R. Bridges, *Three Friends*, 1932. The memoir of Dolben was first printed in 1911, that of Dixon in 1909, and that of Bradley in 1926.

accomplished', had passed on to Williams the business of 'recollating the printed poems and of adding' a few others.[1] We may agree with Williams when he says that his edition, because Bridges had died when the text was with the printer, became 'a memory not only of Gerard Hopkins but also of the poet, his friend, to whom all readers of either owe so great a devotion'.[2] No memoir however finely penned could have done for Hopkins what the editing of his poems achieved so efficiently. Obviously Bridges did not feel any personal vanity or self-satisfaction at having brought out at last the collection of fine and strange poems his Jesuit friend had left him. To the end he remained slightly aloof. But his attitude is perfectly in keeping with his aesthetic views and his private principles: what was too obviously linked with the transient, the merely personal or the intimate did not concern the public at large; but, as a conscious and conscientious artist, he offered them what he deemed the most perfect expression of his thoughts, his moods and feelings, after having carefully sifted out what he considered rash, superficial, unsound or devoid of any musical quality.

Such was Bridges's considered attitude. He never changed it. The fact that he expressed the wish 'that no biography of him should be written'[3] is ample proof that the poet did not want to let the many into his intimacy. His wish has been respected, since no fuller biography exists than the notice in the Supplement of the *Dictionary of National Biography*, 1937. Therefore we know little about him; no member of his family has come forward with more information; and what scanty details we may gather here and there come from Bridges's own poems, from his memoirs of his *Three Friends*, or again from the reminiscences of his friends or his visitors. Indeed, Bridges seems to have fought hard in order to protect his own private world. Thompson[4] tells us that he was ever 'thrusting aside the writer's own emotions except in so far as they might serve as occasional illus-

[1] *GMH Poems*, second edition, 1930, p. ix.
[2] Ibid., p. x.
[3] C. C. Abbott, preface to *GMH to RB*, p.v; E. Thompson, *op. cit.*, p. 1.
[4] *Op. cit.*, p. 105.

tration'. The man had the same determined opposition to any
display of feelings, which explains why his obituarist in *The
Times* could frankly speak of his 'boyish love of brusque personal encounters'.[1] A few incidents in the friendly relations of
Bridges and Hopkins tend to prove that it must have been a
life-long habit. Siegfried Sassoon has given us in his book of
reminiscences, *Siegfried's Journey*, a vivid description of a visit
he paid to the Poet Laureate in 1918, 'in the final week of the
War'. John Masefield was his guide and presenter. The portrait is drawn with a sharp pencil and brings the man who was
then 'remarkably vigorous at seventy-four' into full light. I
think it may help us to understand some essential points in his
character and sensibility.

Having heard that he was liable to be abrupt and even arrogant
towards new-comers, I was rather nervous. But I had loved his
poetry ever since I was twenty, and nothing could have been more
decorously deferential than my state of mind when we entered the
cottage. . . .
My first view of his magnificent bard-like head and fine patrician
features was a pleasantly impressive recognition of the portrait
frontispiece to his Collected Poems. . . .
I departed with a disappointingly unfavourable first impression.
. . . Seen in the light of subsequent experience of him, it was all
quite characteristic. He was proud, self-conscious, and often aggres-
sively intolerant. There was something of the self-contradictory
schoolboy about him. . . . It was, I think, his unrestrained naturalness which caused these somewhat petulant exhibitions of rudeness.
He hated pomposity, and consistently refused to stand on his dignity.
One who knew him well has described him as 'delightfully grumpy'.
. . . His nobility of mind atoned for his inurbanities of behaviour.
. . . In the man there was an unreserved and abundant humanity,
and no one but a fool could fail to love him for it.[2]

'Unrestrained naturalness' may explain much of Bridges's outward abruptness and arrogance. If he was 'delightfully
grumpy', no doubt his 'humanity' atoned for his 'exhibitions
of rudeness', and his friends must have soon discovered that the

---

[1] *The Times*, April 22, 1930. The obituary was misattributed by Thompson
(*op. cit.*, p. 92, to Nowell C. Smith, who (*D.N.B.*, 1937) ascribes it to H. Newbolt.
[2] Siegfried Sassoon, *Siegfried's Journey, 1916–1920*, Albatross, 1947, pp. 98–100.

hard crust protected a soft interior. Such must have been Hopkins's experience. But before we come to understand how Hopkins could always write or speak of his 'dearest Bridges' and address him in the same loving terms, we must try to draw a portrait of Robert Bridges by gathering the few personal traits that can be found, as we have just said, either in his poems, his essays and the memoirs of his *Three Friends*, or in the reminiscences of some of his literary acquaintances. The more we obtain from these various sources, the fitter we shall be to deal with a friendship in which one partner chose to remain for us mute, if not inglorious.

I
Robert Bridges

I. A SELF-PORTRAIT

From what we already know of Bridges's aloofness and of his dislike of revealing himself in his literary works, we cannot expect to find many subjective or intimate reminiscences in his poems and essays. The fact that he left no juvenilia and published his first volume of verse in 1873, in his thirtieth year, is ample proof of his strict control over every line he wrote and decided to publish. Yet we can glean here and there a few traits that may help us discreetly to invade his privacy and thus to know the man a little better.

Prometheus the Firegiver, 'a mask in the Greek manner', and *Demeter*, another 'mask', are far too literary in their imitation of the ancients to offer any personal touch, unless the spirit of wonder and the love of life that breathe through them are considered as revealing a fundamental mood in the young poet. Bridges shared with the Greeks a great love of beauty and art. Deep in his heart he may have wished to be in his own way a 'Firegiver' so that it might be said of him, as of Prometheus:

> Nature had kissèd Art
> And borne a child to stir
> With jealousy the heart
> Of heaven's Artificer. (*Prometheus*, 309–312)

There is one material evidence that Bridges expressed in this classical poem some feelings of his own. In Book III of the *Shorter Poems* the first lyric, 'O my vague desires', is made up of five stanzas, four of which are to be found in the concluding ode of *Prometheus*. They make manifest a joy and a pang of the soul that the poet himself must certainly have experienced.[1]

[1]   O my vague desires!
Ye lambent flames of the soul, her offspring fires:
That are my soul herself in pangs sublime
Rising and flying to heaven before her time.
(*Prometheus*, 1465–8; *Shorter Poems*, Bk. III, No. 1)

Most impersonal is the narrative poem, *Eros and Psyche*, the lovers' story being 'done into English from the Latin of Apuleius'. Can it be the close of an actual day, watched with loving eyes, that suggested the following description given by Psyche?

> . . . For now, though full an hour
> The sun had sunk, she saw the evening light
> In shifting colour to the zenith tower,
> And grow more gorgeous ever and more bright.
>
> (March 24)

If so, many more delicate natural observations could be set down to the interest the poet always took in the marvels of every day:

> The flowers and trees and beasts of the earth; and later
> The skies of day, the moon and the stars of night.
>
> (*Prometheus*, 821–2)

A diffident confession, as revealing as unexpected, is made by Bridges in one stanza. Invisible messengers of the gods have been serving Psyche, and singing to her, accompanied by 'strings unseen and reeds',

> P athetic strains and passionate they wove,
> U rgent in ecstasies of heavenly sense;
> R esponsive rivalries, that, while they strove
> C ombined in full harmonious suspense,
> E ntrancing wild desire, then fell at last
> L ull'd in soft closes, and with gay contrast
> L aunch'd forth their fresh unwearied excellence.
>
> (May 15)

The acrostic expresses the poet's love and reverence for Purcell, the great English seventeenth-century composer. Thus Bridges honours the musician whose 'divine genius' Hopkins deeply admired and to whom he dedicated one of his sonnets, praising him 'that, whereas other musicians have given utterance to the moods of man's minds, he has, beyond that, uttered in notes the very make and species of man as created both in him and in all men generally'.[1] We shall not forget the common admiration of the two poets for Purcell nor the great bond that music, both profane and religious, was between them.

In *The Growth of Love*, a sonnet sequence written much after the fashion set by Mrs. Browning, Rossetti and Meredith, many details of the great experience of love between man and woman must be autobiographical.[2] But the personal element is kept secret and we have no means of telling what the poet alludes to when he speaks of 'sorrow lately learn'd' (Sonnet 9), what spiritual conflicts lie behind his confession of agnosticism

> I stand a pagan in the holy place (Sonnet 23)

or whose face he praises in one sonnet or another, although we know that many of his love poems, written before he met Monica Waterhouse in September, 1882, and became engaged to her in 1884, were composed in praise of other loves.

Through this sequence of fine sonnets[3] we can easily imagine a young man devoted to feminine beauty, ever ready to express with delicacy and gravity the feelings he felt in his heart, but, as it were, anonymously. He speaks, but it is any man speaking to any woman. His ecstasies and his quarrels are those of any lover. We must be content to agree when he says

> My lady pleases me and I please her (Sonnet 30)

although other sonnets tell tales of estrangement, exile or indifference. A few are more circumstantial. We can see Bridges visiting Florence while some English troopers, returning from India, are striding through the streets of the old city,

> Haughtily visiting her holy places (Sonnet 17)

---

[1] *GMH Poems*, pp. 84–85.

[2] In a manuscript note on the history of *The Growth of Love* (formerly in the possession of Kenneth Sisam) Bridges wrote, 'The whole poem is autobiographical, as the title indicates.'

[3] *The Growth of Love* numbered 24 sonnets in the 1876 edition, 79 in the 1889–90 editions. The final edition in 1898 comprised 69 sonnets, of which 41 were new—a fair example of the poet's fastidiousness and careful revision. The numeration in this chapter is that of the final edition.

or see him skating at night on a frozen lake in a

> midnight revelry, that rang
> With steel and flame along the snow-girt ice,
>
> (Sonnet 10)

or again galloping across country 'by field or highway', a happy horseman who avows:

> I ride as one who for his pleasure rides,
> And stroke the neck of my delighted steed,
> And seek what cheer the village inn provides.
>
> (Sonnet 37)

He must have rowed more than once from Henley to Maidenhead,[1] when he was a London medical student, and enjoyed 'an idle June day on the sunny Thames'; but it would be useless to ask him where lie the spots 'of memoried pleasure' and what real people, what chosen vintage or particular cause for merriment made him delight in 'friendship, good wine and mirth' (Sonnet 38).

Most of his *Shorter Poems*[2] are written in the same anonymous vein, although not a few must have been composed under the direct influence of some incident, gay, sad or grave. We hear the lover, the happy bridegroom; we see the physician moved by the 'perfect little body' of a dead child. A snow-fall in London or a ship crowding her white sails, the coming of the nightingales or the 'bold majestic downs', offer him occasions to sing a very personal note. We may notice that he often tells us his spirit was sad when he was young,

> But since I have found the beauty of joy
> I have done with proud dismay.
>
> (Bk. IV, No. 24)

---

[1] The original version of Sonnet 38 gave the names: '. . . The current that our skiff from Henley sped/ To where the Cliefden woods o'er Maidenhead/ Bar its still surface with their mirrored stems'. But even so slight a geographical precision was too much for Bridges; he later abandoned all reference to any town on the Thames.

[2] The numeration of the *Shorter Poems* and of the later collections of lyrics is, unless otherwise stated, that of the one-volume *Poetical Works*, 1953.

He admits that, nurtured by

> the idle dream
> Of [his] boyish day,
>   (Bk. I, No. 1),

he confided to 'poetic sadness' very early in his life, finding pleasure in 'Indolence', accepting his 'sluggish blood' or

> The tender joys, that bless
> My hard-won peace of mind,
> In hours of idleness.
>   (Bk. II, No. 9)

All this reveals the rather romantic young man, the man of leisure, who loved his own fireside 'not least when most alone', but who had to fight against proud dismay, melancholy or spiritual unrest. Although there is nothing very striking in these traits, they may explain how it was that Bridges could be at times in a very grumpy mood.

In spite of his reluctance to speak of himself, in a few poems Bridges does evoke the past and describes incidents of his childhood. There is deep reverence in a poem which is a meditation on the portrait of his grandfather, John Bridges, whom he never knew.

> O high parental claim, that were not but for the knowing,
> O fateful bond of duty, O more than body that bore,
>   The smile that guides me to right, the gaze that follows my
>   going,
> How had I stray'd without thee!
>   (*Later Poems*, No. 13)

John Bridges, a wealthy gentleman-farmer of St. Nicholas Court, Isle of Thanet, had left most of his property to his only son, John Thomas, the poet's father. The estate was sold under the will of the latter, who died in 1853 at the age of forty-seven, when Robert was only nine. At Roselands, Walmer, where the family lived before the death of John Thomas, Robert was certainly happy; he cannot have felt lonely, since he was the

eighth child of a family of nine. But Ernest de Selincourt tells
us that

'as a child, though he loved companionship, his most memorable
hours were passed alone in his father's garden and orchard, in the
cornfields and on the downs beyond, and on the sea-shore at their
feet'.[1]

Indeed, in 'Recollections of Solitude', the poet speaks of

The long light-hearted days that are no more,
(*Later Poems*, No. 1),

and remembers the woods, the meadows, the gardens, the
orchards,
the branching chair of some tall tree,

the sea-shore, the basking downs. He rejoices, when writing
about this southern landscape, some fifty years after he left
Walmer, and grants that

it is happy and true
That memoried joys keep ever their delight,
Like steadfast stars in the blue vault of night.[2]

In *New Poems*, the poet has described the portico, the mossy
terrace, the wooden temple on the mound, the ivied arbour,
where lived the memories of his childhood.

And there 'tis ever noon, and glad suns bring
Alternate days of summer and of spring,
With childish thought, and childish faces bright,
And all unknown save but the hour's delight.
(No. 4, Elegy)

He evokes in the same poem the ships that he saw passing so
near 'in stately motion', the fast-sailing frigate, 'some immense

---

[1] E. de Selincourt, 'Robert Bridges', in *Oxford Lectures on Poetry*, 1934, pp. 207–32.
[2] Did Bridges remember when he wrote those lines in 1903 the following stanza
of Dolben's 'My Treasury'? The images are very similar: 'That treasury of golden
days/ Those bright sweet hours that shine/ Like stars amid a gloomy sky/ Must be
for ever mine.' *Three Friends*, p. 51.

three-decker of the line', and recalls the coming to the 'anchoring ground' of his native harbour-town of 'Napier's fleet unto the Baltic bound', one day in March, 1854, when he was a child of ten. We see him as a boy enjoying all the pleasures of the beach and of the sea:

> 'Twas here I played, and musing made
> My friend the melancholy sea.
>   He from his dim, enchanted caves
> With shuddering roar and onrush wild
> Fell down in sacrificial waves
> At feet of his exulting child.
>   (*Shorter Poems*, Bk. IV, No. 27)

He draws for us a mocking picture of the old schoolmaster at Walmer, who

> Stood over us and from a desk fed us with flies. . . .
>   A dry biped he was, nurtured likewise
> On skins and skeletons, stale from top to toe
> With all manner of rubbish and all manner of lies.
>   (*October and Other Poems*, No. 9)

He describes with charm and pity 'the first visit of compliment that ever I paid', when with his elder sister and Kate, their maid, he went to see Kate's mother, an old woman with the shaking palsy who lived across the downs in the next combe. He, then, was no bigger

> than a mastiff-dog may be, and little of clothing wore
> but shirt and trews and shoes and holland pinafore.
>   (*New Verse*, No. 4)

Like young David Copperfield in the Peggottys' house, he notices every strange detail: the lace-curtain'd panes, the lofty clock with loud, insistent tick, the huge batter'd copper warming-pan, and crockery whimsies ranged on the high mantel-shelf. We see the little boy 'watching furtively' the bland silver-hair'd dame, observing the strange movement of her cotton skirt and 'how her right foot in the air was all a-tremble and jerked/in little restless kicks'.

In a wholly different mood and spirit, Bridges, taking pride
in recollecting the earliest memories of a distant past, reminds
us, with patriotic fervour, that his family had made friends with
the Duke of Wellington, their glorious neighbour at Walmer.
Like Ulysses, speaking 'of the great Achilles whom we knew', he
tells us that he was one of the first to learn of the death of the
Iron Duke on September 14, 1852.

> I had seen his castle-flag to fall half-mast
> One morn as I sat looking on the sea,
> When thus all England's grief came first to me,
> Who hold my childhood favour'd that I knew
> So well the face that won at Waterloo.
>
> *(New Poems, No. 4)*

It is with marked care that Bridges avoids alluding in his
verse to his private joys or griefs and to what lies closest to his
heart. The only poem in which he speaks of his parents is a
sonnet in *The Growth of Love*, where he praises the artist who
made a portrait of his mother. With sadness he notes that

> The smile that charm'd the father hath given place
> Unto the furrow'd care wrought by the son;
> But virtue hath transform'd all change to grace.

He mourns over the tears that his mother shed,

> Tears of love, tears of joy and tears of care, . . .
> Tears of hope, pride and pity, trust and prayer,
> Tears of contrition;

But an ardent filial love makes him worship the face

> Won by the heart my father's heart that won.[1]
>
> (Sonnet 40)

Both language and feeling, through the unexpected inversion,
firmly link together the hearts of his parents whom Death had
parted early. Having said as much and paid his due to those

---

[1] In the Dolben memoir, Bridges has spoken of his mother's 'merry gamesome
spirit'. *Three Friends*, p. 6.

he loved dearly, Bridges refused by deliberate choice to say more.

We realize that much of his aloofness and austerity came from his sense of dignity and his delicacy of feeling. At the same time his fastidiousness originated in an ingrained love of beauteous things, which made him shrink from coarse-grained people and oppose all sentimental appeals and the degrading inquisitiveness of the crowd. His parents' wealth had set him apart from the first in a world of gentlemanly leisure. He was fully conscious of the graces poured upon him by Fortune—

> . . . the pleasant unhinder'd order of our life,
> Our happy enchantments of Fortune, easy surroundings,
> Courteous acquaintance, dwelling in fair homes, the delight of
> Long-plann'd excursions . . .
> (*Poems in Classical Prosody*, Epistle 1)

He had no wish to expatiate upon his good luck, and his prosperous circumstances. The better he knew his uncommon advantages, the less he wished to speak about his easy life, which was so different from the experience of common men. In 1920, in the seventy-sixth year of his age, the poet could well admit:

> For a happier lot
> Than God giveth me
> It never hath been
> Nor ever shall be.
> (*October and Other Poems*, No. 26)

As early as 1890, he could describe the blissful life he led in a quiet tone of contentment:

> The idle life I lead/ Is like a pleasant sleep,
> Wherein I rest and heed/ The dreams that by me sweep.
>
> And still of all my dreams/In turn so swiftly past,
> Each in its fancy seems/ A nobler than the last.
>
> And every eve I say,/Noting my step in bliss,
> That I have known no day/In all my life like this.
> (*Shorter Poems*, Bk. IV, No. 17)

It is true that he devoted himself with great earnestness to the nursing of the sick, when he was a medical student and then a physician in hospitals in London for twelve years. But the fact remains—at which one may marvel today—that he chose his own course of life, followed his own plans, retired from medical practice of his own free will, and all through his life fulfilled his most cherished desires without any check or hindrance, with as little difficulty as a man may expect to find on his way. It is not to be wondered at that the uncommonly smooth running of his life and career made him a solitary man, a man who could dedicate himself to the sole worship of Joy, Beauty and Poetry, and be an artist with an almost unfailing sense of propriety and restraint.

II. THREE FRIENDS: DOLBEN, DIXON, BRADLEY

Dignity and restraint are the sterling qualities of the memoirs which Bridges devoted to the three friends he cherished most. When he speaks of his cousin, the young poet, Digby Dolben, or of the Reverend Richard Watson Dixon, an older poet, or of the Oxford scholar Henry Bradley, he manages to say as little about himself as possible, although he was closely connected with each of them for a few or for many years.

Yet in spite of this limitation, some important points come to light. The captain of one of the Dames' houses at Eton, Bridges admits he was 'terribly serious, determined and of artistic bent'.[1] The 'magnitude of the religious problems . . . was occupying [his] attention'; he and his cousin Dolben 'were in fact Pusey-ites, . . . yet neither of us at that time [in 1863 they were aged nineteen and fifteen] doubted that our *toga virilis* would be the cassock of a priest or the habit of a monk'. Bridges does not remember very clearly how he had come 'to imbibe these notions' and supposes it was 'the purely logical effect of Keble's *Christian Year*, a book regarded in my family as good poetry, and given to us on Sundays to learn by heart'. So Bridges at Eton was a High Church boy. But his temper 'was impatient of controversy' and his personal tendencies led him to poetry and

---

[1] *Three Friends*, p. 9. Quotations in this section and the next, unless otherwise stated, are taken from the book.

'the magic of speech' and not to a spiritual inner life 'of high
purpose and devotion', as was the case with the 'extravagant'
Dolben. Bridges had no sympathy for 'false fancies and affected
sentimentality'. Healthy, strong and muscular, with an
interest in football and rowing, he was immune from such
strange decisions as Dolben's dedication of himself in the Order
of St. Benedict.[1] Dolben's efforts at converting his cousin—
chiefly made through letters, since the parents of both boys,
having no wish to see them indulge these High Church fancies,
prevented their meeting during the school holidays[2]—were of
no avail; but it cannot be doubted that Bridges in his early
terms at Oxford was still bound by friendship and 'religious
conviction' to Dolben. He lagged far behind 'Brother Dominic',
but his interest in Puseyism was still alive. In fact it was this
interest that led to his meeting with Hopkins; and when Dolben visited Oxford in March, 1865, to see the city and colleges,
he met Hopkins who shared with him the same spiritual fervour. Bridges writes: 'He must have been a good deal with
him, for Gerard conceived a high admiration for him and
always spoke of him afterwards with great affection'. Obviously,
Dolben must have found in Hopkins a deeper and more genuine
response to his own eagerness than he could expect to find in
the already more sober-minded and wary Bridges.

Meanwhile, Dolben was planning to found an 'Establish-
ment', some spiritual brotherhood, and, strangely enough, the
head of the community was to be Bridges, who in the memoir
excuses himself for remembering so little about it: 'I might
remember more, had I looked forward to it more confidently.'
But the earnest—though extravagant—young Dolben would
never have dreamt of giving his cousin such high responsibility,
had he had any doubts then about his convictions. It seems that
Bridges was prepared to meet Dolben half-way, to accept
ritualism and the ascetic means of attaining the 'Saintly Life',
so long as it did not lead them to Rome. For Bridges had an
'unconquerable repugnance to the full-blown Roman theo-

---

[1] An Order founded by the Rev. J. L. Lyne in the Reformed Church of England
at Claydon in Suffolk, in 1862.

[2] In August, 1865, Dolben wrote to Bridges, 'They would not let me come to
Rochdale on my way here'. *Three Friends*, p. 68.

logy', as he says, and this repugnance he never dismissed from his mind. He saw Dolben gradually drifting towards the Roman communion, and knew he would have 'Romanized' had not Fate decided otherwise. Dolben was drowned while bathing in the River Welland on June 28, 1867. In the words of Hopkins,[1] 'There can very seldom have happened the loss of so much beauty (in body and mind and life) and of the promise of still more as there has been in his case'. But Hopkins, who had become a Roman Catholic some eight months before, admits that the young poet and Brother of the Third Order of St. Benedict 'had gone on in a way wh. was wholly and unhappily irrational'. Bridges must have shared his friend's strict opinion all the more readily since he was 'drifting fast away' from the old religious sympathies he had held in common with his cousin for a few years.

The concluding paragraph of the memoir clearly reveals, in its style and mood, Bridges's estrangement from Dolben's religious preoccupations. To one whose portrait in Eton College shows 'the saint, the soul rapt in contemplation, the habit of saintly life, of devotion, of enthusiasm for high ideals', he offers the purely aesthetic commentary on his untimely death which an artist, too deeply enwrapped in the 'inexhaustible satisfaction of form', could devise.

It was beautiful and strange that, after all his unceasing mental perplexity, he should die unconsciously—for he must have fainted into the water—without pain, in one of his rare moments of healthy bodily enjoyment: and premature as his end was, and the stroke of it unlooked for, and apparently sudden, yet his last poems show him waiting and expectant, and his last action had all the dignity and fitness of artistic preparation.[2]

Such balanced sentences, polished, rhythmical and full of the magic of language, are scarcely attuned to the spiritual quest of the young poet. Calm beauty of line and artistic style, however noble and graceful, fail when the biographer has to convey the passionate Christian boy. The tragedy of his death, the sacrifice suddenly demanded and accepted in terror and love,

---

[1] *GMH to RB*, Letter XIV, August 30, 1867, pp. 16–17.
[2] *Three Friends*, pp. 104–105.

could have received a more fitting tribute, had Bridges let his heart speak rather than his sense of artistic decorum.

In some subtle way the portrait of Dolben by Bridges is marred by the desire of the draughtsman to tone down his own youthful religious zeal for the High Church cause. Most of the 'ecclesiastical attractions' he and his cousin experienced in their teens appeared to Bridges, at the age of sixty-seven, far more foolish and ludicrous than fifty years before, when he was gradually forsaking the cause and its too devotional friends.

Bridges's other two friends were not, like Dolben and Hopkins, the friends of school or university. They met him in his maturity, and from Bridges's memoirs of them we can gather only a few details of his own character and idiosyncrasies, as well as the quality of his friendship.

It was Hopkins who introduced Bridges to Dixon in 1878. 'I never heard of Dixon until the year 1878, when my friend Gerard Hopkins told me of his poetry'.[1] Dixon was forty-five and Bridges thirty-four. Bridges enjoyed his friendship, which was 'absolutely generous and ideal', and which gave him ample opportunity to discuss poetry and poetical criticism. It was 'a close friendship which was confined to the end of his life'. Dixon, in his undergraduate days at Oxford, had been connected with the Pre-Raphaelite Brotherhood, whose worship of ideal beauty was one of Bridges's essential articles of faith. Theirs was 'a company of enthusiastic spirits, in the flourish and flower of their youth, united in an ideal conspiracy to reform society by means of beauty'. But Bridges, the serious-minded artist, treated them with due severity as light-hearted enthusiasts who did not 'put themselves much about to grasp the facilities which they could command', and who accepted their technical ignorance with a kind of alacrity. (This was a criticism that no one could ever launch against him!) But Bridges, who can scoff at the belief of some Pre-Raphaelites 'that the world could better be regenerated by Painting than

[1] Dixon had been one of Hopkins's assistant-masters at Highgate School in 1861. In June, 1878, Hopkins decided to write to him to express his admiration of *Christ's Company*, a book of poems. There began a fairly regular correspondence between the two poets up to the death of Hopkins in 1889. See *GMH & RWD*, 1935.

by Poetry', pleads in defence of the poets of the Brotherhood. His argument clearly reveals his own traditional notions and there is one sentence that reads like a personal confession.

The common notion that poetry is the one of all the arts which can dispense with apprenticeship—and William Morris's first poems are sometimes cited as an example—arises from not appreciating the effect of the omnipresence of the best models, and the characteristic virtue of books. A boy who has a turn for poetry is acquainted with it from his cradle; and these men were students of literature more than of anything else. They met to read Tennyson and Browning aloud together; indeed, their despised college-lectures were on the classical authors of antiquity, whose masterpieces are the grammar of literary art; and these were almost the only masterpieces with which they were familiar.[1]

We gather from this that Bridges possessed an early awareness of his poetical gifts, a sense of the virtue of books and of the literary importance of the classical authors of antiquity. This explains part of his own confidence and authority, as well as his attitude towards his friend's poetical works.

For the editing of Dixon's poetry Bridges acted on the same principle as he did for Hopkins's. In both cases the consistency of his policy is obvious. He let time slowly prepare a public for their poetry.

I had always hitherto refused [to edit a selection of Canon Dixon's poetry], or had rather deferred doing this office for my friend, because I could not see in the public taste the sign of any feeling that would welcome the book, or even regard it with the respect necessary to its acceptance.

When 'indications of a more favourable attitude' began to appear, he was ready to undertake the necessary edition of the poems.

If Dixon's poems lack finish and 'cannot be defended against the charge of inequality', and if the younger poet is fully aware of their defects and deficiencies, the man himself is, in the words of Professor Abbott, 'greater than his verses'.[2]

---

[1] *Three Friends*, pp. 115–16.
[2] Introduction to *GMH & RWD*, p. xxxi.

Bridges liked in him his gentleness, his air of nobility, 'his insight, clear judgment and memory', as well as 'his good temper, humour, patience, tenderness and sympathy'. He wrote of 'this great ingenuous being' whose Christian virtues were 'propagating themselves around him in a natural state like healthy plants'.[1] He certainly revered him and deemed his affection a priceless gift. He felt, as deeply as Hopkins did, the unobtrusive influence of a man who had both beauty of character and sanctity of mind.

Must one regret that almost no letter was kept of the correspondence between the two friends? Was the humility of Dixon so thorough that he seldom gave full scope to his own views and thoughts and expected Bridges always to take the lead in the choice of subject-matter or of detailed criticism? Was there in his letters, as there was in his speech, a 'convincing sincerity' with nothing 'expansive or avenant' in it? Both poets loved Nature and delighted to depict its moods and seasons and incidents with quiet passion, a rich mastery of words and an exquisite ear for the delicate sounds of syllables. There was a Wordsworthian touch in Dixon, as both Bridges and Hopkins observed.[2] No doubt the letters exchanged by Dixon and Bridges would have been most illuminating and would have offered much of the interest evinced by the letters of Hopkins and Dixon. But Bridges will keep on thwarting our simplest wishes. We cannot find any good reason for his destroying both sides of the correspondence; we can only infer, from his known habits, that he came to his decision after a careful consideration of the matter.[3] All students of English poetry

---

[1] *Three Friends*, p. 147.

[2] 'Dixon in his earlier and later work often philosophized in Wordsworth's manner,' says Bridges in the memoir (p. 134), and he quotes Hopkins who said 'that he did not think that there was any one who had so much of Wordsworth's insight into Nature as he had' (p. 133).

[3] In the preface to *GMH & RWD*, Professor Abbott says, 'The letters written by Gerard Hopkins to Canon Dixon came into the possession of Robert Bridges about two years after Dixon's death'. His own letters to Dixon he may have obtained at the same time. He 'carefully arranged' in a large book the letters of his two friends. He acted differently with his own, and must have destroyed Dixon's letters some time after 1908, when he quoted one or two of them in the memoir. *Three Friends*, pp. 122 and 146.

must regret it, since they have to rest content with the memoir, a heartfelt and noble testimony to a friendship about which Bridges could write these fine lines:

> Man hath with man on earth no holier bond
> Than that the Muse weaves with her dreamy thread.[1]
>
> (*New Poems*, Eclogue I)

With Henry Bradley, the philologist, Bridges found many congenial common interests; but they were those of elderly men and their mutual sympathy was never on simple affection-ate terms. Bradley gave scholarly help when Bridges launched his own phonetic script—a scheme to which he devoted much of his time in the last thirty years of his life, and on which he held strong views.[2] Bradley's co-operation was again a valuable asset when Bridges organized the Society for Pure English in the years immediately before and after the First World War.[3] No doubt there were in Bradley some traits of character that particularly appealed to the poet. Bradley was a family man, who loved children; so did Bridges. Both men, apart from their intellectual occupations, made their domestic affections 'the centre and first interest' of their lives. Both were fond of long walks through the countryside. Neither was of a social dis-position though they were 'quick to make personal ties'. If Bradley had not Bridges's physical vigour, yet his presence was 'resolute and responsive', just as much as the Poet Laureate's. Their religious and philosophical views formed a strong bond. When Bridges writes, 'He would not perhaps have resented being called an Agnostic. . . . I should have described him off-hand as a fairly orthodox Peripatetic with a kindlier feeling than I had towards German Idealism',[4] the words could well serve to describe the author of *The Testament of Beauty*. Then,

[1] A poem, published in 1899, commemorating the visit Bridges paid to Dixon in 1879. 'The sentiment is from life, but the incidents and scene are fictitious.' *Three Friends*, p. 120.

[2] Bridges invented a phonetic alphabet and had a special type designed and cut for the edition of his *Collected Essays*. See S. Nowell-Smith, 'The Phonotypes of Robert Bridges', *Alphabet and Image*, No. 5, September, 1947.

[3] The S.P.E. was founded at Chilswell in 1913. The first tract appeared in 1919; from 1920 to 1930 Bridges wrote or contributed to nearly all tracts published.

[4] *Three Friends*, p. 198.

Bridges, who certainly was from his early undergraduate days ready to let no one 'presume to tell him what he should like or dislike', always enjoyed the friendship of men who were 'profound and sound critics in all literary matters'; and Bradley was such a man, to say nothing of Dixon or Hopkins. The following sentences, written in praise of Bradley, rival Bridges's own taste and moral attitude.

His literary style was a perfected logical statement of the matter in hand, unmistakably conveyed in convenient and simple grammar, with keen sensitiveness to the consonance, association and dignity of the words employed. . . . He had the true artist's esteem for honesty, and contempt for aesthetic affectations.

The qualities Bridges admired in his friend were those he cherished most in his own style and his aesthetic creed. There was between these two scholarly Oxford gentlemen a sympathy which went as deep as the natural affection of two Eton College boys and the friendship of the poets of Yattendon and Warkworth. So, when Bridges, taking up the moving words of A. W. M. Baillie—who said that one of his greatest regrets in no longer believing in a second life was that he wanted so badly 'somewhere, somehow, to meet Gerard Hopkins again'[1] —writes at the end of his memoir of Bradley:

And difficult as it is with our sorrowful experience to face with any comfort the prospect of a general resurrection, yet there is none of us who would not desire to meet his old friends again, and cannot picture the joy of it. I myself would risk a good deal on the chance of meeting Henry Bradley: indeed all my memories of him are so pleasant that I can almost imagine the delight of his company enduring *in eternum,*

we must consider the wish as the most sincere the poet could express and as the highest compliment he could pay. We realize that no man was so near his heart as Henry Bradley. To Mrs. Bradley, he wrote after the death of his friend: 'As you know, I loved him very deeply and reckon him among the few men with whom I have had full friendship without any intel-

---

[1] *Further Letters*, Additional Note K, p. 449.

lectual or moral reserve'.[1] In all fairness Bridges could not say so of Dolben, the extravagant Puseyite, or of Dixon, the grave historian of the Church of England and the 'medieval' poet, still less of Hopkins, the Jesuit.

Whether he chose to do so or not, Bridges describes in the three memoirs three main stages of his own life. Through Dolben, we see the young Etonian, captain of his house, the Corpus Christi undergraduate with a veiled but definite High Church devotion, who went to Oxford expecting to take Holy Orders and left it an agnostic, neither Dr. Pusey nor Canon Liddon succeeding in holding sway over his soul. By choosing the career of a physician, his philosophical speculations took him to the camp of the Broad Churchmen, to which men like Arnold of Rugby and Charles Kingsley had given fame and honour.

Through Dixon, we see the poet of maturer years, the artist who leaves medical practice to devote himself wholly to poetry, prosody and language, and is drawn towards an older poet, whose quiet worship of Nature—but not his medieval fantasies —he admires.

Through Bradley, we see him elderly and donnish, secure in his own literary views, enjoying his phonetic hobby or his steadfast defence of pure English, while his mellow scepticism bathes in the classical and gentlemanly atmosphere of the old university, remaining all the time slightly aloof and aristocratic in his contempt for the outside world, yet full of human kindness.

These three portraits allow us to draw, somewhat vaguely perhaps, but not inaccurately, a portrait of the man Bridges was. But we miss many lively details of his outward aspect, his ways with people. A more direct likeness, drawn by those who knew him well, must be added to this unostentatious self-portrait.

III. AS OTHERS SAW HIM

Neither Dolben, Dixon, Bradley nor Hopkins has left any description of Bridges. The only remark that might suggest that

---

[1] *Correspondence of Robert Bridges and Henry Bradley, 1900–23*, 1940, p. 187.

Hopkins admired his friend's physical beauty is made in very general terms; in the same vague terms he praises beauty of the mind and the beauty of character. But the compliment is unmistakable, if it is very quiet. 'I think then no one can admire beauty of the body more than I do, and it is of course a comfort to find beauty in a friend or a friend in beauty'.[1] In order to understand the enthusiastic admiration Bridges aroused in spite of himself, we may recall that Percy Simpson and S. K. Ratcliffe could not take their eyes off him and thought him 'the possessor of the most *beautiful* face ever seen in a man'.[2]

He must have been a beautiful man from youth to old age. The majority of the descriptions we possess were written by friends who knew him in the last decade of the nineteenth century—such as the artist Sir William Rothenstein—or in the last twenty years of his life. But many traits of character, thus revealed, evidently belonged as much to the young man as to the old gentleman.

When the obituary notice in *The Times*, published the day after the poet's death, April 22, 1930, spoke of his 'great stature and fine proportions, his leonine head, deep eyes, expressive lips, and a full-toned voice, made more effective by a slight, occasional hesitation in his speech,' we may suppose that such physical traits were already his when he was at Corpus Christi in 1863, and were even more impressive. We can better understand the friendships he was graced with all through his life when we read,

His extraordinary personal charm was, however, due to something deeper than these; it lay in the transparent sincerity with which every word and motion expressed the whole of his character, its greatness and its scarcely less memorable littlenesses. . . . Behind them was always visible the strength of a towering and many-sided nature, at once aristocratic and unconventional, virile and affectionate, fearlessly inquiring and profoundly religious.

Rothenstein, who made several drawings of him and knew him well, speaks of 'a grandeur about him' and a 'bearishness which hid a warmth of friendship'.[3] He adds, 'He had a rich and

[1] *GMH to RB*, Letter LXIV, October 22, 1879, p. 95.
[2] E. Thompson, *op. cit.*, p. 91.
[3] W. Rothenstein, *Men and Memories, 1900–22*, 1932, pp. 210–11.

masculine interest, ardent, searching and learned, yet again with something finally simple and childlike which was one of his endearing qualities'. *The Times* obituary describes the poet's 'childlike delight in his own powers and special advantages'. His 'boyish love of brusque personal encounters', there mentioned, may well have been a life-long habit, quite in keeping at any rate with his decision, taken, as we saw, in the early 'sixties, to let no one tell him what he should like or dislike. His contempt of convention could go beyond limits, as the following anecdote related by Compton Mackenzie proves in an amusing way.

I remember that once in the middle of a tirade against the imbecility and illogicality of the old public-school Latin Primer pronunciation, he picked up a volume of Herrick which was lying on my table. 'Why do you read this r-rot?' he growled with that slight stammer of his. 'Because I like him among the best of poets.' He opened the volume haphazard and read:

> 'Her eyes the glowworm l-lend thee,
> The shooting stars attend thee.'

Then he shut the volume with a snap and tossed it to the other end of the room. 'What infernal r-rot,' he growled. 'What eyes has a glowworm to lend anybody!'[1]

We can easily understand why Sir Walter Raleigh, who was an active member of the Society for Pure English and a great friend of Bridges, called him 'grumpy' in a letter to Lady Elcho, but 'delightfully grumpy'.[2] Describing Bridges's conversation and explaining his abruptness and frank views, Raleigh makes some perceptive remarks:

He mentions thing after thing which is commonly believed and says that of course it's not so. He's always right. His intellect has been so completely self-indulged that it now can't understand rubbish. He has never obeyed anyone or adapted himself to anyone, so he's as clear as crystal, and can't do with fogs.

Here again we notice the independence of spirit and the total

---

[1] C. Mackenzie, *Literature in my Time*, 1933, p. 134.
[2] *Letters of Sir Walter Raleigh, 1879–1922*, 1926, vol. ii, pp. 390–91.

surrender to his own likes and dislikes. The man trusts himself, because he has been searching out the truth by himself and has come to his own judgment without any help. Solitude, egotism, a clear sense of the power of his intellect, self-will and an aristocratic individualism have led him to a candid self-reliance and a great liberty of tone and manner towards other people. George Gordon tells us that Bridges was a 'selective and capricious reader'.[1] His character and his brusqueness seem to vouch for it, and give an air of truth to Compton Mackenzie's humorous report.

Legend related, I do not know with how much truth, that Bridges had never read any of Keats until he was asked to write an introduction for the edition of his poetry in the Muses' Library, after which he produced what is perhaps, and indeed I will not qualify it, what *is* the finest piece of poetic criticism in the English language.[2]

A legend no doubt!—but a legend that illustrates the poet's indifference to anything that he had not seen, felt, appreciated and judged personally; it emphasizes the freshness of his approach, not burdened with the views and judgments of others.

Sir Henry Newbolt certifies that the 'grumpy poet' was not a recluse.

He really did enjoy the society of the younger men, like Binyon, Yeats, and myself. . . . He received us with the most flattering kindness and generosity; and his boyishly bluff humour made acceptance easy for us. But he never allowed our visits to disturb his accustomed way of life, or our conversation to lead him on to ground which was uncongenial to him.[3]

We may sum up all these different aspects of Bridges in a phrase, which we borrow from Gordon: 'He was first of all a private gentleman . . . He grew up, through the kindness of fortune, unwarped by the struggle of living, with none of the inevitable vices of a profession'. He was an athlete, a hard-working and hard-worked physician,[4] a scholar, a sensi-

---

[1] G. S. Gordon, *Robert Bridges* (Rede Lecture, 1931), 1946, p. 19.

[2] C. Mackenzie, *op. cit.*, p. 135.

[3] H. Newbolt, *My World as in my Time*, 1932, p. 189.

[4] See R. Bridges, *Collected Essays*, XXX, pp. 267–97, 'An Account of the Casualty Department'.

tive poet of beauty and joy, a leisured country gentleman, finally 'a great Victorian and . . . the last of his race',[1] who certainly took to heart and lived according to the famous ideal set forth by Tennyson in *Oenone* (1832):

> Self-reverence, self-knowledge, self-control,
> These three alone lead life to sovereign power.

A recent anonymous critic writes: 'To be with him was to recognize a great and lovable man as well as a poet—a fastidious aristocrat, staunch in his affections, outspoken in his loyalties'. Such a man could well enjoy lasting friendships and we may already understand, from all this external evidence, why Hopkins rejoiced in his 'dearest Bridges'.

IV. THE BASIS OF HIS FRIENDSHIP WITH HOPKINS

At first glance one might well wonder at the friendship that sprang up between the two young men when they met for the first time at Oxford in the late autumn of 1863. Physically the differences were great. Bridges was a tall, strong, muscular boy, who took an active part in the athletic life of his college.[2] Hopkins took little or no interest in sports, although he enjoyed long walks in the countryside. Bridges was handsome, Hopkins was not.[3] Much has been made of Hopkins's statement that no one can admire 'the beauty of the body' more than he does. Herbert Read, we remember, suggested as an unconscious or semiconscious basis of the friendship some physical attraction on the part of Hopkins. But the aesthetic cult of physical beauty that was prevalent in the 'sixties sufficiently explains Hopkins's remark, without our having to go to dark recesses of the soul. To Hopkins it was always fitting—though 'dangerous', as he

---

[1] So says Arthur Waugh in an article on Bridges in the *Fortnightly Review*, June, 1930.

[2] In 1867 Bridges stroked the Corpus boat in the Eights and in a regatta in Paris during the Exposition Universelle.

[3] The photographs of the two young men in *GMH to RB* offer a striking contrast. Hopkins's features are delicate, soft, dreamy and, apart from the strong chin, rather feminine. Bridges's are more strongly delineated, with firm lips and a determined look. Daniel Sargent pointedly stresses the obvious external differences. 'They did not outwardly seem made for intimacy, for Bridges had the mien of an *athlete* and Hopkins the mien of an *aesthete*'. (*Atlantic Monthly*, August, 1943, 'The Charm and the Strangeness'.)

himself pointed out in the same letter, and six years later in the sonnet, 'To what serves mortal beauty?'—that beauty of mind and beauty of body should go together. And he rejoiced to find both in Bridges.

Bridges was certainly drawn towards Hopkins by his sensitive mind, his fine intelligence and his integrity of spirit. The muscular beauty of Hopkins lay there; his was a clear, direct intellect, determined to be frank, sincere and outspoken. But their first bond was their common Puseyite viewpoint and their common religious ideal. We shall see that Hopkins, when Bridges arrived at Oxford, took over Dolben's eager defence of ritualism. Since both students had thought of becoming priests of the Church of England, they must soon have come under the spiritual direction of Dr. Pusey and Canon Liddon, who were, in the university as well as in the country, the leaders of all churchmen who wished 'to restore the dignity of the priest in the minister'.[1] Though this spiritual link was soon to break, it had been deep and strong enough to remain as an invisible chain. Whatever changes would come over them a great passion had once been in their hearts. They never could forget that it had brought them together.

Both friends were also under the influence of the Pre-Raphaelite cult of Beauty; they still kept their schoolboy admiration for Tennyson;[2] Walter Pater was Hopkins's tutor; they shared a passion for Nature, for Beauty and for Poetry. At Nature they looked with keen, observant eyes, enjoying the

---

[1] G. M. Young, *Early Victorian England*, 'Portrait of an Age', 1934, p. 476.

[2] The earliest poetical fragments of Hopkins written in the late summer of 1862 bear evidence of Tennyson's style cleverly imitated. As to Bridges, the following incident is worth recording: 'On June 10, [1863] Tennyson received a letter from young Robert Bridges, . . . then a sixth form boy at Eton, thanking him for the gift of his portrait and autograph. Bridges had just recited at Eton "speeches" a passage from *The Princess* and, as he was personally quite unknown to Tennyson, naturally assumed that the gift was the consequence of this. "I hope," he wrote, "you will excuse my troubling you with my thanks, which I owe you the more, being an entire stranger. Had I known you personally I could hardly have wished a greater honour; as it is, I could have no greater".' Tennyson's answer kindly set matters right. He was not responsible for the sending of his portrait; some friend of his was, to whom he had sent Bridges's thanks. It would have been a vain thing in him to have sent his portrait to a stranger, but he desired Bridges to accept 'the assurance that since you like to have my portrait, I like that you should have it'. Charles Tennyson, *Alfred Tennyson*, 1949, pp. 344–5.

sight of the humblest flower, the play of sun on water, the graceful ease of lofty trees. Beauty, the beauty of body, of line, of form, of expression, of language and style, they gravely worshipped. But it was of great consequence for them that they should consecrate their lives to an artistic cult that did not separate them from their worship and love of God. Hugh I'Anson Fausset has shewn that if the two friends were drawn towards aestheticism, it was because 'it had begun as a counter-movement to the growing rationalism'.[1] If Hopkins's problem was 'integrating his craving for beauty in a spiritual vision',[2] so was Bridges's. One went to Roman Catholicism, the other turned finally to Plato and the Symposium. But since they must *praise*, poetry was for them the only means of giving God, Nature and Beauty the appropriate homage and reverence.

Another trait common to both must not be overlooked; their seriousness of purpose. They were not to look at Nature in a vague sentimental mood, nor to glorify Beauty in uncertain abstract terms, nor to write poetry indifferently, being content to follow and do as their great predecessors had done. Their age was one of a powerful aesthetic revival and of the vindication of art for its own sake;[3] but it was also an age of science and of strict rules, and there was in the two young poets the strong purpose of using their own gifts, and of strengthening their passion with the most perfect technique they could master through reflection, scholarship and experience.

On such firm bases, the friendship of Bridges and Hopkins could have developed with the years and become the deepest joy of their lives, even if, relinquishing all thought of entering the ministry of God in their national Church, each of them had gone his own way in a professional career. As long as their different religious attitudes remained, within the fold of the Church of England, simply due to their different temperaments, nothing could break the literary and aesthetic sympathies that drew them together. Both knew their kinship, both were certain of their earnestness, both admired their respective

[1] Hugh I'Anson Fausset, *Poets and Pundits*, 1947, p. 108.
[2] *Ibid.*, p. 109.
[3] See A. J. Farmer, *Le Mouvement esthétique et décadent en Angleterre, 1873–1900*, 1931, pp. 22–27.

intellectual gifts and were ready to help each other. But the conversion of Hopkins to Roman Catholicism was to give their friendship the tragic quality and the permanent flaw that neither of them could have expected or imagined. A full friendship without intellectual or moral reserve suddenly became impossible, in spite of their instinctive affection for each other. Even though the step taken by Hopkins appeared as the logical consequence of his spiritual evolution and the honest acceptance of an intimate experience, Bridges could not understand it, being unable to fight down the Protestant suspicion of Rome which lay deep in him and even grew stronger with time. George Gordon has given a clear summing up of the case:

> Hopkins's youthful conversion to Romanism surprised few of his friends; . . . but the decision, so characteristic of him, to press the point home, to push the argument to extremity, and, by becoming a Jesuit, take the hardest path—this was felt to be another matter. Intimacy was for a time intimidated; Bridges drew back; and, though they sometimes met, six letters in as many years seem to have been all that passed between these later voluminous and eager correspondents. This was a barrier which by its nature could never be wholly removed. . . . The range of their friendship, though never the force of their affection, was proportionately restricted.[1]

We shall find in Hopkins's letters many proofs of the disharmony due to the spiritual chasm that opened between them in 1867. The lack of understanding on Bridges's part will even at times go beyond what could be expected. The Roman "superstition"[2] was too much for him, and the Society of Jesus was a

[1] G. S. Gordon, *The Discipline of Letters*, 1946, pp. 169–170. ('G. M. Hopkins and R. Bridges', a Lecture from the Chair of Poetry in the University of Oxford, June 7, 1938.) As a matter of fact, after Hopkins had entered the Jesuit novitiate at Roehampton in September, 1868, and until normal correspondence was resumed early in 1877—an interval of eight years and five months—Hopkins wrote six letters and did not even get an answer to every one of them.

[2] Bridges's old family house at Walmer was sold after his father's death and became a convent. In *The Summer-House on the Mound* the poet recalls the fact in these lines:

> A priest has there usurped the ivied mound . . .
> Within the peach-clad walls that old outlaw,
> The Roman wolf, scratches with privy paw.
>
> (*New Poems*, No. 4)

But Hopkins in *The Wreck of the Deutschland* had written, 'And Luther . . . beast of the waste wood'! (Stanza 20)

system he loathed and for which he never ceased to rebuke his friend. Yet, in spite of it all, nothing could destroy the old associations born in college rooms or in chapel. When poetry and music renewed in them an inclination which had been slumbering in their hearts, the feeling of attachment and love towards each other flared up and remained to the end alive and burning high.

Undergraduate friendships are always strong. They endure in spite of distance or of widely different interests. This common rule proved true for Bridges and Hopkins. Their university memories overcame all possible causes of estrangement. Other concerns were to create new bonds between them. They found in their love of poetry, in the discussion of technical intricacies of prosody and metre, and finally in their interest in music, sacred and profane, capital reasons for entertaining a fairly regular correspondence. The poems they wrote attracted their mutual criticism, appraisal and admiration. In the exchange of letters concerning their own poetical works they both found help and encouragement; it sustained or restored self-confidence, while introducing a discipline, friendly but exacting, into their audacities of style or prosody.

To end these general considerations on a literary friendship which we are about to study more closely, let us emphasize that the affection and confidence of the two friends in each other were enriched by the very differences that they could discover in themselves. Each drew from the other some of the qualities he lacked. We shall see how Hopkins helped Bridges to find his own poetical rhythm and fought against his somewhat narrow views, literary and moral. And Bridges by his rebukes prevented in some measure the 'erring on the side of oddness' that was Hopkins's weakness; his unfailing interest in his friend's poems, even when he least understood the poet or the verse, sustained the daring creator of 'sprung rhythm' whenever he felt

> . . . so haggard at the heart, so care-coiled, care-killed,
> so fagged, so fashed, so cogged, so cumbered,
>
>   (*The Golden Echo*)

that he lost all confidence in himself.

The mystery and beauty of their friendship lies there. Just as Hopkins introduced Bridges to Dixon and Patmore, and spoke highly of his friend's poems whenever he had an opportunity, so Bridges kept, with 'far fonder a care' than that of Hopkins's co-religionists, the Catholic poems of a Jesuit priest, and was finally responsible for editing the 'lov'd legacy' that had 'lain coy in my home', till time—in his conscientious opinion—was ripe for their introduction to the general public. Bridges may have been wrong in keeping them so long as a secret and strange treasure, but literary history registers the great success of the *Poems* in the last thirty years, and the time chosen by Bridges for publishing the small book he introduced and annotated in 1918 was certainly most favourable.[1] What we positively miss is the memoir he should have written of Hopkins. But it appears from a fairly recent testimony, which few critics have called attention to, that Bridges had actually contemplated writing such a memoir and publishing a selection of the poems almost immediately after Hopkins's death. Let us quote George Gordon's words in full:

I have seen the letters addressed to Provost Daniel of Worcester—proposing as early as August 20, 1889, within a month or two of Hopkins's death, that he should print at his press a memoir of Hopkins, with a selection from his poems. 'It will be a unique volume,' he wrote. On October 11, he reports that he can send the poems any day and the memoir possibly by January. Why this project fell through I have no knowledge; at any rate some hindrance occurred, and Bridges had to take other and more gradual ways of making known to a public unacquainted even with his name the most revolutionary poet of his day, and, at first sight, by far the most uncouth.[2]

There is no present means of discovering why the project fell through. There may have been difficulties about the copyright between the Society of Jesus and Hopkins's family; there were such difficulties when the poems were ultimately published,

---

[1] Critics in the 'thirties, following Herbert Read's lead, thought it necessary to disparage Bridges whenever they praised Hopkins. One may prefer Hopkins both as man and poet without being unfair to Bridges.

[2] G. S. Gordon, *op. cit.*, p. 182. See also *infra*, pp. 156–9.

and it was a delicate matter. Or Bridges may have changed his mind. Some day the real explanation may be given by those who know it. Did the few who had read Hopkins's poems in 1889—Edmund Gosse and Coventry Patmore were among them[1]—prevail upon Bridges to postpone their publication? Perhaps Bridges refrained because dignity and gentlemanly feelings forbade him to stress his strong opposition to Hopkins's religion and odd prosody; besides, all the essential facts would be found in the letters of his friend which he had carefully preserved. As for his own feelings, his introductory sonnet, composed at Chilswell in January, 1918, expresses them with sufficient clarity, tenderness, power and beauty.

[1] See *GMH to RB*, p. 295, and *Further Letters*, p. 351.

II

Two Oxford Undergraduates

Hopkins won a scholarship to Balliol College in the autumn of 1862. He went to Oxford for the Easter term, 1863. Bridges went from Eton to Corpus Christi for the following Michaelmas term. They did not know each other before they met at the university. Hopkins was the eldest son of a family of nine; his father was an average-adjuster in the City; and the family lived in Hampstead in easy circumstances. Bridges's father had died in 1853, leaving a widow and nine children. In 1854, when Robert went to Eton, Mrs. Bridges had married the Rev. Dr. J. E. N. Molesworth, vicar of Rochdale in Lancashire. The Bridges family lived in affluence.

Both families were moderate High Church, but the two boys were not so moderate by the time they reached Oxford. Bridges's Puseyite convictions must have developed at Eton, but they always remained strictly Anglican. We infer from his later interest in Church music that he was more concerned with the aesthetic revival of liturgy than with a return to Catholic tradition. Yet it is clear that he had been well instructed in the ideas and convictions propagated since 1833 by the Tractarians, and that he shared their views. In his memoir of Dolben he writes:

The magnitude of the religious problems which we had been led up to face was occupying our attention; it involved both our spiritual and practical interests in life. A sectarian training had provided us with premises, which, so long as they remained unquestioned, were of overwhelming significance: they dominated everything: the logical situation was appalling: the ordinary conventions of life were to us merely absurd.[1]

[1] *Three Friends*, p. 9.

This passage, even though it provides us only with the bare facts, is clear enough. A 'sectarian training', given to him by Puseyite clergy, stressed the 'illogical situation' of the Established Church, governed by Crown and Parliament which were no longer united in the Christian faith, and turned the 'ordinary conventions' of Christian life into 'absurdity'. Bridges characteristically adds, 'We regarded the claim of the Church in the same way as Cardinal Newman had elaborated it in his writings.'

Obviously Bridges held the views elaborated by Newman as an Anglican clergyman,[1] before he resigned the vicarage of St. Mary's in September, 1843. But as he says that he himself 'never read any controversial books', it is quite possible that his opinion was only reflecting the opinions of his group. The fact remains that he was then in full sympathy with the Apostles of the Oxford Movement. As a boy he had read Keble's *Christian Year*, a book of devotional poetry 'regarded in my family,' he writes, 'as good poetry and given to us on Sundays to learn by heart'.[2] This book, published in 1827 and sub-titled 'Thoughts in Verse for the Sundays and Holydays throughout the Year', could give in its own quiet way a deep sense of Catholic liturgy. But *The Christian Year* did not turn all the Anglicans who read it into High Church people. So the really effective influence must have come from such Eton friends as Dolben, Muirhead, Manning, and principally Coles,[3] who even at that early age was a great devotee of the Oxford Movement. These young men formed a real brotherhood full of zeal and piety. Does not Bridges speak of his frequent visits to St. George's Chapel,

[1] In 1862 Newman had still to wait seventeen years for his Cardinal's hat. Bridges is alluding to the *Tracts for the Times*, 1833–41, in which Newman, together with Keble and Pusey, had developed the spiritual claims of the Catholic Church, which he wanted the Church of England to uphold and defend against the errors of Protestantism and Popery. Such was the practical theory of the *Via Media* that Newman had evolved in his lectures on the prophetical office of the Church in 1837. But from the end of 1839 he had lost faith in his own formula, though he firmly believed that the Church of England was a living branch of the universal Catholic Church, in the same way as the Catholic Church in France or Italy.

[2] *Three Friends*, p. 10.

[3] V. S. S. Coles, 1845–1929, preacher, missioner and spiritual guide, Principal of Pusey House from 1897 to 1909, was one of the leaders of the Catholic revival in the English Church, and a close friend of Hopkins, Liddon, Dean Church and Bishop Gore.

Windsor, where it was his custom 'to go on short after-fours and sit in the north aisle or organ-loft, stealing out at the end of the anthem in time to be not very late for five o'clock school'?[1]— a proof that the schoolboy was more than punctual in his daily prayers and cared for such quiet moments of devotion as the Chapel Royal would afford at Evensong.

Although Bridges does not say so, we cannot doubt that when he arrived at Oxford he joined the group of undergraduates gathered round Canon Liddon,[2] one of the brilliant clergymen who kept the flame of Puseyism burning, and who gradually steered the High Church of the nineteenth century into the Anglo-Catholicism of the present day. Pusey himself was a noble figure who attracted many of the young men who confessed to him. Dolben and Coles are names that come up in the very first letter of Hopkins to Bridges, dated August 28, 1865. Liddon is not named but there is evidence that Bridges knew him well.[3] So did Hopkins, for it was Liddon who earnestly tried to prevent him from taking 'the final and last step' to Rome. Within five days, from October 16 to October 20, 1866, he wrote no fewer than four long urgent letters,[4] pleading the cause of Canterbury. No clergyman would have written with so much authority and sympathy had he not been on intimate terms with the young student, had he not felt at the same time that his spiritual responsibility was fully involved.

The earliest letters we possess from Hopkins to Bridges prove that after two years at Oxford they were quite good friends. At the beginning of the long vacation in 1865 Hopkins had been to Manchester on a visit to one of his college companions, Edmund Geldart. Bridges had invited him to Rochdale, which is only ten miles away, but his letter had reached Hopkins

---

[1] *Three Friends*, p. 12.

[2] H. P. Liddon (1829–90), preacher, chaplain and spiritual guide, Vice-President of St. Edmund Hall, Canon of St. Paul's, served under Dean Church. Gave lectures on the New Testament every Sunday evening for ten years from 1859 to 1869, at St. Edmund Hall and Queen's.

[3] In a comment on a letter from Dolben, who in November, 1865, was trying to find a tutor in order to prepare for a Balliol scholarship. Bridges deplores the difficulty he encountered in discovering a suitable tutor for his cousin. 'Canon Liddon was hunting with me,' he adds, which shows the part played by the clergyman in the practical life of his young disciples. *Three Friends*, p. 81.

[4] *Further Letters*, pp. 400–404.

after some delay. With no other trace of humour than the mere statement that he had left Manchester 'more than a month' before, Hopkins writes, with genuine feeling, 'Else nothing cd. have been so delightful as to meet you and Coles and Dolben'. Was Bridges holding with his friends a plenary meeting of Dolben's society of 'Canons and Brothers of the Holy Name'? Hopkins's answer was taken as a future acceptance and Bridges, being still very keen on having his friend at Rochdale, renewed his invitation a year later. Unfortunately Hopkins, who was in Sussex, was going to join his parents at Shanklin in the Isle of Wight and had given up 'all idea of going to the north'. Bridges, however, was not to be denied; he wrote back and repeated his invitation a week and again a fortnight later. On August 4 Hopkins answered that 'I should like nothing so much as to stay at Rochdale, more especially (if one can say that) when you hold out the possibility of Dolben being there'. On August 26 he writes: 'I am most happy to come any day in the first week of September which you like to name'.[1] Bridges had suggested that they might read together, and though at first the suggestion had sounded 'very odd' to Hopkins, it may have helped him to take his favourable decision. We shall see that, however genuine and great was his pleasure in visiting Bridges and meeting Dolben again, there was another personal reason that had led him to accept the invitation of his Lancashire friend.

II. HOPKINS'S VISIT TO ROCHDALE

Hopkins went to Rochdale in the first week of September, 1866.[2] He must have reached Bridges's home, Dr. Molesworth's vicarage, on Saturday, September 1. He was back in London on September 21. As the two friends had intended, they read Greek. Hopkins was to take 'Greats' in the spring of 1867 and Bridges in the autumn of the same year. Their different methods of reading Herodotus prevented them from

---

[1] *GMH to RB*, Letters III and IV, p. 3.

[2] In his Dolben memoir (p. 91), Bridges writes: 'Meanwhile in *August* of that year Gerard Hopkins came to me at Rochdale, and stayed, I think, some weeks'. The month was *September*.

working together for more than a few days. By recording this
little detail Bridges throws light on their respective temperaments. Hopkins 'was so punctilious about the text and so enjoyed loitering over the difficulties that I foresaw we should
never get through and broke off from him to go my own way.'[1]
The scrupulous seriousness of Hopkins, always most eager to
understand and explain, contrasts with Bridges's slight irritation and his wish to go over the text at a faster pace; he is
determined to act independently if need be. But of course they
did not devote the whole of their time to such serious matters,
and we gather from one letter that they spent an afternoon
'filling the aquarium'.[2] They spoke of poetry and music, and
discussed at length the design of a flagon and stopper which
Bridges wanted to offer to his brother-in-law, the Rev. William
Henry Glover, rector of Thorndon in Suffolk.[3] Hopkins was
asked to design the stopper and to have it done by the well-
known architect, George Edmund Street. He acted according
to plan and all his letters from September 22 to December 26
deal with his difficulties, which were increased by his own hesitations and fears of doing wrong.

The days spent by Hopkins at Rochdale were among those
he cherished most in his memory. His letter of thanks ends with
the words, 'Believe me, dear Bridges, with the utmost gratitude
your very affectionate friend.' And when a year later another
invitation to Rochdale was sent to him, he refused in most
delicate terms: 'But the very pleasure I had in my stay last
year is part of the reason why I do not wish to make another,
if you can understand.'[4]

We might not understand such a wish to keep as a perfect
memory the short and sole sojourn he made at Dr. Molesworth's vicarage, if we did not know the deeper reasons he
had for being so grateful to Bridges. It so happened that his
stay at Rochdale coincided with his great spiritual ordeal.
Some time before, he had come to his secret final decision to go

---

[1] *Three Friends*, p. 91.
[2] *GMH to RB*, Letter VI, p. 6.
[3] *Ibid.*, Additional Note C, p. 307.
[4] *Ibid.*, Letters VI and XVI, pp. 8, 19.

over to Rome, and the journey to Lancashire was the occasion of his meeting Newman at Birmingham Oratory to decide on the day of his reception into the Roman Church. So all the time he was with Bridges he was weighing in his heart the terrible consequences of his conversion. In his journal for July 17 is written, 'It was this night I believe but possibly the next that I saw clearly the impossibility of staying in the Church of England, but resolved to say nothing till three months are over.'[1] This note must be set side by side with the remark made to the Rev. E. W. Urquhart: 'In fact as I told you my conversion when it came was all in a minute'.[2] And the month of July is corroborated by his postscript to an earlier letter sent to the same correspondent on September 24.

Although my actual conversion was two months ago yet the silent conviction that I was to become a Catholic has been present to me for a year perhaps, as strongly in spite of my resistance to it when it formed itself into words, as if I had already determined it.[3]

Therefore Bridges greeted under his roof a friend who in his heart knew that he was a convert and wished to keep for some time yet the secret of his decision. For Hopkins the situation was an awkward one. But the other secret step he had taken made it even more awkward.

On August 28, the very day he was writing to Bridges that he expected to arrive on Saturday, September 1, Hopkins had written to Dr. Newman, asking for an interview at Birmingham on his way to Lancashire, and expressing his anxiety to become a Catholic.[4] To Bridges he had merely said:

If Saturday would suit you, I shd. leave home on Friday and sleep at Birmingham where I have some business I must manage to do at some time while I am in the north, most conveniently I think then.[5]

But Dr. Newman was abroad at the time and could not answer before September 14. It was only on the return journey from

---

[1] *GMH Journals*, p. 146.
[2] *Further Letters*, Letter XII, October 4, 1866, p. 27.
[3] *Ibid.*, Letter XI, September 24, 1866, p. 27.
[4] *Ibid.*, Letter IX, pp. 21–22.
[5] *GMH to RB*, Letter V, August 28, 1866, p. 4.

Rochdale to London that the young Balliol student met the famous convert of 1845 and decided with him when and where he would be 'received'.

One may easily imagine in what spiritual unrest, anxiety and tremor Bridges's friend was during the three weeks of his stay. He was in a 'painful confusion of mind about my immediate duty'; he had admitted as much in his letter to Dr. Newman. But he was determined to conceal it; he had no wish to disclose to Bridges his own state of mind. He also wanted to tell no one of his conversion till he was received.[1] Such a policy tended to prevent any counter action on the part of his parents and to avoid unpleasant or distressing scenes. With Bridges, until his going to Birmingham 'made it impossible any longer to conceal it', Hopkins deliberately kept silent, in spite of their intimacy, because his situation was delicate as the guest of a clergyman of the Church he had decided to leave. He had no intention of giving pain and alarm to Dr. and Mrs. Molesworth. He was well aware that the parents of young Puseyites were careful not to let their sons be 'corrupted' by Romanizing enthusiasts or possible converts. When Digby Dolben had asked Mrs. Molesworth whether he could join Bridges's brother in Yorkshire, if his tutor accepted charge of him, he had promptly received a negative answer, framed in kind but firm terms. Hopkins was certainly right when he wrote to his friend as an apology for his silence, 'It would have been culpably dishonourable and ungrateful, as I said before, not to have done one's best to conceal it.'[2]

Although Bridges, as we shall see, did not realize it at first, Hopkins's deliberate reticence testifies to his moral delicacy towards his friend, and proves his love for him. As a convert, it cannot be doubted that Hopkins had in his heart a strong desire to see his nearest friends become Catholics. But not at any cost. Any conversion to Catholicism meant both for the proselyte and for his relatives a time of distress and sorrow.

---

[1] He tells his friend Urquhart in a letter dated September 20, but under pledge of secrecy. (*Further Letters*, p. 24.) Bridges was under the same pledge. Hopkins was to announce his conversion to his parents by letter at the time of his reception.

[2] *GMH to RB*, Letter VI, p. 6.

By all Anglicans—and perhaps more so by High Church people—the decision was looked upon as scandalous. Practically it meant a complete severance of intimate bonds. Blood often spoke less strongly than religious prejudice; feelings ran high. Even before he had decided to 'Romanize', Dolben could exclaim pitifully in a letter to his cousin, 'It is somewhat sad to find oneself differing more and more entirely from all one's relations in every religious thought and feeling.'[1] No wonder he could write when despondency prevailed over him, 'Sometimes I feel so tired of it all, which is so wrong'.[2] Hopkins had the same gruelling experience. He was not prepared to act as an irresponsible proselyte.

To another great friend, Urquhart, whom he believed to be on the verge of conversion, Hopkins could write with frankness,

I most earnestly hope you will delay no longer. There is nothing I need say in the way of argument, and I wish too not to say anything. It wd. be presumptuous of me to say more than this—that I am hoping for your conversion and expecting it and of course I do not omit to pray for it.[3]

But in this particular case both friends knew perfectly where they stood. Besides, Urquhart's position was quite independent. He could act more freely and, as he was five years older than Hopkins, the appeal could impress him without necessarily swaying his opinions as a mature man, well able to judge and decide for himself.

In Bridges's case, conditions were wholly different. There was the known position of his parents, their inclination and his own to avoid discussion on all religious subjects,[4] and what he himself describes as a 'plain blurting disposition'[5] which must have made it rather difficult to unbosom oneself to him. What-

---

[1] *Three Friends*, p. 75.

[2] *Ibid.*, p. 63.

[3] *Further Letters*, Letter X, p. 23.

[4] *GMH to RB*, Letter VI, p. 6. Speaking of a Mr. Walford, formerly a junior master at Eton and now a member of the Birmingham Oratory, Hopkins writes: 'How glad he shd. be to see you on yr. way to Oxford, . . . and of course he wd. avoid all religious subjects, I am sure.'

[5] *Ibid.*, p. 9.

ever wishes he might entertain, Hopkins knew he must not express them. And he plainly says so: 'You see the point of what was on my mind at the vicarage was chiefly this, that my wishes about you cd. not be gained except at your own and [Dr. and Mrs. Molesworth's] trouble and grief.'[1]

Bridges 'did not know what was the matter'[2] with him but he did not ask questions. He may have wondered what 'business' his friend wanted to do at Birmingham; he may have had his own guesses at the sort of visits Hopkins proposed to pay there, but he dared not ask anything. Naturally enough, when Hopkins told him the reason why he had had to stop at Birmingham on his way back to London, Bridges felt 'surprised and sorry'. He could not understand his friend's complete silence; he felt that it shewed a lack of confidence, ill repaying his own kind-heartedness. Twice in the course of a week, on September 22 and 28, Hopkins had to explain his attitude:

You were surprised and sorry, you said, and possibly hurt that I wd. not tell you of my conversion. . . . I was never sorry one minute; it wd. have been culpably dishonourable and ungrateful, as I said before, not to have done one's best to conceal it. . . .[3]

You seem so puzzled at my silence: I want you to understand that it was fr. no natural reticence, which is not in me, but fr. the plain conviction of the unkindness and—to use the word which I fancied people wd. give it—treachery of letting you know. And please believe it was meant for a real silence: having decided not to tell you I meant you not to know: hints or constructive conclusions wd. have been both weak and mean. Though you call yourself 'of a plain blurting disposition' I think you wd. however agree that silence is an excellent discipline and especially during the process of conviction (this of course is neither here nor there to my silence at Rochdale)—indeed you have several times said as much. In fact it occurs to me that you are unusually reticent and certainly have a great respect for reticence.[4]

[1] *Ibid.*, Letter VIII, p. 7.
[2] *Further Letters*, Letter XI, to E. W. Urquhart, September 24, 1866, p. 26. '[Bridges's] kindness at that time when he did not know what was the matter with me I perpetually thank God for.'
[3] *GMH to RB*, Letter VI, p. 6.
[4] *Ibid.*, Letter VIII, p. 9.

He insists on the deference due to his hosts; it was for him a point of honour. It would have been wrong to disturb the peace of these good people who had every confidence in him: he could not betray them. He also pleads for silence as a positive virtue and tries to win Bridges by reminding him that he is not a loquacious fellow, and that he is respectful of other people's reserve and privacy.

As a matter of fact, it is this very quality that must have endeared Bridges to Hopkins while he was at Rochdale in the throes of his conversion. For a highly sensitive, scrupulous, restive temperament like that of Hopkins, Bridges's puzzled but discreet silence, the outward show of unconcern that concealed his real warm-heartedness, must have been most welcome. A brief unobtrusive remark proves that Hopkins deeply appreciated his friend's circumspection: 'Pray do not apologize for yr. absence: indeed one is so glad when people put one on such terms that they allow one not to incommode them—if you follow that involution of speech.'[1] It was this reserve and concealed kindness which inspired Hopkins with a deep and lasting gratitude: 'I can never thank you enough for your kindness at that time'; it gave to their friendship its firmest foundation.

When Hopkins speaking of his visit to Rochdale wrote, 'The happiness it has been the means of bringing me I cd. not have conceived', it must have been quite clear to Bridges that his friend considered his invitation as the indirect cause of his final decision. 'And now I have even almost ceased to feel anxiety'. For ever Rochdale and Bridges would be linked in his memory with Birmingham and Dr. Newman. All unawares, Bridges had smoothed the path that led his friend to Rome, and soothed his restless mind by offering him the quiet retreat of an Anglican vicarage and his unassuming company. It was a boon Hopkins would never forget.

III. THE PARTING OF THE WAYS

Bridges had some merit in acting so kindly. His friend's

---

[1] *Ibid.*, Letter VIII, p. 9. The next three quotations are taken from Letter VI, pp. 4–8.

conversion to Romanism meant the loss of a real fellowship with a spirit seemingly well attuned to his own. Whatever the future held in reserve, something was gone that could never be found again. However devoted they might be to each other, their intimacy was gone. Paradoxically, Rochdale had seen their friendship ripen and deepen, but at the same time be crippled for ever. Hopkins was a friend both found and lost at the same time.

In September, 1866, Bridges had kept enough of his old religious sympathies to understand—at least for a brief period—why Hopkins, with a good dozen other university students, was going over to Rome. But he had begun to lose interest in religion and to regard it with a certain moral superiority.[1] After the first shock of surprise, he could not help teasing the new convert in his letters. He asked Hopkins what he thought of the quiet way he had taken his disclosure. But had he taken it really so quietly? Was he not using his alleged indifference as a wet blanket to damp Hopkins's enthusiasm? And when he pretended to doubt the reasons offered by Hopkins to justify his silence at Rochdale, or deliberately interpreted them erroneously, was he not using irony and mockery both to neutralize Hopkins's passionate earnestness and as an act of self-protection? As an Englishman and an Anglican Bridges could tolerate Hopkins's scandalous religious convictions as passing whimsies; he certainly hoped that one day his friend would revert to saner views. Irony and indifference were two methods that could be used, alternately or simultaneously, in order to prevent Hopkins from settling himself in his new faith without more ado. This may not have been fully conscious as a policy, but when it was deliberate, it may have been considered as cruel kindness.

Hopkins on his own side was not unaware of Bridges's disposition. For a man who generally went straight to the heart of the matter, it is remarkable how he fought shy of religious problems when speaking or writing to Bridges. He must have

[1] Was it at the university or much later, as a letter of February, 1875, seems to imply, that Bridges began to read Hegel? The German philosopher could not have been wholly unknown to him in 1866, and his logical pantheism may have appealed to Bridges, together with his magnifying and extolling of pure conscience. In this system the human mind is the apex of the whole creation.

realized very early that it was a vain endeavour. But, when necessary, he spoke with complete frankness, showing his friend that he could not be deceived or misled. Here is, for instance, the answer he makes to Bridges's outward show of indifference and wrong construction:

And then you ask what I thought about your taking my disclosure quietly. If I had thought the things which you put, could I have written as I did or meant to? But of course you know I thought nothing of the sort. You will force me to express again what I wanted you to believe before.[1]

The allusion might be difficult to catch if Hopkins had not, immediately under this last sentence, drawn a kind of mock commercial name-plate which clearly shows what he means.

Trumpery,
Mummery and G. M. HOPKINS Flummery
Designer.
☞ Removed to the other side of the way. ☞

He thus frankly if somewhat cynically admits that no convert to Romanism could escape the suspicion of hypocrisy, falsehood, nonsense and intrigue. But at the same time he wishes his friend to abandon such an unkind supposition.

Again, in order to prevent Bridges from taxing him with unfairness for having kept his decision to himself, he remarks quite candidly, 'You never said anything that gave me any reason to think you were being converted.'[2] He thus stops all false pretence on the part of his friend and sets things in their right proportion. And as the years went by, Bridges gave him ample reason to think that his Christian faith was becoming less and less dogmatic. Yet, although they went their opposite ways, they tried hard not to break the bonds of their friendship.

In the first years that followed Hopkins's reception into the Roman Church, it was Bridges who persistently tried to keep in touch with Hopkins. He did not allow himself to lose sight of

---

[1] *GMH to RB*, Letter VIII, p. 10.
[2] *Ibid.*, p. 9.

him. They may not have seen much of each other at Oxford, while Hopkins was preparing for Greats and the thought of it was like a mill-stone round his neck.[1] But we notice that Bridges sent his friend two invitations at a short interval, one during the long vacation in August, 1867, and the other three months later for the Christmas vacation. Each time Hopkins refused. He was assured of Bridges's kindness, but it was impossible for him to go to Rochdale in September, since he was going to Edgbaston to join the staff of teachers in Dr. Newman's Oratory.[2] In December the shortness of the vacation made it difficult for him to manage both a visit to Rochdale in the north and the Christmas festivities at home in London. He took pains in his second refusal to write affectionately.[3] He had no desire to avoid his friend.[4] When Bridges took Greats, he wrote twice, showing real interest in his success and even offering last-minute advice. On November 19 he wrote from the Oratory, 'Greats begin on Thursday [21st], I believe. If you will be properly composed and confident I have no doubt that you will do well.'[5] Bridges took a second class in Greats, and it is amusing to note that Hopkins, writing to him some time before the examination, had prophesied, 'A 2nd is the class I have always imagined you wd. get: mind it is a good one.'[6]

Early in January, 1868, Bridges left England with Lionel Muirhead[7] for a long tour in the Middle East. They were to visit Egypt and Syria. Hopkins's letters clearly show that the two friends, knowing they were not going to meet for a fairly long time, did their best to see each other in the weeks preceding this long tour. Hopkins asked Bridges to stop at Birmingham on his way home from Oxford, after degree day at the

[1] Letter XV, p. 18: 'Is not the thought of Greats like a mill-stone round your neck now? It was to me.'

[2] Letter XIV, p. 17: 'On the 10th of next month I shall go to Edgbaston; on the 17th their school begins.'

[3] Letter XVII, p. 20: 'I still think I had rather not come to Rochdale in the vacation, if you will allow me to make the refusal. But I thank you very much for the offer.'

[4] Letter XIV: 'I may be in Oxford next term for a day or less when of course I shall come to you'.

[5] Letter XVII.

[6] Letter XVI, November 12, p. 20.

[7] Muirhead was a Balliol man and a painter in water-colours. Bridges dedicated to him Bk. IV of his *Shorter Poems*.

end of the Michaelmas term. Later, having failed to see him in the Midlands, he wrote from Hampstead on Christmas Eve, inquiring,

When exactly and where shall you be in town? for I shall be here—at least as a head-quarters—till about a week—well until you sail at all events, so if you will let me know we can meet, that is you can come here.[1]

Bridges wrote back, giving his address for the brief period he would be in London. But his time being very short, he gave Hopkins an appointment at noon on January 8; unfortunately the latter could not come, his aunt having kept him. He felt truly disappointed. 'I am now at Croydon and shall not be able to see you therefore before you go. I am very sorry indeed for this: it is the great inconvenience of my invitations and that comes of the short holidays.'[2] And Hopkins added: 'This note accordingly is to say good-bye'. He only meant to bid Bridges God-speed and a prosperous journey; but he knew at the same time that when Bridges came back, six months later, his own situation would be definitely different. Teaching at the Oratory at Edgbaston did not suit him, and he had decided to end the uncertainty he was in 'about the future'. During a retreat at Easter he was to see whether he had 'a vocation to the priesthood'. This he told Bridges, asking him not to repeat it. He was also to choose between the Benedictines and the Jesuits. At the end of his retreat he came to the decision to become a Jesuit priest.

We do not know how Bridges reacted to the news. He must have been eager to know what Hopkins had resolved, for in the latter's journal[3] we read, 'June 24 [1868]—Letter from Bridges, who is now home.' Hopkins answered on June 27, and his letter must have been a great shock to one who, as we know, had an unconquerable prejudice against the Roman Church and therefore must have shared much of the horror with which his contemporaries regarded Jesuits.[4] But besides the shock,

---

[1] Letter XIX, December 24, p. 21.
[2] Letter XX, January 9, 1868, p. 22.
[3] *GMH Journals*, p. 168.
[4] In the introduction to *GMH to RB* (p. xlv) Professor L. Abbott writes: 'To

Bridges may have felt some puzzled attraction. He was given the opportunity of discovering an unknown land and observing a strange phenomenon. As a scientifically-minded spectator, he could well be interested. Hopkins, at any rate, did not want his going into the Jesuit novitiate at Roehampton to break links or to prevent all possible meetings. Since Roehampton was in south-western London, friends living in the great metropolis could pay him visits from time to time. In the very letter in which he told Bridges of his future position, he made his wish known in the clearest possible way: 'My address will then be Manresa House, Roehampton, S.W. and perhaps sometime when you are in town you might come and see me: it is quite near, and easy of access by Putney or Barnes.'[1]

It was in fact an invitation; having made it on the eve of a tour through Switzerland, Hopkins repeated it as soon as he came back to London, giving his address again and emphasizing that Roehampton was 'easily accessible'. He could have written a long letter, for having failed to see Bridges, who had come to London while he himself was on the Continent, he certainly had much to say. But he wanted his friend to come and see him, and so he wrote, expressing doubts about his own future ability to write or answer letters: 'But I hope we shall meet soon and for that reason I need not write much.'[2] One feels that Hopkins is anxious to remain on the friendliest terms with Bridges; he wants him to be convinced that, even if a few material difficulties may restrict their correspondence, their communication can remain as close as ever. Nothing can shake or sever their intellectual and artistic affinities.

Such was the hope entertained by Hopkins. It may have been wishful thinking. The strict rules of the Society might well curb his warmest desires; his studies, his own spiritual discipline, the absence of permanence in his location would certainly prevent his devoting much time to visitors or correspondents. Nevertheless he insistently urged Bridges to come and see him whenever he was in town, and he clearly did so

Bridges the priesthood raised an insuperable barrier: he had, and rightly [*sic*], a profound distrust of the Society of Jesus'.

[1] Letter XXI, June 27, p. 23.
[2] Letter XXII, August 7, p. 24.

because Bridges on his part had shown that he wanted to keep up friendly relations. Neither of the two young men could be blind to the obvious: they had come to the parting of the ways. The paths they were to follow would lead them away from each other. But in spite of everything they both tried to sever as few bonds as they could help.

The remarkable fact is that, from the evidence we possess, Bridges appears to have vied with his friend in his efforts to keep up their close personal relationship. As early as November, 1867, Bridges sent Hopkins his photograph;[1] it may look boyishly sentimental, but it reveals a feeling of affection. He also asked Hopkins about Southey's *Doctor*, a prose work in which the Romantic poet gathered all sorts of light and serious literary information, mixing legend, history, facts and fables. It was Bridges's roundabout way of letting his friend understand that he is slowly making up his mind to become a doctor. And Hopkins does not fail to take the hint.[2] Far more revealing is the addressing of Hopkins by his Christian name. This form of endearment, which was once briefly dropped but afterwards never abandoned, may simply prove that, unlike Hopkins, who felt that Bridges's surname was prettier than his Christian name, Bridges preferred his friend's Christian name. It certainly suggests a growing affection and the realization that, at the very time when he was seeing less and less of him, Hopkins was holding an important place in his heart. Does it mean more than that? Does it express, in some subconscious way, a masculine-feminine relation between two minds, one virile and balanced, the other sensitive and flexible? It is impossible to answer with any assurance. Subconsciously a masculine-feminine relationship may have existed; but since, according to shifting circumstances, either one mind or the other would seek help and guidance, the relationship itself was ever shifting, and no reliable or enlightening conclusion can be drawn from it.

[1] Hopkins may have sent his 'likeness' to Bridges in late summer, 1868. In a letter to his mother, dated September 10, 1868, he asked her to send his photograph to a friend at the Oratory. *Further Letters*, p. 105.
[2] *GMH to RB*, Letter XVI, November 12, 1867, p. 19: 'After what you tell me about the *Doctor* are you not beginning to think more particularly about what you are going to be? I want to hear about this'.

The only positive element is a mutual tenderness. 'Dearest Bridges' faithfully echoed 'Dearest Gerard'.[1] And there is no better explanation of it than of Montaigne for his friendship with La Boétie. They knew they could confide in each other; they knew that there existed between them an unexplained, unexplainable but absolute love. Their mutual tenderness was a mutual trust. Every letter of Hopkins brings a new proof that he spoke freely and intimately: his feelings, his passing moods, his uncertainties, his fits of sadness were never concealed. Bridges may not have been so free in disclosing his thoughts and impressions, but we may surmise that he was far more frank with Hopkins than with any other friend, and this may well explain the burning of his own letters when he decided to let the general public know as little of himself as he possibly could.

Having been invited to visit Hopkins at Roehampton, if he could not see him before he entered the novitiate, Bridges managed to pay a farewell visit to Hampstead on August 25, a fortnight before Hopkins left his home for Manresa House. In the journal of 1868 we read the following note:

August 25.—Fine; cold wind. Bridges came up and Rover bit him. After this we went down to town together and talked in Hyde Park.[2]

In 1869 Bridges, who had started on his medical studies and was residing in London, paid his friend a visit or two. He went to Roehampton some time in April, but failed to see the young Jesuit novice, for 'at the time the community was unluckily in a three days' retreat'.[3] Such ill luck did not deter Bridges from his intention to see Hopkins in his new surroundings. In Octo-

[1] Hopkins used the words 'Dearest Bridges' in the letter of November 12, 1867, for the first time. 'Dearest Gerard' begins the only letter left by Bridges (May 18, 1889: *Further Letters*, Appendix III, p. 433). In his introductory sonnet Bridges apostrophizes 'Gerard'.

[2] *GMH Journals*, p. 187.

[3] *GMH to RB*, Letter XXIII, April 29, 1869, p. 25. Abbott in a note to the letter gives an entry of the journal of 1869: 'A penance which I was doing from January 25 to July 25 prevented my seeing much that half-year'. This might lead us to suppose that Hopkins had more or less condemned himself to solitude. But his penance—as the context clearly shows (*GMH Journals*, p. 190)—concerns his love of looking at nature and at various delicate details of land and skyscape.

ber, the same year, he sent a note saying he would come the next Sunday, but Hopkins answered that Sunday was not really suitable—'I shall be able to be but a short time with you'[1]—and suggested Saturday afternoon. From a letter to his mother[2] we know that Hopkins saw his friend on Monday, October 18. So there was at least one meeting at Roehampton. But we cannot say whether they met or not at other times during the next eighteen months. And yet Bridges, as we know, was a medical student in London,[3] and opportunities for paying visits to Manresa House must have been numerous. Did he take advantage of them? Once again we cannot answer with any assurance.

There is one certainty. The next letter from Hopkins is dated April 2, 1871, and so there is a gap of a year and a half in the correspondence. Hopkins has been at Stonyhurst in Lancashire for the last six months, and his letter implies the existence of some kind of estrangement for which he is ready to take the blame.

I hear nothing whatever of you and the fault is certainly mine. I am going to address this to Rochdale, because you may have changed your lodgings in town . . . I shall not write more now, indeed I have nothing to say. Please tell me all about yourself. I am sure I must have behaved unkindly when you came to Roehampton.[4]

When did they meet last at Roehampton? Was it really on October 18, 1869? What did they discuss? What possible reasons can Hopkins have had to 'behave unkindly', unless they touched upon some controversial religious point? Although Hopkins feels 'sure' about his own unkindness, this may be simply a scruple of conscience, as was often the case with him,[5]

---

[1] *GMH to RB*, Letter XXIV, October 14, 1869, p. 26.

[2] *Further Letters*, Letter XV, p. 107.

[3] Bridges signed on as a student at St. Bartholomew's Hospital medical school on November 6, 1869, giving his home address as the Vicarage, Rochdale, and his London address as 25 Great Ormond Street. There seems to be no justification for the assertion (first made in *St. Bartholomew's Hospital Journal*, May, 1930, p. 138, and repeated by Professor Abbott) that he was entered in 1871.

[4] *GMH to RB*, Letter XXV, April 2, 1871, pp. 26–27.

[5] On his return from Rochdale in September, 1866, Hopkins had concluded his excuses for his silence with a severe and unreasonable self-criticism: 'This will

without any real cause. Bridges, immersed in his medical studies, may well have found so much interest in his new life and his new friends that silence, in spite of Hopkins's misgivings, would be a natural consequence.[1] As a matter of fact, Bridges had given such an excuse to his friend when he had seen him at Roehampton. The letter Mrs. Hopkins received from her son establishes this. As it provides at the same time a remarkable testimony of Hopkins's feelings towards Bridges, the whole paragraph must be quoted.

The day before yesterday, Bridges called here: he is now in town reading medicine (at 35 Great Ormond Street) and if you thought he wd. like it and you liked it yourself you might, I think, ask him to Hampstead some time—he was a great friend of mine and very kind to me and is very nice in himself, as I believe you know. I shd. say however that he says he always tries to refuse invitations to dinner now in order not to interfere with his professional reading.[2]

This passage is of great importance. It testifies to the earnestness with which Bridges has embarked upon his medical studies; it also reveals Hopkins's intention to bring his friend into his family circle and thus create new bonds of intimacy, or at least to keep in touch with him through his near relatives. In his praise of Bridges he gives two reasons for their great friendship: Bridges's past kindness to him, and his 'niceness' in himself. But why does he write, 'He *was* a great friend of mine'? Is he thinking of the years at Oxford, or the three weeks spent at Rochdale, and comparing in his heart the warm intimacy of yesterday with the more conventional friendliness of today? It may have been a mere slip of the pen, but it betrays a subtle feeling of change and dispossession. The green lawns and meadows of colleges and vicarage were fast receding from the two young men, but they left imperishable memories.

make it plain how I feel that wherever I go I must either do no good or else harm', a plain exaggeration. (Letter VI, September 22, 1866, p. 7.)

[1] Between 1867 and 1874 Bridges made several long tours abroad, and these absences may also partly explain his silence.

[2] *Further Letters*, Letter LV, October 20, 1869, pp. 107–108.

III

Oppositions and Misunderstandings

I. BRIDGES'S POLITICAL VIEWS

When Bridges and Hopkins were walking along the paths of Hyde Park or in the garden of Manresa House, what were the themes of their conversation? We can imagine the earnest Jesuit novice and the self-controlled student discussing poetry and prosody, or music. They would have carefully avoided religious problems, but it is quite possible that they discussed social questions. We know that Hopkins always had a strong interest in philosophy, and that in controversial matters he was alive to the fact that 'strong persuasion is nothing when you do not know what is really said by the other side'.[1] In his journal he liked to record the more important political and social events, either in order to keep in touch with the outside world or to ponder over the sad fate of nations and men.[2] For instance, he carefully transcribed the principal dates of the Franco-Prussian War in 1870–1, the insurrection of the Commune and its suppression, the capture of Rome by the troops of Garibaldi, and such uncommon or striking incidents as the death of a fasting girl, the first sitting of a negro in the American Congress, and the Tichborne trial.[3] Hopkins could also read in *Blackwood's Magazine* an article entitled 'The Battle of Dorking, Reminiscences of a Volunteer' which gave an account, supposedly told fifty years later, of the defeat at Dorking of an English army, composed chiefly of volunteers, by invading Prussian forces— a strange amalgam

---

[1] *Further Letters*, Letter XLVIII to his mother, October 20, 1866, p. 99. He uses the argument against his family. As Anglicans they have never examined the claims of the Roman Church: he has.

[2] See *GMH Journals*, pp. 202–203 and 217–18.

[3] For the trial for perjury of Arthur Orton, claimant to the Tichborne title and estates, see J. D. Woodruff, *The Tichborne Claimant*, a book that even in 1957 must carry the sub-title, 'A Victorian Mystery'.

of prophecy and propaganda which shocked British opinion at the time and was stigmatized by Gladstone as a piece of 'alarmism'. In his journal, Hopkins wrote, 'The Battle of Dorking and the fear of the Revolution make me sad now.'[1] Hopkins was keenly aware of the sordidness of things, of the squalor of towns and the misery of the poor. Although he was to have more immediate acquaintance with them later in life, as a parish priest in the busy districts of the industrial towns of Lancashire, his teachers at Roehampton and the Jesuit preachers who came to Manresa House cannot have failed to prepare him for the miserable conditions in which factory workers were often to be found. Bridges himself, as a future casualty physician, knew he would come into direct contact with the poorer classes. Already in the Children's Hospital in Great Ormond Street he must be meeting with pain and distress.[2]

In the early 'seventies social and political problems loomed large. There was social agitation in Europe. The influence of the Communist Manifesto, published in 1848, was slowly developing; its socialist revolutionary ideas were attractive to the underpaid workers. The hope of triumphing over the ruling classes was strengthened by the international status they had given to their organization. In 1864 the International Working Men's Association had been founded in London, and all workers hoped that world-wide union would give more driving-force to their movement. Here and there rebellions flared up and were quashed by Governments, which acted violently from fear as much as from anger or in self-defence. The Commune insurrection in Paris had been a terrible experience, frightening most people, and bringing both hope and despair to the lower classes. In England the Government was discussing the Irish problem with a view to quieting the Fenians. Ruskin had begun to publish in monthly instalments his letters addressed to the 'Workmen of England', and his denunciations, if at times inconsistent, were pugnacious and satirical. As

[1] *GMH Journals*, August 6, 1871, pp. 213 and 413.

[2] In 1878 Bridges was to publish in the *St. Bartholomew's Hospital Reports* 'An Account of the Casualty Department', giving a graphic description of the hard, almost inhuman work the physicians on the staff were put to. See *Collected Essays*, No. XXX, pp. 264–97.

Trevelyan points out, there was no strong movement of socialism, but growing discontent with the spirit of *laissez-faire*.[1]

Obviously, such problems could not leave Bridges and Hopkins totally indifferent. If their attitudes had depended only on their earlier education, they would have been almost identical. They certainly shared with Ruskin the opinion that industry and factories were destroying beauty and corrupting both rich and poor, but the views they held were conservative. Their respective studies, however, were to colour their views deeply.

All through his life Bridges, with his scientific and logical training, reacted strongly against socialism and defended his own conceptions of law and order. The views he expressed in his 'Epistle to a Socialist in London' in 1903,[2] and in *The Testament of Beauty* a quarter of a century later, can be regarded as representing his most constant political opinions.

For him 'all our study endeth emptily in full doubt', and considering that it was 'never intended for mortal fancy to compass . . . the divine intention', he concludes that,

> from first purposes unknown
> None should seek to deduce ideal laws to be liv'd by.
> (Epistle II, 10–11)

From the wealth, abundance and generosity of Nature, he deduces that

> the symmetric allotments
> Where nothing exceedeth, nothing encroacheth, nor assaileth,
> (*Ibid.*, 209–210)

are unthinkable. He refuses the stern regulation of the socialist and asks:

> What madness works to delude you,
> Being a man, that you see not mankind's predilection
> Is for Magnificence, Force, Freedom, Bounty . . .
> (*Ibid.* 220–22)

[1] G. M. Trevelyan, *English Social History*, 1948, p. 558.
[2] In *Poems in Classical Prosody* (*Poet. Works*, pp. 423–36). The 'Epistle' was first published in *Monthly Review*, July, 1903.

Pleading for equality, on the ground that it is just, is a dangerous thing:

> Should that once come about, then alas for this merry England,
> Sunk in a grey monotone of drudgery, dreamily poring
> O'er her illumin'd page of history, faln to regretful
> Worship of ancestors, with nought now left to delight her,
> Nought to attain, save one nurst hope, one ambition only—
> Red Revolution, a wild Reawakening, and a Renaissance.
> (*Ibid.* 264–9)

Revolution spells hope in the possibilities of change. But can Man be changed?

> If man's propensity is vain,
> Vulgar, inane, unworthy; 'tis also vain to bewail it:
> Think you to change his skin? 'Twere scale by scale to regraft it
> With purer traditions; and who shall amend the amenders?
> (*Ibid.* 285–8)

Taking such traditional pessimistic views for granted, Bridges advocates his own quiet way of living, his middle-way—

> I, that feeding on Ideals in temperat' estate
> Seem so wealthy to poor Lazarus, so needy to Dives.
> (*Ibid.* 319–30)

In the 'Epistle' and in the second book of *The Testament of Beauty*, Bridges illustrates his point by comparing the modern socialistic or communistic system to a bee-hive, and the moral lesson included in the comparison is clearly drawn in the lines that close the long passage of the *Testament*.

> I say 'tis plain, that (if the things
> be comparable) then with the beehive compared
> the New-world slave-plantations wer abodes of bliss.
> (Selfhood, 439–41)[1]

Bridges never accepted the 'sophistry' of Communist theories. Nowell C. Smith speaks of his 'high disdain of any sort of

---

[1] *RB Poet. Works*, p. 606.

communism',[1] but it is more than that. It is utter distrust and spirited mockery. He cannot 'prefer so blindly the race to the unit', and 'as artist' he approves

> Far other ideals than what seem needful in action.
>
> (Epistle II, 422)

Bridges's views and arguments against Communism need not be discussed. He shared the prejudices of his class, and the principles he set forth were to be expected from an individual artist who always cared more for liberty within a certain hierarchical order of things than for equality and democratic levelling:

> —a doctrin kindly at heart, that cajoleth alike
> diffidence of the ruler and conceit of the crowd,
> who in collusion float its credit; and awhile
> their ship of state runneth like the yacht in the race
> that with full bellying sail, for lack of seamanship,
> seemeth to forge ahead while it loseth leeway.
>
> (Ethick, 253–8)[2]

There was in him the traditional lack of confidence in the rule of the people, and his classical and aristocratic upbringing drew him away from 'the madding crowd'. If we want to understand his reaction to the new socialist ideal as well as to any notion or system, we can turn to the poem entitled 'Johannes Milton, Senex',[3] in which it is possible to read his own philosophy and method. It is the philosophy of an honest sceptic, who, being unable to see and know God, to apprehend His wisdom and His eternal purpose, determines to trust his own spirit, after having tested all systems and arguments and 'reproved' all that seemed to him unworthy.

> Therefore will I be bound to no studied system
> Nor argument, nor with delusion enslave me,
> Nor seek to please Him in any foolish invention,
> Which my spirit within me, that loveth beauty
> And hateth evil, hath reprov'd as unworthy.

---

[1] N. C. Smith, *Notes on 'The Testament of Beauty'*, 2nd edition, 1931, p. 17.

[2] *RB Poet. Works*, p. 664.

[3] *Poet. Works*, p. 439, *Poems in Classical Prosody*, No. 6. The poem was written in 1903 or 1904.

This may well present itself as the profession of faith of a
doubter and a cynic. Yet Bridges kept a sense of piety and duty
which gives to his free thinking the grave tone of worship.

> But I cherish my freedom in loving service,
> Gratefully adoring for delight beyond asking
> Or thinking, and in hours of anguish and darkness
> Confiding always on His excellent greatness.

II. HOPKINS'S RED LETTER

The subtle balance struck between indifference to all systems and the 'loving service' of God and Beauty is one of the
peculiar traits of Bridges's intellect. A spirit of reverence and a
spirit of doubt dwell in him in quiet company. He distrusts
Man and his inventions; he 'adores' and 'confides in' God:
thus can he solve with no great qualms his own problems. All
parties and all churches are suspect to him; they can only
arouse his utter mistrust or his taunting mockery. Keeping
himself free from all possible errors, he stands apart, grateful
and phlegmatic.

Not so with Hopkins. He had made a definite choice and
sided with one Church. Politically, in the early eighteen-seven-
ties he was deeply stirred by events on the Continent and particularly in France. Fighting against his own conservative
views, he was turning towards the social problems of his day
and trying to understand them. Bridges could afford to remain a staunch individualist. Hopkins, as a Catholic priest,
could not. His letter to his friend on August 2, 1871, giving his
frank opinion about Communism—he was later to call it his
'red letter'—clearly shows how differently the two men felt
on this grave matter.

One may wonder why Hopkins ever broached the subject,
choosing Bridges as his confidant, when he must have known
that his friend could not accept his views at all. It was a psychological blunder and the only excuse we can find for it is his
gradual loss of touch with Bridges. As it is quite possible that
they had not met or corresponded for more than eighteen
months, resuming an exchange of letters may not have been **an**

easy affair at a time when they realized how far Stonyhurst lay from London.

Hopkins had written in April, 1871. To his complaint, 'I hear nothing whatever of you', and to his request, 'Please tell me all about yourself,' Bridges evidently answered with a long letter, giving reasons for his silence and all necessary information about himself. He responded fairly promptly; we know that he wrote his letter in May. Hopkins, who always took some time before replying, wrote again in August.[1] It is important to note that it was some sly remark, possibly some play upon words, made by Bridges in his letter, that set Hopkins on his provocative declaration. The allusion in the letter is obscure: we can only surmise that Bridges spoke of the International humorously or teasingly, for Hopkins, adopting a similar tone, wrote:

> I feel inclined to begin by asking whether you are secretary to the International as you seem to mean me to think nothing too bad for you but then I remember that you never relished 'the intelligent artisan'.[2]

We may infer that Bridges had contrasted his own life with that led by Hopkins, opposing perhaps the materialistic ways of the world to the pious and secluded existence of his Jesuit friend. The words in inverted commas may be an expression used by Bridges in his letter; but it is difficult to understand his determined opposition to the 'intelligent artisan' unless he had been referring to the social problem and the men who, in the Workers' Unions, were trying to obtain full recognition of their statutes and activities by the Government.

Indeed there were ample reasons for a young man living in London to touch upon such questions. Parliament was discussing the new Trade Union Bill that was to be passed the same year. The Education Act of 1870 had provided for new Board Schools for the children of the poorer classes, and no doubt those schools would help many boys to become 'intelligent artisans'. Bridges may also have alluded to the Paris Com-

---

[1] *GMH to RB*, Letter XXVI, August 2, 1871, p. 28, 'I can hardly believe this is August and your letter dated May'.

[2] *Ibid.*, p. 27.

mune, crushed ruthlessly by Thiers late in May. Even if Hopkins had not mentioned Bridges's strong opposition to the Socialists, we could assume it, knowing as we do what were his deep-rooted prejudices. We can therefore easily imagine Bridges's dismay when he read his friend's letter and came to the strange admission, 'Horrible to say, in a manner I am a Communist.' It must have seemed to him sheer extravagance and reprehensible irresponsibility.

It is only fair to say that Hopkins's reasoning was forcible and offered a clear view of the whole problem. At the same time it made the necessary reservations and admitted possible corrections. His main points were as follows:

I must tell you I am always thinking of the Communist future. The too intelligent artisan is master of the situation I believe. Perhaps it is what everyone believes, I do not see the papers or hear strangers often enough to know. It is what Carlyle has long threatened and foretold. . . . He preaches obedience but I do not think he has done much except to ridicule instead of strengthening the hands of the powers that be. . . .

However I am afraid some great revolution is not far off. Horrible to say, in a manner I am a Communist. Their ideal bating some things is nobler than that professed by any secular statesman I know of (I must own I live in bat-light and shoot at a venture). Besides it is just. I do not mean the means of getting to it are. But it is a dreadful thing for the greatest and most necessary part of a very rich nation to live a hard life without dignity, knowledge, comforts, delight, or hopes in the midst of plenty—which plenty they make.

They profess that they do not care what they wreck and burn, the old civilization and order must be destroyed. This is a dreadful look-out but what has the old civilization done for them? As it at present stands in England it is itself in great measure founded on wrecking. But they got none of the spoils, they came in for nothing but harm from it then and thereafter. England has grown hugely wealthy but this wealth has not reached the working classes; I expect it has made their condition worse.

Besides this iniquitous order the old civilization embodies another order mostly old and what is new in direct entail from the old, the old religion, learning, law, art, etc., and all the history that is preserved in standing monuments. But as the working classes have not been educated they know next to nothing of all this and cannot be expected to care if they destroy it.

The more I look the more black and deservedly black the future looks, so I will write no more.[1]

The true diagnosis of the situation, the explanation—not the justification—of the blind, destructive power of the uneducated masses, the clear exposure of such conservative critics as the ageing Carlyle who offered few or no practical suggestions but

most inefficacious-strenuous heaven-protestations, caterwaul, and Cassandra-wailings . . . *too* dubious moonstone-grindings and on the whole impracticable-practical unveracities,

—in short, every argument in the letter distinctly proves that Hopkins had been pondering over this dramatic situation and its far too easily detectable consequences. He had certainly not read Marx; his own political views were not socialistic but he was not going to shut his eyes to the bare facts. Both in the name of justice and in favour of a more sensible social and economic policy, Hopkins utters a protest which does him honour as a man and as a priest.

Did Bridges consider this moving letter as a blatant effort on the part of his friend to 'force emotion into theological channels'[2] and to give to his radical views the moral warrant of his Church? No doubt Gerard was a dear friend, if somewhat unpredictable. But really, from Puseyism to Romanism, then to the Society of Jesus, and now to Communism, this was going too far! He must show him that he was not prepared to stand any nonsense. He considered the letter as a proof of wrong thinking and in very bad taste. He disliked these pessimistic views. Anything that could foster class hatred, as the letter certainly could, was to be checked. Therefore he decided not to answer. Hopkins would remember that his friend held totally different views, and more sober ones. His silence would clearly

---

[1] *Ibid.*, pp. 27–28. In the original the whole argument is given in one long paragraph. To stress the process of reasoning, each new consideration is given a new paragraph above.

[2] This phrase Bridges used in his preface to his friend's poems to describe his 'mannerism'. It may serve here as a direct expression of his feelings. See *GMH Poems*, p. 204.

mean that he was not interested in such sermons, with which he had no patience.

And so from August 2, 1871, to January 22, 1874, that is for practically two and a half years, there was no exchange of letters. It remained for Hopkins to take the first steps towards resuming a correspondence that really seemed no longer possible. When he wrote again, he did not refuse to acknowledge his blunder, feeling certain that his 'red opinions' had 'disgusted' Bridges. He reminded his friend that 'he had little reason to be red', and pleaded that he had said 'nothing that might not fairly be said'. He gently rebuked Bridges for his long silence—'It seems to show a greater keenness about politics than is common'—and tried to make him realize his oversensitiveness. 'I think, my dear Bridges, to be so much offended about that red letter was excessive.'[1] It *was* excessive; but Bridges's stern and narrow attitude was to remain a warning for Hopkins. He was to remember that some topics or problems were not to be touched upon by him. Henceforward, whenever he discussed certain moral or religious or political matters with Bridges, he did it with the utmost care so as not to hurt him. In most cases he merely gave his opinion frankly, but never sought to turn it into a lesson or into advice, unless advice was definitely asked for.

III. 'STIRRING THE RELUCTANT FIRE'

The 'red letter' incident was the major incident in the literary friendship of Bridges and Hopkins. It could have broken it irredeemably. In fact in the long period between October, 1869, and February, 1877, Hopkins wrote only four letters and, very likely, received only as many answers. The intervals between those letters were one-and-a-half years, two-and-a-half years, and again two years. One must admit that few friendships would have remained alive on such scanty nourishment. It tends to prove, as we had occasion to show, that the bonds of friendship which linked the two men were so strong as to be impervious to the destructive action of time, distance and opposite views. But it is true, as Professor Abbott has remarked, that

[1] *GMH to RB*, Letter XXVII, January 22, 1874, p. 29.

when there was a danger that communication might cease, 'fortunately Hopkins faced the task of stirring the reluctant fire'.[1] As an excuse for his few letters, Bridges said he objected to their being opened before they reached Hopkins. He interpreted as an act of suspicion towards himself a general regulation which is meant as a personal sacrifice on the part of any Jesuit living in a community. He had to obtain from his friend a conciliatory explanation: the envelopes were torn half-open, but practically no letter was ever read by a superior.[2]

From February, 1877, to April, 1889, the correspondence between Bridges and Hopkins was essentially a correspondence of poets and literary men. Their letters treated a great variety of subjects, as we shall see in our next chapters. The tone was always serious, but there is no restraint and mutual confidence is complete. During those twelve years Hopkins wrote 143 letters or post-cards, which gives an average of ten to twelve letters a year. To no other friend did Hopkins write so regularly and so intimately. In the same period of years, he wrote only thirty-eight letters to his parents, twenty-nine to his good friend Baillie, and forty-one to R. W. Dixon, while from August, 1883, to May, 1888, he wrote twenty-six to Coventry Patmore. The figures speak for themselves; they show beyond doubt that no one could compete with Bridges for the first place in Hopkins's heart. To no other did the Jesuit poet show so much warmth and tenderness of sentiment.

Being dutifully obedient to the orders of his superiors—he humorously spoke of himself as 'Fortune's football'[3]—Hopkins went from Roehampton to Stonyhurst, thence to St. Asaph in North Wales, thence to various parish churches in Oxford, Liverpool and Glasgow, back to Roehampton and Stonyhurst, and finally to Dublin, where he was to spend the last five years of his life as a Professor of Greek at the Catholic University

---

[1] *Ibid.*, Introduction, p. xliv.

[2] *Ibid.*, Letter XXIX, February 24, 1877, p. 32. Owing to the rarity of letters exchanged, Bridges had ceased to call Hopkins by his Christian name, as he used to do. In a postscript to this letter Hopkins asked him to resume the old habit.

[3] Letter CVI, July 26, 1883, p. 183: 'But I have long been Fortune's football and am blowing up the bladder of resolution big and buxom for another kick of her foot'.

College. In spite of these frequent changes of residence he tried to meet Bridges whenever an opportunity occurred. Such pleasant occasions were few and far between. Let us record them now, for they offer a more lively image of a friendship which, unfortunately for the persons concerned, had to rely most on the written page.

At once we notice that both friends seem to have been quite willing to meet, though with less eagerness than might be expected. They sent each other invitations, accepted them, but seldom succeeded in following them up. Through a certain indifference to possibilities or a passive acceptance of things as they were, they never met regularly. The last twelve years of their friendship offer a tale of opportunities missed, and of brief encounters leaving food for regret. And during those short visits, there often took place some small incident, arising from a slight misunderstanding, as if they were to be reminded that no friendship ever runs smooth and that they had 'certain sensitive places'[1] on which they must not touch. There certainly was on either side a definite shrinking from any meeting that might impair their mutual affection or shake their confidence, an anxious avoidance of explanations that might make intimate oppositions too glaring. But it is true that apart from their preference for safer and quieter encounters through the medium of letters, their busy lives and their common shyness are sufficient to account for the infrequency of their meetings.

Twelve meetings in the course of twelve years is a small record indeed. Is it not remarkable—and rather surprising—that Hopkins, who spent a year at Roehampton teaching rhetoric from September, 1873, to August, 1874, never once mentions a visit to Bridges although his journal records many excursions to London, a stay at his parents' house at Hampstead and meetings with many other old friends? Yet when Bridges sent him an invitation a year later, when Hopkins was at St. Asaph in North Wales, the answer rings with a true note of regret:

[1] In Letter LXXVI, June 28, 1881, p. 133, Hopkins writes, 'As for being able to ruffle me if you chose, no doubt if you touched me on certain sensitive places you would not only ruffle but deeply wound'.

But if you had sent me such an invitation last year, when I really was at Roehampton, what a pleasure it would have been and what a break in the routine of rhetoric, which I taught so badly and so painfully.[1]

It is plain that, had he merely expressed such a wish, the invitation would have come a good many months earlier. But in 1874 Hopkins was still uncertain about the feelings of his friend towards him.

The situation was quite different in 1877. As soon as he knew that he was to spend a fortnight with his family at Hampstead, Hopkins sent a post-card to Bridges. 'I hope to be in town for a fortnight or so from the 25th. Shall I be able to see you?'[2] Bridges concealed his pleasure by giving to his invitation the excuse of having been solicited. He got the following answer:

I was not so brazen as to give myself a tacit invitation to stay with you, as your note seems to imply. Parentage of course will 'put me up', up at Hampstead. But since you say I am to come for dinner, and that at 7, and I am unwilling to be out late, it will be necessary, I think, for me to avail myself of your offer and sleep that night. I look forward, I need not say, to seeing and hearing your treasures (poetical and musical) and yourself.[3]

Bridges was then living at 52 Bedford Square with his mother, Mrs. Molesworth, who had come to join her son in London after the death of her husband in April, 1877.[4] The two friends met certainly once or twice, since in a letter written before returning to North Wales Hopkins thanks Bridges for his 'kind entertainments' and regrets that he will have 'no opportunity of seeing you again either at your house or here'.[5] Bridges may have gone to Hampstead, but it is far from certain. As we have already noticed, most of the invitations came from Bridges; and this might suggest merely that Hopkins, in spite of his

[1] Letter XXVIII, February 20, 1875, p. 30.
[2] Postcard XXXIII, July 18, 1877, p. 41.
[3] Letter XXXIV, July 23, 1877, p. 42.
[4] Letter XXXII, June 13, 1877, p. 41: 'I am very glad your mother is coming to live with you and shall have all the more reason to visit you—if ever that day should come.'
[5] Letter XXXVI, August 10, 1877, p. 43.

parents' kindness towards him, could not act quite freely. But it seems that Bridges, for some unknown reason,[1] fought shy of paying visits to the Hopkins family at Hampstead.

> By the by I should have told you that I would long ago have asked you to dine and sleep here (the latter now impossible) but I thought, and think, that you would not care.[2]

This casual remark made by Hopkins, who was undoubtedly willing to return his friend's kindness, implies that he is aware of certain fixed limits beyond which Bridges will not go. Being independent and doing what they pleased when they pleased was in fact a tacit rule with both men.

In 1878, Hopkins being a preacher at the Jesuit Church, Farm Street, Bridges went to hear him. He was then about to leave London for the Surrey hills[3] and seems to have lingered a few days more in town in order to see and hear his friend. Curiosity must have played no small part in his decision to stay; hearing Hopkins preach was too unexpected an opportunity to be missed. He duly went to Farm Street on Sunday, August 4, and gave his impressions with a pinch of salt. It appears that the preacher hesitated once or twice through loss of memory. Bridges thought it was nervousness. Hopkins wrote:

> I was very little nervous at the beginning and not at all after. It was pure forgetting and flurry. The delivery was not good, but I hope to get a good one in time. I shall welcome any criticisms which are not controversy. I am glad you did not like the music and sorry you did not like the mass.[4]

Did Bridges go to hear others of his friend's sermons at Farm Street? We have no means of knowing. But he certainly had occasion to discuss rhetoric and the art of preaching with him,

---

[1] Had Mrs. Hopkins invited him, as her son had suggested? Had Bridges declined the invitation? Did the three Misses Hopkins frighten the eligible bachelor?

[2] Letter XXXV, August 8, 1877, p. 43.

[3] Hopkins's letters of July and August, 1878, tend to prove that Bridges was often in town. He may have gone to Surrey for a short period in July or for the weekends.

[4] *GMH to RB*, Postcard XLVI, August 8, 1878, p. 57.

for they met two or three times at Bedford Square in July and August.

We learn, from passing remarks in a letter of 1882 and in a letter to R. W. Dixon, that in 1879 the two poet-friends—for by then poetry and prosody had become their central subjects of discussion—met in Oxford and took a walk along the Cowley Road;[1] and again in 1880 they saw each other during the summer season. In 1881 Bridges was severely ill with pneumonia, and hearing this on July 2, Hopkins promised a visit, if nothing hindered him, on July 6[2]—a visit which he paid.

He had reason to hope that the illness would not be very serious, for Bridges's constitution was strong and healthy. But it did turn out to be serious; Bridges recovered very slowly and had to go to Italy and Sicily for the winter months. After the complete restoration of his health he retired from medical practice, as he had long meant to do, in order to dedicate himself entirely to poetry. He left London in September, 1882, and went to live with his mother in the delightful Berkshire garden-village of Yattendon. But before he left London he took advantage of Hopkins's return to Roehampton[3] and visited him there on June 4 and 8.

No encounter of Bridges with Roman Catholic rites was a simple or plain-sailing adventure. His instinctive dislike of ceremonies, that to him seemed so near to superstitious worship, he could ill conceal even in front of his friend, whom he was ready to tease though unwilling to hurt. Hopkins's kindness during his illness had touched him. He could not hide from himself that Hopkins's latest letters were most affectionate; they betrayed joy at his recovery and revealed the dismay and anguish that his possible loss would have meant to the lonely priest-poet who cared for his affection. He could not be indifferent to such tender and cheerful words as,

I hope, my dear heart, you are now really better; not better, well; strong, vigorous, lusty, beefish, as apt to pull an oar as to turn

---

[1] Letter LXXXV, June 10, 1882, p. 148.
[2] Letter LXXVI, June 28–July 3, 1881, p. 133.
[3] Hopkins was at Roehampton from October, 1881, to August, 1882, for his 'tertianship', a year of spiritual retreat.

GERARD HOPKINS, 1880

a sonnet with the best in either kind. And we may now shortly hope to meet. For I suppose I shall be at Roehampton tomorrow.[1]

He had answered as soon as he was back in London, and had asked his friend to propose a suitable day. Hopkins had suggested May 18, Ascension Day, 'in the afternoon, the earlier the better'.[2] Finally Bridges came on Sunday, June 4, accompanied by Bertie Molesworth, the son of his eldest sister. The Jesuit's heart 'warmed towards' the boy[3] but he had not expected his visit and although he said to Bridges, 'If you were to bring him again I shd. be glad to see him,' he could not help expressing his disappointment: 'It cannot be denied nevertheless that the presence of a third person is a restraint upon confidential talk.'

Was it a slight feeling of irritation that made him refuse to let Bridges buy a few peaches which he had noticed in the garden of Manresa House? Did Bridges in a playful mood offer to steal them? At any rate he made Hopkins feel 'wretched'.[4] In the *Testament of Beauty* Bridges has given his own version of the incident, and it may well be, as he says, that the scrupulous priest did not want to indulge the taste of the sweet plushy fruit, a sacrifice for which his lay friend could find no good reason.

> And so,
> when the young poet my companion in study
> and friend of my heart refused a peach at my hands,
> he being then a housecarl in Loyola's menie,
> 'twas that he fear'd the savor of it, and when he waived
> his scruple to my banter, 'twas to avoid offence.
> But I, upon thatt day which after fifty years
> is near as yesterday, was no stranger to fear
> of pleasure, but had grown fearful of thatt fear.
> (Ethick, 433–41)

---

[1] Letter LXXXI, April 3, 1882, p. 143.

[2] Letter LXXXII, May 15, 1882, p. 144.

[3] Letter LXXXIII, June 5, 1882, p. 145. Bridges's sister Maria Elizabeth had married (Sir) Guilford Lindsey Molesworth in August, 1854, two months before her mother married his widowed father.

[4] Letter LXXXVII, September 27, 1882, p. 152. Hopkins gives a spirited description of Stonyhurst College and ends 'and, what caps all, if I were shewing it you, as I hope to do . . . you could not make me wretched now by either stealing or buying fruit', a direct allusion to the incident three months before.

When the poet wrote those lines some forty-five years later he had had time to reflect on the deeper meaning of Hopkins's attitude. Although he did not share his friend's asceticism, he could explain it, in all fairness to his delicate feelings.

>   yet since
> the sublimation of life whereto the Saints aspire
> is a self-holocaust, their sheer asceticism
> is justified in them; the more because the bent
> and nativ color of mind that leadeth them aloof,
> or driveth, is thatt very delicacy of sense,
> whereby a pinprick or a momentary whiff
> or hairbreadth motion freëth the detent of force
> that can distract them wholly from their high pursuit.
>
>   (*Ibid.* 441–9)[1]

But on that June day in 1882 he had been shocked, and must have shown it.

Coming again to Manresa House four days later, on June 8, he was to be far more deeply shocked. It was Corpus Christi Day, a festival in honour of the Eucharist. Hopkins had written the day before: "Tomorrow, Corpus Christi, you must not come: I shd. be engaged'.[2] The Jesuit knew that Bridges, if he happened to be present at the procession, would prove incapable of understanding the ceremony; he did not wish to annoy him to no purpose, nor to be wounded by any critical remarks he might make. But Bridges came. And he made remarks. And Hopkins had to be patient and explain. It was a brief piece of theology, which he must have known all the time was lost on his friend.[3]

But there was, behind Bridges's disparaging remarks, another matter of much greater concern to Hopkins. The friend who was dearest to him spoke as if these rites and ceremonies had no meaning for the 'housecarl in Loyola's menie'. How could he entertain such thoughts? How could he be so cynical towards a man whose earnestness and deep faith must be plain to him?

---

[1] *Poet. Works, The Testament of Beauty*, p. 669–70.
[2] Letter LXXXIV, June 7, 1882, p. 147.
[3] Letter LXXXVI, June 16, 1882, p. 149.

Was it, we may ask, because, having once regarded Hopkins's conversion as extravagant and lacking in common sense, Bridges believed that his whole religious life was stamped with the same marks of oddness and absurdity? Or was it some sub-conscious hope that his friend would one day abandon these foreign habits, so alien from what he considered as the sensible national traditions of England? Or again was this overt cyni-cism the expression of a man who, with many of his contem-poraries, believed that Christianity could only exist as make-believe? Possibly one could answer all three questions in the affirmative. At any rate, the attitude of both men is most re-vealing; we plumb the depth of the spiritual gap between them. Hopkins's defence of his own earnestness ends with a lesson and a warning that Bridges certainly remembered years later.

It is long since such things had any significance for you. But what is strange and unpleasant is that you sometimes speak as if they had in reality none for me and you were only waiting with a certain disgust till I too should be disgusted with myself enough to throw off the mask . . . Yet I can hardly think you do not think I am in earnest. And let me say, to take no higher ground, that with-out earnestness there is nothing sound or beautiful in character and that a cynical vein much indulged coarsens everything in us. Not that you do overindulge this vein in other matters: why then does it bulk out in that diseased and varicose way in this?[1]

'Strange and unpleasant' though it was, Bridges's mental attitude towards the religion of his Jesuit friend could not change. Whatever smacked of Christolatry or Mariolatry or Jesuitism 'disgusted' him. The more he cared for the poet or the man in Hopkins, the more he wished to show him that he did not care for the world he lived in and for its principles. But one feels at the same time that Bridges knew he had strong prejudices and wanted to keep them. Hopkins, who, as a priest, cared deeply for the spiritual welfare of his friend, always touched on this prickly matter with diffidence, and only after much hesitation.[2] He was aware that Bridges would not only

[1] Letter LXXXV, June 10, 1882, p. 148.
[2] See Letter LI, January 19, 1879, p. 60 ('You understand of course that I desire to see you a Catholic . . .'), and Letter LII, January 29, 1879, p. 64 ('So with hesitation and fear I wrote').

be unwilling to listen to argument or exhortation but would almost automatically construe his meaning 'all wrong'. Once or twice he vented his grievance, but at the same time he resigned himself to his melancholy fate.

And indeed how many many times must you have misunderstood me not in my sonnets only but in moral, social, personal matters! It must be so, I see now. But it would embitter life if we knew of the misunderstandings put upon us; it would mine at least.[1]

Even when he rebuked him for being 'so unreasonable towards me' he could, no doubt for the sake of their friendship, leave things as they were, brushing aside the logical consequence of his protest. 'To think a man in my position is not in earnest is unreasonable and is to make difficulties. But if you have made them and can solve them, by a solution which must be wrong, no matter.'[2] Again and again when we read Hopkins's letters and try to guess at what his friend had written, we come to the conclusion that Bridges, looking down upon his correspondent's religion, acted the superior man—an attitude frequently met with on the part of Anglicans towards Roman Catholics up to quite recent times. Bridges, for instance, never failed to score points, when occasion offered, even if he knew that it would make his friend miserable. When a common acquaintance and one of Hopkins's most intimate friends at Oxford, William Addis, left the Church in 1888—he had been 'received' into the Roman fold in October, 1866—Bridges told Hopkins he was 'glad'. To which, Hopkins could only answer, 'But why should you be glad? Why at any rate should you burst upon me that you are glad, when you know that I cannot be glad?'[3] Silence and tactful reserve were the best policy.[4] They had in fact agreed to disagree from the very beginning. Yet they must at times have felt what Hopkins expressed in one of his last

---

[1] Letter C, March 26, 1883, p. 177.

[2] Letter XCIII, November 26, 1882, p. 163. Before the passage we quote, Hopkins had clearly stated: 'When I reproached you for treating me as if I were not in earnest I meant, and I mean now, to open up no further question.'

[3] Letter CLXIII, October 20, 1888, p. 298.

[4] In April, 1881, Hopkins had sent, among comic poems, an epigram on the Church of England, to which Bridges had objected. See Letters LXXIV, May 14, and LXXV, June 16, 1881, pp. 129–31.

letters, 'I am sorry to hear of our differing so much in taste. I was hardly aware of it. (It is not nearly so sad as differing in religion.)'[1]

When in 1884 Hopkins left Stonyhurst for Dublin, few oppotunities remained for the two friends to meet. In the summer vacation of 1884 the Jesuit professor of Greek did not leave Ireland. The year after, although he did come to England, and even went to Hastings to spend a few days, possibly a week-end, with Coventry Patmore, he 'did not attempt to see' Bridges. The latter had married in September, 1884,[2] and the diffident Hopkins did not wish to intrude on their peaceful happiness at Yattendon. But he was quite willing to visit his friend and his wife in their secluded village,[3] and in 1886 and 1887 he was able to accept their invitation. In their company he spent Thursday, May 6, 1886, a 'delightful day', leaving 'fragrant' memory.[4]

His last visit was almost certainly on Thursday, August 24, 1887. The letter of thanks seems to have been written as soon as he was back with his family, in their summer residence at Court's Hill Lodge, Haslemere.[5] Bridges had offered to come to Haslemere a few days before, but the house was full and he could not be given a bed.[6] Thus the two friends showed an equal desire to see each other, as if they vaguely felt that Fate was offering them their last opportunity. Little did they know then that within twenty-two months death was to part them for ever.

Although in his letters Hopkins had often complained of his bad state of health, his nervous prostrations, and his 'languishing', Bridges could not believe that the attack of typhoid fever would so easily and so rapidly destroy his friend's life. By some

---

[1] Letter CLXVI, September 25, 1888, p. 290.

[2] The Waterhouses had moved to Yattendon in April, 1881. Robert Bridges married Mary Monica Waterhouse there on September 3, 1884. Oddly enough, Robert had asked Gerard, the Jesuit, to be his best man.

[3] A year earlier Hopkins had decided to go to Yattendon; but he inadvertently took a through train, and 'was whirled past' at Pangbourne. See *GMH to RB*, Postcard CIX, September 11, 1883, p. 186.

[4] Letter CXXXIII, June 1, 1886, p. 225.

[5] Letter CLI, August 25, 1887, pp. 258–60.

[6] Letter CL, August 11, 1887, p. 258.

strange piece of luck, his last letter to Hopkins escaped destruction. The feelings of deep concern and kindness expressed in it offer ample proof of the strong bonds of friendship that no distance and no opposed beliefs could sever. We must quote it in full since it is the only occasion we have to see how Bridges answered his friend's letters and to hear, ever so faintly, the tone of his voice.

Yattendon

DEAREST GERARD,

I am so sorry to get a letter from one of your people telling me that you are ill with fever. And yesterday I sent you off a budget of notes on Milton's prosody. And when I last wrote I never mentioned your ailing tho' you told me in your letter that you interrupted it to lie down.

What is this fever? F. Wheeler says that you are mending. I hope you are recovering properly; let me have a line. I wish I cd. look in on you and see for myself.

You must send me a card now and then, and one as soon as possible to let me know about you.

Meanwhile I must be patient.

I think that if you are really mending Miltonic prosody will be just the sort of light amusement for your mind. I hope you are well enough already—and will make a quick recovery and complete for wh. I pray. Yr afft.

R.B.

May 18, '89

5 minutes before the letter came I was writing your name for the binder of the 'Growth of Love' to send you a copy.[1]

Almost the whole gamut of friendly feelings is to be found in this last message: anxiety, concern, the physician's earnest inquiry —'what is this fever?'—and regret at being unable to help with his own medical knowledge—'I wish I cd. look in on you'. There is apology for not having mentioned his ailing when he had last written, and good wishes for a speedy recovery, and prayers offered; there is the urgent appeal for better news, and loving care expressed in a tone of subdued passion—'meanwhile I must be patient'. And there is the poetical bond, the critical advice required (represented, to humour the patient, as 'light amusement'), and the gift of a volume of sonnets.

[1] *Further Letters*, Appendix III, Letter M, p. 433.

This last message of true affection, which reached Hopkins a few weeks before he died, must have brought him one of his last great joys. As he lay dying, Hopkins may have reflected that in spite of disagreements, conflicts and misunderstandings —fleeting shadows—there had burned in two noble hearts a strong fire of love. And the letters and poems he left would ever bear witness to it.

IV

Two Poets Discuss Each Other's Verse

I. BRIDGES INVITES CRITICISM

Had there been no other bond of friendship between Bridges and Hopkins than that of Oxford memories, we may doubt whether their friendship would have succeeded in triumphing over their many psychological, moral and religious differences. We may grant that their being aware of such differences helped them either to brush them aside, or to accept them as an immutable state of things; but even if we admit that the two friends were on the whole 'reasonable' about their opposed opinions and tried to tone them down, though with little success, we cannot see how their correspondence would have been so important and so regular, had there not been other strong links between them. They were friends because they enjoyed each other's company and each other's letters, but also because they had a common interest in literature, poetry and music.

Both Bridges and Hopkins had friends who were nearer to their hearts. Alexander Wood,[1] Edward Bond and Mowbray Baillie were warmly loved by Hopkins; so were Henry Wooldridge and Lionel Muirhead by Bridges. But we have nothing to learn from these smooth-running friendships, which belong to the pleasant private world of quiet feelings. Such friendships are essential to the life of any man; they are part of the air he breathes, but they do not make history. One might object that the letters of Hopkins to Baillie are not merely friendly letters; they deal with a scholarly subject—philology. But their philology is at once a little too technical for the general reader and not

---

[1] For Alexander Wood see *GMH Journals*, p. 321, and 'More Light on Gerard Hopkins', by J. H. Crehan, in *The Month*, October, 1953.

technical enough for the expert; the interest is not wide enough, and if Hopkins's inquiries were made in earnest, they kept an amateurish character of which both he and his correspondent were quite aware.

With Bridges the case was different. Hopkins and he were interested in poetry, literature and music. Their lives were partly or wholly involved in these artistic matters and problems. We have strongly—and we deem rightly—emphasized the instinctive attraction which was the secure bedrock of their friendship. But they set above it, and apart from it, an artistic and literary curiosity, a will to learn from each other or at least to be fully acquainted with each other's achievements, and this was as deliberate as their avowed intention to remain free from any conscious imitation. The problems they dealt with were never indifferent or superficial. Their entire relationship throve on this intellectual and aesthetic intercourse and on the exchange of frank and sometimes blunt criticism.

At Oxford, and at Rochdale, the two friends had spoken of poetry and music. Hopkins was the poet and Bridges the musician. One wrote sonnets, the other melodies; and if one asked, 'When you are next writing will you send yr. airs?',[1] the other, in his turn, asked for copies of poems to be pasted in his book.[2] It seems that in the late 'sixties Bridges was chiefly interested in music and that he did not as yet write much poetry. In 1874 Hopkins could inquire, 'Did I ever before see anything of yours? say in Coles' book? I cannot remember',[3] which implies that, before Bridges published his first book of poems, his friend knew practically nothing of his poetical gift; on the other hand he felt sure of his musical competence, since as early as November, 1867, he had written—with a touch of humour but without any tinge of irony—'I have begun the violin and if you will write a trio or quartet I will some day take the first or second part in it.'[4]

---

[1] *GMH to RB*, Letter XII, December 22, 1866, p. 15.

[2] Letter XXII, August 7, 1868, p. 24: "I cannot send my *Summa* for it is burnt with my other verses . . . I kept, however, corrected copies of some things which you have and will send them that what you have got you may have in its last edition'.

[3] Letter XXVII, January 22, 1874, p. 29.

[4] Letter XV, November 1, 1867, p. 18.

During the long estrangement of the years 1871–7 neither the Jesuit nor the medical student knew what his friend was doing. It took them some time to discover that while each had been devoting the best of his time to his calling—medicine and the ministry—they had both in their spare time written poetry or prepared to experiment in new rhythmic patterns.

On January 17, 1874, there appeared in the *Academy* a review by Andrew Lang of 'a Mr. Bridges's poems, Robert Bridges the title shewed. And the characteristics the writer found in the poems were true to' . . . the man Hopkins knew.[1] It is interesting to note that the critic mostly praised the poet for his indifference to modern tendencies:

It could scarcely be gathered from his book that he has ever read Mr. Tennyson or Mr. Swinburne; and he sees things as clearly, speaks as simply, feels as truly, as if the modern demand for research and subtlety had never been heard.[2]

If Hopkins could detect his friend from such remarks, as well as from the few lines that were quoted, it stresses the fact that already Bridges's classical tendencies, both as man and artist, were remarkable. At least the influence of the classics was certain, and Hopkins, who knew of his friend's preference for the poetry of the ancients, had no hesitation about the author. And yet he wrote, 'Given that you write and have changed . . .' —which in a mild form is the expression of a genuine surprise. He certainly expected Bridges to write music rather than verse; but if he chose to write verse, form and theme could only be classical. To Hopkins it was a sudden and unexpected discovery. And it was a godsend too, as he frankly admitted in his letter. 'To have seen these gave me an occasion to write again'. He was not slow to seize the opportunity, for he wrote his letter within a week of reading the review in the *Academy*; it was obviously the best means to try and patch up their silent quarrel over Communism. Bridges could not but be pleased that his friend had noticed the appearance of his book of *Poems*; and the

[1] Letter XXVII, January 22, 1874, p. 29.
[2] The main passages of Andrew Lang's criticism are quoted by Abbott in *GMH to RB*, Note F, p. 308.

mild rebuke he received at the same time for not having answered the 'red letter' could lead him to assume a less stringent attitude and consent to resume correspondence. But in spite of Hopkins's affectionate move, Bridges was determined to remain silent for some time yet. Moreover he appears to have had for a considerable length of time no intention of speaking of his poems. In his letter Hopkins had been wary; he had not passed any remark on his friend's verse and had not even expressed the wish to obtain a copy. He did not know how Bridges would react to his letter, and did not want to offer any cause for displeasure. He could not tell whether the publishing of this small book of fifty-three poems was the indulgence of a passing fancy. How could he have guessed that it represented the first fruit of a rich crop that would be harvested for more than fifty-five years, bringing fame and the laureateship? Knowing that he was writing to a man who was 'unusually reticent', Hopkins waited for the time when his friend would choose to be more confiding and less self-reliant.

It took three years to bring Bridges to the conviction that Hopkins would be a trustworthy critic of his poems, a conviction that grew upon him without any external interference. It must have been clear to him, once he decided to persevere in the writing of poetry, that Hopkins's literary judgment as well as his classical culture would help him to come to a better appreciation of his own taste and preferences. Bridges, who, as we know, 'never obeyed anyone or adapted himself to anyone', sent his poems to Hopkins not in order to secure influential criticism but to whet his own critical acumen. Besides it must be remembered that when he first sent his *Carmen Elegiacum* and the twenty-four sonnets of *The Growth of Love* in February, 1877, he did not know or even suspect Hopkins to be writing verses then, for he imagined his friend to be, in his secluded world of theological studies, utterly lost to literature. But living in a religious Society, admittedly indifferent— though not averse—to new currents of thought, taste and fashion, Hopkins could perhaps understand, with more sympathy than many of his contemporaries, a poet who deliberately refused to follow the Epicurean aesthetes of his day, and who in his careful elaboration of traditional themes did not make a bid for popularity. Bridges was certainly alive to the fact, and it helped him to overcome his hesitations, which died hard. Professor Abbott would have us believe that Bridges's long silence—a two years' silence between February, 1875, when he invited Hopkins to his rooms in Maddox Street, and February, 1877, when he renewed the invitation—was due to his 'fear that his letters were read by others'.[1] But although Hopkins took the objection seriously in order to prove to his friend that it was groundless, and that it was 'quite unreasonable and superstitious to let it make any difference', since the envelope was just torn half open and the letters never taken out, it was in fact the poor excuse Bridges had chosen to give in order to hide his lasting sense of grievance and his slowness to relent and make things up.

It is possible that Hopkins's frank avowal, 'I can do nothing more than say how much I like to hear about you,'[2] which was a proof of friendly feeling and a definite appeal, gradually worked upon Bridges and made him realize that a literary correspondence would be profitable to him as well as to the Jesuit. The letter from Hopkins in 1875 brought ample proof that there were few questions on which they might agree. Merely to show, perhaps, that in spite of his classical tendencies in poetry he was fully aware of modern philosophical tendencies, Bridges had told his correspondent that he was reading Hegel in the original; to which the latter had answered that he 'had no time to read even the English books about Hegel', and that after all he could—'at all events a little'—read Duns Scotus, for whom he cared 'more even than Aristotle and more *pace tua* than a dozen Hegels'. Duns Scotus and Hegel stand poles apart; obviously no useful discussion could arise from this unexpected encounter of medieval scholasticism and modern German idealism. What field was left for their common investigation apart from literature? On poetry and prosody and literary criticism they might still disagree, but disagreement could be profitable. It could bring a flow of valuable suggestions. Since argument about wider issues was impossible, or rather un-

---

[1] *GMH to RB*, p. 31, note 3.
[2] *Ibid.*, Letter XXVIII, February 20, 1875, p. 30.

necessary, owing to their rigid philosophical and religious views, the ground was clear for literary or technical discussions in which each correspondent could send a stimulating analysis of reasons for praise or blame. The two friends finally acted on the conviction expressed one day by Hopkins when he urged Bridges to send his poems to Canon Dixon, adding that it was his own interest: 'for a poet is a public in himself'.[1]

A public they soon could ill dispense with. But whatever the motive that induced Bridges to send his 'pamphlets'—and it may have been just an interest in the remarks a priest could make on secular verse—it gave Hopkins deep and lasting pleasure. To one who knew the positive quality of his own critical and creative powers and who, even if he accepted that they should be used sparingly, vaguely hoped for some quiet acknowledgment of his literary penetration and balanced judgment, it was like the lifting of a veil. It restored for ever confidence and friendship, and it immediately brought their correspondence to an intellectual and artistic level it had not yet known. Bridges, who disliked pretty speeches and superficial compliments, got what he wanted—a frankness verging at times on rudeness, but refreshing; a kindness in the personal appreciation that seldom failed to encourage him. Later, when Hopkins's achievement as an original poet and the excellence of his critical comments as a prosodist became conspicuous, Bridges fully realized the quality of his friend's judgment; but he cannot have been slow to acknowledge—at least to himself —the authority with which the critic spoke. Indeed it is remarkable to see how, from the very first letters in which Hopkins gives his opinion on Bridges's poems, he expresses himself with a masterly propriety. There is no conceit, no pride; the remarks are always to the point; but under the kindness or the abruptness lies the virile self-conviction of a teacher—a teacher who, it must be remembered, not only came to read all the poetry Bridges wrote, but who was asked by two other poets, Dixon and Patmore, to read, revise and offer suggestions for new editions of their poems.[2] The two poets who shared with

[1] Letter LI, January 19, 1879, p. 59.
[2] See *GMH & RWD*, Letters XIV, XVI, XVII, XIX–XXI, and *Further Letters*, CLXVII–CLXXVI.

Bridges the friendship of the Jesuit priest-poet trusted in the soundness and delicacy of his moral and artistic judgment. They carefully noted his remarks, and acted upon them when they thought it advisable. Bridges, as we shall see, did not fail to use his friend's suggestions whenever he considered them beneficial. But he was careful to avoid any influence that might dominate him. The advice he obtained from Hopkins was always weighed, sorted, sifted, sometimes accepted, more often rejected. But in the course of this task, and although the poet was on his guard—being helped in this by his critic, who ruthlessly hunted out 'echoes' of his own poems—the influence went deeper than either friend imagined.

II. HOPKINS CRITICIZES BRIDGES

February, 1877, was a significant date in the two poets' lives. Had Bridges not decided to send his poems to his friend and ask for his appreciation, Hopkins might have remained silent about his own work. As it is, Bridges's confidence led him to ask for his fellow-poet's frank opinion of his experiments; this meant a constant interchange of manuscripts or books of poems, and a painstaking consideration of little details. For greater convenience we shall study Hopkins's criticism before we turn to Bridges's. Although they reacted upon each other, and alternately took precedence of all other topics or receded in the background, a separate examination will help us to understand better what Bridges asked and obtained, what he gave in his turn, and the benefit Hopkins himself derived from it.

It is amusing to notice how Bridges, who up to 1877 had been a poor correspondent, answering at long intervals, at unexpected times, and always rather briefly (if we are to judge from Hopkins's letters which generally seem to follow suit), suddenly turns into a man who brooks no delay, being obviously eager to know his friend's opinion of his poems. Hopkins has to write almost at once, merely to say that the real answer will come some time later for it has 'yet to be written'. And the answer he sends one month after having received the poems leaves St. Asaph for London only because Bridges has complained of his delay in writing. Very often, in the course of their correspondence, Hopkins will apologize for answering belatedly; he has been overworked or ill. Given each in turn, or sometimes both at once, these were unfortunately genuine excuses; but it is also true that Hopkins liked to take time over a manuscript[1] or over a letter.[2] So, when he did not care to wait, Bridges insisted on having an immediate answer. 'I cannot say much on [*Nero*] if I am to answer you at once', complains the critic; but his letter runs to 1,400 words and covers four printed pages.[3] And he deals with lines, words, the lyrical or dramatic beauty of a piece or a play, and the larger literary problems, in the most simple and direct manner, never taking anything for granted, and praising in order to obtain from his friend more discipline, a more exacting artistry.

The first book of *Poems*, published in 1873, Bridges did not send to Hopkins. In fact, the Jesuit Father first came upon a copy quite by chance at his uncle's.[4] But almost all the other poems and plays written by Bridges between 1877 and 1889 were seen by Hopkins either in manuscript or in book-form. We may draw up the full list of those early works.

1873. *Poems*, dedicated to H. W. Wooldridge.   (a)
1876. *Carmen Elegiacum*, dedicated to Patrick Black.   (b)
1876. *The Growth of Love.*   (c)
1879. *Poems*, by the Author of 'The Growth of Love'.   (d)

(a) This edition contains 53 poems. Only 17 of them are to be found in Bk. 1 of *The Shorter Poems* (1890) and 1 sonnet in *The Growth of Love* (1889).

(b) A Latin poem on the history of St. Bartholomew's Hospital.

(c) A poem in 24 sonnets; no author's name.

(d) This edition contains 19 poems. 13 of them are to be found in Bk. II of *The Shorter Poems* (1890) and 3 sonnets in *The Growth of Love* (1889).

[1] He keeps *Prometheus the Firegiver* from June 5 to November 4, 1882, and 're-views' it again between November 29 and December 4. *GMH to RB*, Letters XCIII–XCV, pp. 161–6.

[2] Letter LXXI, begun on January 20, 1881, concluded and sent on February 8, pp. 116–24.

[3] Letter CXXVI, March 24, 1885, pp. 208–12.

[4] Letter XXXVI, August 10, 1877, p. 44, postscript: 'At my uncle's last night I found your first volume, which he had come to know at Rome and lent about to his friends'. Rome points to uncle George Giberne whose wife, *née* Maria Smith, was Hopkins's cherished aunt. See *The Listener*, January 24, 1957, 'Remembering Gerard Manley Hopkins', by Lance Sieveking.

1880. *Poems*, by the Author of 'The Growth of Love,' third
series. (e)

1883. *Prometheus the Firegiver*. (f)

1884. *Poems*. (g)

1885. *Nero*, Part I, dedicated to Thomas Barlow. (h)

1885. *Eros and Psyche*. Dedicated to the Celestial Spirit of
Henry Purcell by an Unworthy Lover. (i)

1889. *The Growth of Love*. (j)

1889. *The Feast of Bacchus*, dedicated to C. H. Daniel. (k)

1890. *Palicio*, dedicated to William Bridges. (l)

1890. *The Return of Ulysses*, dedicated to C. H. H. Parry. (m)

1890. *The Christian Captives*, dedicated to Mandell Creighton. (n)

1890. *Achilles in Scyros*, dedicated to Samuel Gee. (o)

1890. *The Shorter Poems* (p)

(e) Out of 20 poems, 5 are to be found in Bk. III of *The Shorter Poems* (1890) and 13 sonnets in *The Growth of Love* (1889)—only 10 in the final edition of 1898.

(f) Subtitle, 'A Mask in the Greek Manner'.

(g) This edition contains 24 poems, 7 of which had not been published before; 6 of the 7 are to be found in Bk. III of *The Shorter Poems* (1890).

(h) Subtitle, 'An Historical Tragedy of the First Part of the Reign of the Emperor Nero.'

(i) Subtitle, 'A Poem in Twelve Measures: The story done into English from the Latin of Apuleius'. The measures cover the twelve months from March to February and there are as many stanzas as there are days in the month. The romantic dedication to Purcell must be noticed.

(j) This edition contains 79 sonnets. Of the first (1876) edition 14 sonnets out of 24 have been retained after considerable alterations; the final (1898) edition contains 69 sonnets only. This sonnet-sequence was for more than twenty years the treasure-chamber of Bridges's best sonnets, which he kept revising, adding new ones and ruthlessly cancelling others.

(k) Subtitle: 'A Comedy in the Latin Manner, and partly translated from Terence.' Dated Yattendon, June, 1885.

(l) Subtitle: 'A Romantic Drama in Five Acts in the Elizabethan Manner.' Dated Yattendon, 1883.

(m) Subtitle: 'A Drama in Five Acts in a Mixed Manner.' Dated Yattendon, 1884.

(n) Subtitle: 'A Tragedy in Five Acts in a Mixed Manner.' Dated Yattendon, 1886.

(o) Subtitle: 'A Drama in a Mixed Manner.' Dated Yattendon, August, 1887.

(p) This edition contains four Books. The poems of Bk. I and Bk. II had been printed in earlier pamphlets. Bk. III contains 19 poems (11 from earlier books), and Bk. IV contains 30 (all new). Bk. V was published in 1893; it contains 20 poems, finally reduced to 19 in 1894. Each book in the 1894 edition of *The Shorter Poems* was dedicated to one of Bridges's great friends—to Wooldridge, 'to the memory of G.M.H.,' to R.W. Dixon, Lionel Muirhead and M. G. Knight.

The plays and poems published in 1890, the year after Hopkins's death, were written between 1883 and 1887 and must be mentioned since most of them are under discussion in Hopkins's letters. It is difficult to say whether Bridges regularly sent his friend all his books, and impossible to say whether he showed him all his manuscripts when they chanced to meet in London or at Yattendon. In February, 1879, Hopkins duly received the new pamphlet of *Poems*, and in October, 1880, not only *Poems, Third Series*, but another pamphlet, 'first series, second edition', containing 19 poems from the original volume of 1873. In 1882 *Prometheus the Firegiver* was submitted to him for revision and in 1885 the same careful revision was required for *Eros and Psyche*. *Nero, Part I*, was under scrutiny in 1884, as well as *The Return of Ulysses*. *The Feast of Bacchus* had to wait for more than six months before Hopkins could read and criticize it, owing to the pressure of his work in the year 1886–7. Other works are not mentioned, so that we cannot consider Hopkins as a systematic critic of his friend's works. But he never failed to read, and to give his frank opinion of the poems he read.

The *Shorter Poems* published in 1890 gathered within their four Books the best lyrics Bridges had written between 1873 and 1890. Those in Book I were his final selection from the volume of 1873; those in Book II from the pamphlet of 1879; those in Book III from another pamphlet, published in 1880, and from a small volume printed by the Rev. C. H. O. Daniel in 1884. All the poems in Book IV were printed in 1890 for the first time,[1] and although it is possible that Hopkins saw some of them in manuscript, none of them is discussed in his letters. On the other hand, many poems in the first three Books are remarked upon. What sort of criticism does Hopkins offer?

It is the criticism of one who admires and praises, while paying careful attention to details of form and rhythm and making suggestions or asking for alterations in the most direct manner. Sincere admiration and outspoken comment go hand in hand. The beginning of the letter in which he gives his first impressions of the pamphlet of 1879 will serve as a perfect example of Hopkins's manner.

---

[1] Bridges gives these facts in a note at the end of the 1890 volume, p. 87.

DEAREST BRIDGES,

Your precious little volume is to hand—also to head and heart, breathing genius everywhere, like sweet-herbs. I shd. like to criticize it in detail throughout, but that may not be. Something however I must say.

The jewel of all, *judice me*, is no. 2. That is a lovely poem. But nevertheless I must tell you that the first verse appears to me to be faulty. It wd. seem to be divided between the two speakers, as the rest of the piece. If so the first two lines shd. be in italics. And if so then *lay* should be *lies*. Also *Silence!* should be *Hush, hush* or *O hush!* If however it is really the inmate who speaks, then the question will be an ironical, not an earnest one, and mean: How can love awake that has lain asleep so long? and if so this shd. be brought out, as by: Should love again awake. . . ? But the other sense is smoother, besides that otherwise the question seems absurd, for the longer the sleep has been the nearer must the waking be; if it *is* sleep and not death . . .[1]

The opening words praise the poet in no vague terms and stress the delicacy of his poems; but there is matter for criticism, and although Hopkins seems to exclude the possibility of doing so, he immediately finds fault with the first lines of No. 2, gives reasons, suggests emendations, provides other words, and, argues about the logical sequence of thoughts.[2] He is not trying to be more subtle than Bridges; he simply shows him a way of giving more cogency to the poem. In this particular case Bridges followed his advice, as will be seen by setting side by side the 1879 and 1890 versions.

1879	1890
	MUSE
Will Love again awake,	Will Love again awake
That lay asleep so long?	That lies asleep so long?
Silence! ye tongues that shake	POET
The drowsy night with song.	O hush! ye tongues that shake
	The drowsy night with song.

Of course Bridges did not always follow Hopkins's advice.

---

[1] *GMH to RB*, Letter LIV, February 22, 1879, pp. 67–68.

[2] Anne Treneer in 'The Criticism of Gerard Manley Hopkins' (*Penguin New Writing*, No. 40, 1950, pp. 98–115) writes truly: 'Sometimes on receiving a poem from Bridges he would become as active imaginatively as if it were his own poem'.

But considering his abrupt temper, his 'grumpiness', and a self-confidence that verged on conceit,[1] we must say that Hopkins had a singular power over him, whenever his suggestions referred to style, prosody and rhythm. It is surprising to notice that the critic is little concerned with the meaning of the short lyrics. When in his opinion the meaning is 'bad', that is to say morally reprehensible, he will not fail to say so;[2] he will even appear very finicky about some anodyne comic verses.[3] But generally speaking the thought or the sequence of thought interests him less than the 'workmanship' or 'the richness of phrase'. All the shorter poems are graceful songs of love, or praise Nature clearly and gently, as in the 'Elegies' of Book I; they quietly mingle the delicate beauty of a rose or a poppy, or the tender notes of a linnet courting his lady, with the happy or melancholy thoughts of a lover. The 'Spring Odes' of Book II invite the reader to the sluggish joys of the country or to the hard-won peace of mind of the town fireside. These are the songs of 'vague desires', of 'indolence', of the sweet delights of love. One can well imagine Father Parkinson, the Jesuit Superior of St. Aloysius, Oxford, reading them 'murmuringly out over tea, with comments and butter'.[4] Such poetry was simply and quietly going in the opposite direction to Swinburne (whose *Poems and Ballads*, second series, had appeared in 1878), and Hopkins praised it for that very reason. He liked

the constant music . . . the freshness and buoyancy and independence

---

[1] Letter XXX, April 3, 1877, p. 34: 'The sonnets . . . make me proud of you (which by the by is not the same as for you to be proud of yourself: I say it because you always were and I see you still are given to conceit; witness your fussing about the 'Romana venustas' epigram . . .).'

[2] Letter LIV, February 22, 1879, p. 69: '*Elegy* . . . the piece is beautiful and full of music. The meaning is bad.' Bridges had written:

> Nay, were my last hope quenched, I here would sit
> And praise the annihilation of the pit.
>   (*Shorter Poems*, Bk. II, No. 10.)

[3] In a humorous Ode, later discarded, Bridges had described an 'old salt' whose 'seaward cottage' had been wrecked by the sea, and who,

> Seeing the "Anne", his boat, was lost
> And Anne his wife was saved alone,
> Slipped from his moorings, and has gone . . .

Hopkins commented, 'The vulgar verses about Anne leave a bad taste'.—Letter LIV, p. 71.

[4] *Ibid.*, p. 68.

I find in your poems, marked with character throughout and human nature and not 'arrangements in vowel sounds' as Mallock says, very thinly costuming a strain of conventional passion, kept up by stimulants, and crying always in a high head voice about flesh and flowers and democracy and damnation.[1]

Because Bridges obviously seeks originality in being composed, graceful and classical, Hopkins is most strict in his criticism. He insists that 'the meaning shd. be felt at once'[2] and hunts down ambiguous expressions. Of one sonnet, he writes,

I cannot make out, do what I will, who is that conqueror? It might be Love, it might be Death, it might be Time, but there are reasons against each.[3] 'Yet has no secret with the soul pourtrayed' means, I suppose, 'Yet has no secret in common with the there pourtrayed soul', but it is a very ambiguous phrase. It reads as if it meant something it cannot mean.[4]

Even the real value of a demonstrative adjective is carefully looked into:

I will say that I think it wd. be better to write 'one irrevocable day'. 'That . . . day' is ambiguous: you mean *ille dies*, the particular day which in fact did, etc.; I took it for *is dies*, a day such that, whenever it shall come, it is doomed to etc.[5]

More than anything else, he warns Bridges against 'echoes'. In the 'Hymn of Nature' he finds 'lines that distinctly echo Milton, I mean distinct passages; and Tennyson too'. In the same letter he says that the 'Elegy' is unequal,

[1] *Ibid.*, pp. 72–73.

[2] *Ibid.*, p. 72.

[3] Letter LXX, October 26, 1880, p. 113. The reference is to *Poems, Third Series*, 1880, No. XIX, a sonnet ('These days, even as men see them, dull and slow') which Bridges never reprinted.

[4] *Ibid.* The line appears in the 1880 pamphlet, No. XIII. Bridges made no alteration (except 'hath' for 'has') in *Poet. Works*, where the poem is Sonnet 39 in *The Growth of Love*.

[5] Letter LXIV, October 22, 1879, p. 94. The line was printed accordingly in the 1880 pamphlet; and the sonnet was reprinted with major emendations and without the ambiguous line in *The Growth of Love*, 1889 and in the final edition (1898) where it is No. 41.

because, as I told you and I now maintain my past judgment, there are two lines in it echoing Gray's: *they do it, they will do it to every ear, it is a great fault to do it, and they do it.* They are not at all the best lines and they can be easily changed and yet they echo lines which are held to be of faultless and canonical beauty. The subject and measure shd. of themselves have put you on your guard. Gray's poem may be outdone but, if you understand, it cannot be equalled.[1]

The underlined words, the repetition of 'they do it', and the judicious remark at the end of the passage stress the strong opposition of the critic to anything that savours either of plagiarism or of conscious transposition. In his considered opinion the great masters of the past can be admired but they cannot be imitated and it is useless to try to equal them; one must do otherwise[2] or else the only way out of the difficulty is to outdo them, and that is not an easy task. Had Hopkins lived, what would have been his criticism of the poems of T. S. Eliot or Ezra Pound which deliberately use 'echoes' as a literary and poetical device? He might have repeated what he said about Bridges's historical play, *Nero*: 'The echos [*sic*] are a disease of education, literature is full of them; but they remain a disease, an evil'.[3]

Obviously the writer of those words cared for originality above all things and was irritated by the burden of literary memories. Bridges on the other hand enjoyed the company of the classics, and had learnt his art at their feet. All the plays he wrote between 1883 and 1890 were either translated from the Greek or imitated from Greek or Latin authors. *Prometheus the Firegiver* is a mask in the Greek manner. *The Feast of Bacchus* is partly translated from Terence, who had borrowed the plot from Menander. *The Return of Ulysses* dramatizes the chief scenes in Homer's *Odyssey*. A passage in *Achilles in Scyros* is copied from Calderon's *El Principe Constante*, a play from which Bridges borrowed the subject of his *Christian Captives*.[4] No one borrowed more consistently or more freely. Quite naturally he

[1] Letter LIV, p. 69.
[2] Letter CLXVI, September 25, 1888, p. 291. 'The effect of studying masterpieces is to make me admire and do otherwise.'
[3] Letter CXXIV, February 6, 1885, p. 206.
[4] The above facts are to be found in notes at the end of the plays. See *Poetical Works*, 1895–1905, Vols. III–VI.

also tried his hand at translating sonnets of Michelangelo into English verse, and Hopkins was attracted in spite of an ingrained aversion for that exercise.

> I should be very glad to see your prose of Michelangelo's sonnets and also your verse, for though I do not like verse-renderings of verse (according to the saying, *Traduttore traditore*) yet I think you could do them if anyone can.[1]

A guarded compliment! But Bridges may have smiled when reading the passage, for Hopkins himself had his try at verse-renderings of verse, translating Horace and Latin hymns into English and Shakespeare's songs into Latin and Greek.[2]

Far more revealing among all this rich and varied criticism are the emendations suggested. They all seek to instil more grace and more power and rhythm into Bridges's verse. A few instances chosen from among many will suffice.

Bridges had written,

> Rich hues have marriage made
> With sweet unmemoried scents.
> (*Shorter Poems*, Bk. II, No. 13)

Hopkins suggested a different rhythm; instead of regular trimeters, a contrast of trimeters and dimeters might give more lightness and freshness to the lyric, which he said was 'very charming, though not fully filed'. He went on:

> Could you not end something like:
>
> > Sweet hues have marriage made
> > With as sweet scents—
>
> or　　　　　With sweeter scents—
>
> and　　　Thy death be that flower's death
> 　　　　　And sky thy tomb—?[3]

---

[1] Letter LXII, August 14, 1879, pp. 88–89.
[2] See *GMH Poems*, pp. 182–8, 196–200.
[3] Letter XLV, July 16, 1878, p. 56.

Bridges did not accept the suggestion, which would have destroyed the smoothness of his song, and have implied a wholly different conception of the theme.

Generally speaking, Hopkins's suggestions tend towards a more spirited movement, as though he wanted the poet to react against the too easy flow of his lines. There is a significant passage in a letter where he criticizes one of Bridges's finest lyrical poems, which as it stood could not be much improved. All the remarks tend to give it a more dramatic turn and a more personal touch. Let us quote the poem[1] in order to understand more clearly the text of the letter.

> O my vague desires!
> Ye lambent flames of the soul, her offspring fires:
> That are my soul herself in pangs sublime
> Rising and flying to heaven before her time:
>
> What doth tempt you forth
> To drown in the south or shiver in the frosty north?
> What seek ye or find ye in your random flying,
> Ever soaring aloft, soaring and dying?
>
> Joy, the joy of flight!
> They hide in the sun, they flare and dance in the night;
> Gone up, gone out of sight; and ever again
> Follow fresh tongues of fire, fresh pangs of pain.
>
> Ah! they burn my soul,
> The fires, devour my soul that once was whole:
> She is scattered in fiery phantoms day by day,
> But whither, whither? ay whither? away, away!
>
> Could I but control
> These vague desires, these leaping flames of the soul:
> Could I but quench the fire: ah! could I stay
> My soul that flieth, alas, and dieth away!

The poem was sent in manuscript to Hopkins in January, 1881: four of the five stanzas were included in *Prometheus* in

---

[1] *Shorter Poems*, Bk. III, No. 1 (*RB Poet. Works*, 1953, p. 264). It is not possible to reconstruct the exact text sent to Hopkins in manuscript.

1883, and all five in *Poems*, 1884. Here is what the critic had to say about it in 1881.

I have a very great deal of you to answer. To take the last first, the poem 'O my vague desires' is a very noble piece, as fine, I think, as anything you have yet done. It is 'all road' very remarkable. The rhythm too is correct and strong. I make a few suggestions. (1) The rhythm of line 4 wd. be a little improved by something like 'arising' instead of 'rising'. (2) Would it not be a better stroke to have instead of 'for ever soaring . . . dying? O the joy of flight!' something like 'You ever soaring aloft, soaring and dying Flames of joyous flight'? (3) I would have 'Ah! they burn my soul, *My* fires, devour my soul (or 'spirit'?) that once was whole'. (4) The word you were in search of instead of 'phantoms' must be 'gledes'— and then you would continue 'day after day'. (5) Why should not the last short line have three feet like the others, as, 'Could I but control'? 'Could I control' has only two. (6) The next one is the only rhythmically bad one: both rhythm and feeling are bettered by 'My vague feelings, my leaping flames of soul'. So too in the next line I would have 'my fires'. (7) The last line might perhaps, but I am not sure, be improved by 'still flying alas!'[1]

A few suggestions indeed! In fact the compliment at the beginning would never lead us to believe that so many improvements could be necessary. But Hopkins cares for consistency and directness. In his first version Bridges had probably written line 8,

For ever soaring . . .

with the stress on the second syllable.[2] Therefore Hopkins asks for 'Arising and flying' in line 4, which offers the double advantage of stressing the second syllable and creating an amphibrach pattern for the rhythm of the line. The second suggestion seeks to link the second and third stanzas instead of keeping each as a separate unit. The third and sixth suggestions tend to underline the autobiographical character of the poem, no doubt

---

[1] Letter LXXI, January 26, 1881, p. 117.
[2] Such is the reading in the choric ode in *Prometheus* (1883). The two different versions are still to be found in *Poet. Works*, 1953 (pp. 46–47 and 264), which suggests that such rhythmic considerations, dear to Hopkins, were of less importance to Bridges.

more vividly than Bridges wished. The fourth suggestion is most typical of Hopkins. He would like the poet to use the common phrase 'day after day'; 'phantoms' must then give way to a shorter word; and the word he offers is uncommon, archaic and obsolete—'glede' or 'gleed', meaning fire, flame, beam or ray. It is far too strange a word for the vocabulary Bridges uses in the poem. It would jar. The final suggestion asks for present participles in the last line to echo the participles in line 8; assuming that this line in the manuscript contained, as in the printed text, the archaic third person singular—'flieth', 'dieth'—the suggestion made is also a way of getting rid of such forms, which Hopkins disliked. In the event the only suggestion that Bridges did retain—in the *Shorter Poems* text—was the fifth, which pointed to an oversight and restored the three stresses in the first line of the last stanza. Thus we see how carefully Hopkins reviewed his friend's poems, and how some of his objections were typical of his own temperament, which as we know was far more fiery than that of Bridges.

Yet at times Bridges, who as early as April, 1879, asked Hopkins whether he might make use of his suggestions,[1] did follow the hints given. He even took over whole lines that Hopkins had written to improve upon his own. For a sonnet in *The Growth of Love*, first printed in *Poems*, 1879, Hopkins rewrote ten lines out of fourteen in his own style; he admitted it was 'd——d impertinence',[2] but Bridges adopted the emended first tercet which gave to the third line more point in its abruptness and dramatic exclamations.

> O cruel jest—he cries, as some one flings
> The sparkling drops in sport or shew of ire—
> O shameless, O contempt of holy things.[3]
> (*Growth of Love*, No. 43)

In another sonnet Bridges, describing his beloved, had first written:

[1] *GMH to RB*, Postcard LVI, April 8, 1879, p. 76. 'May you use my suggestions? But why else do I make them. If you will do me the honour.'
[2] Letter LIV, February 22, 1879, p. 70.
[3] Bridges had written in his first version:
> . . . The sparkling drops in sport or scornful ire;
> O shameless, brute contempt of holy things!

> 'Tis joy the foldings of her dress to view
> And all she doth is past expectancy.[1]

Hopkins did not like the inversion, nor the weak verb, 'doth'. He made various suggestions at long intervals, in April, 1877, in February, 1882, and again in October, 1886, after he had sent Bridges a Latin rendering of the sonnet, which he knew by heart.[2] His own manner can easily be detected in this:

> Her fall of fold is daylight in my view.

The alliteration is evocative of the rich silk dresses of the time. Later, Hopkins turned to another image. He wrote:

> I shall never rest till you change the third line in the sonnet 'In all things beautiful': it weakens and disfigures an otherwise perfect work. Can you not say something like:
>
> As but to watch her folds fall how they do,
> And all { her ways are / that comes is } past expectancy—?

In 1886 he repeated that the line was a weak one in a masterpiece and that he had wished for something like

> 'tis joy to watch her folds fall where they do,
> and all that comes is past expectancy.

His insistence[3] triumphed over the poet's possible hesitations, and Bridges's final version practically adopted Hopkins's last wish:

> 'Tis joy to watch the folds fall as they do,
> And all that comes is past expectancy.

---

[1] *The Growth of Love*, 1879, Sonnet V, cf. *Poet. Works*, p. 202.

[2] *GMH to RB*, Letters XXX, April 3, 1877, p. 35; LXXX, February 1, 1882, p. 141; and CXL, October 31, 1886, p. 243.

[3] Another typical instance of Hopkins's insistence is to be found in his objection to the word 'domeless' in the first line of *Prometheus the Firegiver*. From 1882 to 1886 he kept on asking Bridges to choose a better word. In the 1898 edition, 'ætherial' took the place of 'domeless'. See Letter XCII, p. 159, note 2.

One more example may serve to shew how close Hopkins could come to his friend's process of poetical composition, and how true was the remark he made once, that 'it is just as if I had written [the poem] myself and were dissatisfied'.[1] At the same time, it demonstrates that Bridges fully trusted the artistic insight of his critic and could use his advice to the best advantage. He had written for *Poems*, 1880, a pleasant song on a very old theme.

> Thou didst delight my eyes:
> Yet who am I? nor best
> Nor first nor last to test
> Thy charm, thy bloom to prize.

Hopkins immediately saw that 'test' was a make-rhyme and a rather unpoetical word. He made the following suggestions.

Talking of perfection, could you not get rid of *test* in 'Thou didst delight'? Look here: rhyme on *first* and *durst* and you will get something very good. I dare not tell you my thought, for it wd. be to defeat my own purpose, but do it yourself, simple, suitable, and sweet.[2]

And Bridges did it, improving the prosody as well as the graceful ease of the lyric.

> Thou didst delight my eyes:
> Yet who am I? nor first
> Nor last nor best, that durst
> Once dream of thee for prize.
>   (*Shorter Poems*, Bk. III, No. 12)

Thus unobtrusively Hopkins left his stamp on a few of his friend's poems. He may have been responsible for corrections or improvements that we do not know about, for he discussed Bridges's poems orally when he was shewn them in manuscript, or he may have made notes on manuscripts or first editions that Bridges later destroyed. There is no means of interpreting the following passages from letters written in December, 1884, when Hopkins was reading *Eros and Psyche*:

[1] Letter LXIV, October 22, 1879, p. 94.
[2] Letter LXXX, February 1, 1882, pp. 142–3.

I have been some days annotating as desired, either gilding or else refining gold. [*Footnote :* I shall not be long.][1]

There is one stanza about Psyche's sister falling like a stone. In suggestion it is one of the most brilliant in the poem but in execution very imperfect, and therefore I have been freer there than anywhere else.[2]

Yet these remarks prove clearly that the critic's work of revision went very far. It is hardly rash to suggest that the emendations in the letters are very few compared to those that are unrecorded or no longer extant. Considering the evidence we have of his careful annotation of Dixon's and Patmore's poems,[3] we must assume that Bridges's poems and poetical plays received comparable attention. We shall have confirmation of this when we come to Bridges's attempts at 'sprung rhythm'. Hopkins took his task as a critic in great earnest, and he was most exacting. In fact as early as October, 1879, that is less than two and a half years after he had started revising his friend's poems, he had drawn from him a bewildered query which shows that for a short period Bridges doubted his own gifts. The hypercritical Hopkins had almost destroyed his self-confidence; but he was soon to restore it.

You ask whether I really think there is any good in your going on writing poetry. The reason of this question I suppose to be that I seemed little satisfied with what you then sent. . . . But you are to know, indeed very likely you experience the same thing, I see your work to its very least advantage when it comes to me on purpose to be criticized. It is at once an unfinished thing, in my eyes, and any shortcoming or blemish that in print I should either not notice or else easily digest with the excellence of the context becomes a rawness and a blot, to be removed before my mind can even sit down to receive an impression of the whole or form a final judgment about it. . . .

You seem to want to be told over again that you have genius and are a poet and your verses beautiful. You have been told so, not only by me but very spontaneously by Gosse, Marzials, and others;

[1] Postcard CXXII, December 17, 1884, p. 201.
[2] Letter CXXIII, January 1, 1885, pp. 202–203.
[3] See *GMH & RWD*, 1935, and, for the correspondence between Hopkins and Patmore, *Further Letters*, 1956, pp. 295–393.

I was going to say Canon Dixon, only, as he was acknowledging your book, it was not so spontaneous as Gosse's case. You want perhaps to be told more in particular. I am not the best to tell you, being biassed by love, and yet I am too. . . . If I were not your friend I shd. wish to be the friend of the man who wrote your poems. They shew the eye for pure beauty and they shew, my dearest, besides, the character which is much more rare and precious . . .[1]

This may be the letter of a man 'biassed by love'—and indeed in a very noble way it is a beautiful love-letter—but it is sincere and intelligent praise.

Hopkins knew he was praising his best friend but he also felt certain that his praise, and just the sort of praise he was giving, was fully justified. Bridges knew at the same time that the praise he received was always accompanied with strictures upon his defects or artistic weaknesses. By skilfully blending compliment and disapproval Hopkins obtained a hearing, and helped his friend to a greater mastery of his style. Bridges did not turn a deaf ear to such remarks about *The Growth of Love* as, 'In general I do not think you have reached finality in point of execution, words might be chosen with more point and propriety, images might be more brilliant etc.'[2] Nor could he be indifferent to such judgments as these:

I saw that *Ulysses* was a fine play ; . . . nevertheless, perhaps from my mood of mind, I could not take to it, did not like it, beyond a dry admiration.[3]

The Menandrian period appears to me the dullest and narrowest world that one could choose to lay an action in, a jaded and faded civilization; moreover I have a craving for more brilliancy, more picturesque, more local colour: however you austerely set these things aside and I am to take the play [*The Feast of Bacchus*] for what it is. In its kind then, which has for me no attraction, and in its metre, which has for me no beauty, I think it a masterpiece. The language is a strong and chaste English; it is, I suppose, for us much what the French admire in *Télémaque* and in Racine's plays.[4]

[1] *GMH to RB*, Letter LXIV, October 22, 1879, pp. 93–96.
[2] Letter XXX, April 3, 1877, p. 35.
[3] Letter CXXIX, May 17, 1885, p. 216.
[4] Letter CLI, August 25, 1887, pp. 259–60.

Here is frankness indeed! The differences of mood and taste are not concealed; they are indeed emphasized by the writer to make his criticism less disagreeable. At the same time there is admiration for a style which, in spite of Hopkins's dislike of it, is acknowledged to have fine qualities. In fact Hopkins hits the mark when he discovers in his friend's poetry the stamp of classicism—not the classicism of the Augustan Age, but that of the French tradition, with its clarity, its economy of means, its fine language. There was little irony but genuine eulogy in the exclamation that followed a compliment on Bridges's style, 'Style seems your great excellence, it is really classical. What fun if you were a classic!'[1] It is for us to derive an ironical pleasure from an unexpected situation: romantic Hopkins helping Bridges—at times in spite of himself—to become a classic.

III. BRIDGES CRITICIZES HOPKINS

The first letter in which Hopkins, on request, criticized Bridges's poems was written on April 3, 1877. With it were sent two sonnets for which their author, although he did not say so, wished to have his friend's appreciation. Thus began the reciprocal valuation of their poems, and, in the words of a competent judge, 'Bridges became for a long period the most influential and controversial critic of Hopkins'.[2]

'Controversial' is certainly correct; 'influential' needs qualification. The superlative implies other critics, and we must remember that (apart from men like Edmund Gosse, Hall Caine and Andrew Lang, who had occasion to see and pass judgment on some of Hopkins's sonnets),[3] Dixon and Patmore also read and criticized the Jesuit poet. Since we are only concerned with Bridges, we shall merely give Pick's excellent summary of the attitudes of Dixon and Patmore, which are far easier to re-

---

[1] Letter LXX, October 26, 1880, p. 111.

[2] John Pick, 'Gerard Manley Hopkins', in *The Victorian Poets, A Guide to Research*, Harvard, 1956, pp. 196–227.

[3] It was through Bridges that these critics became acquainted with a number of Hopkins's poems. Gosse alone appears to have appreciated their originality. See *GMH to RB*, Letter LIX, April 22, 1879, p. 79, 'I do warm to that good Mr. Gosse for liking and, you say, "taking" my pieces.'

construct than Bridges's because we possess their side of the correspondence.

[Of the three poets who constituted his public] the least of these was the one who was most understanding and appreciative; for Dixon read the poems with 'delight, astonishment, and admiration'.[1] He found them 'amazingly original'. He urged immediate publication. He felt the 'power' of *The Wreck of the Deutschland*, a poem which came to be a test for each of Hopkins's friends. Dixon perceived that something in Hopkins's life and character gave his poems 'a rare charm', 'something that I cannot describe, but known to myself by the inadequate word *terrible pathos*—something of what you call temper in poetry: a right temper which goes to the point of the terrible; the terrible crystal'.[2]

Very different was the reaction of Patmore, a fellow-Catholic and experimentalist in verse, who preferred those poems that were least typical of Hopkins and most nearly approximated what he called 'the ordinary rules of composition'. Patmore granted that the obscuring 'novelties' in time might become 'additional delights'[3] but yet 'I do not think I could ever become sufficiently accustomed to your favourite poem, *The Wreck of the Deutschland*, to reconcile me to its strangeness'.[4]

It must be borne in mind that Patmore was sixty-one when he read Hopkins's poems for the first time, and was not a man who could easily accept a style so utterly dissimilar to his own. Dixon was forty-six, and he was more ready to admit a style unlike his own because his mind was more supple and more keenly alive to the qualities that lay beneath the apparently rough surface of the poems.

With Bridges the case was altogether different. He and Hopkins were of the same age, and could make allowance for differences. But the one was gradually turning into a professional poet, while the other gave to poetry what little spare time his religious life and his scrupulosity allowed; so that when Bridges read Hopkins's poems in 1877 he looked upon them as the wild experiments of an amateur, and also as further evidence of his

[1] *GMH & RWD*, Letter VIA, April 5, 1879, p. 26.
[2] *Ibid.*, Letter XXA, October 26, 1881, p. 80. 'The terrible crystal' is from Ezekiel, 1, 22. (See *N. & Q.*, June, 1956, p. 267a.)
[3] *Further Letters*, Letter CLXXVID, March 20, 1884, p. 353.
[4] J. Pick, *op. cit.*, p. 201.

friend's religious singularity. Both form and theme, in the pieces submitted to him, came as a shock, and it took him a long time to overcome this first disturbing impression. He always considered it a duty to react against Hopkins's oddities and to prevent him from going too far in his mannerisms and obscurities, even though he was not slow to recognize in him a genuine poet and a great one. Most critics have reproached Bridges with a lack of understanding of Hopkins's genius, and have considered it a pity that the Jesuit poet met with such an unsympathetic response from his best friend. But it should be remembered that Bridges, although he tried to bully Hopkins out of his whimsicalities, admired him and knew how to praise him. Dixon bears witness to this. In 1882, when urging Hopkins to go on writing poetry, he added, 'Bridges struck the truth long ago when he said to me that your poems more carried him out of himself than those of any one.'[1] If the poet of *The Growth of Love* had been blind to 'the health-breathing and purely powerful' poetical faculty of the author of *The Wreck of the Deutschland*, he could never have been 'carried out of himself' by his poems and would never have spoken so highly of them to Dixon or to Patmore.[2]

The story need not be retold here how Hopkins, after having sent his friend two sonnets in his new rhythm (he had warned him, 'And don't *you* say *my* lines don't scan'),[3] decided to show him *The Deutschland*—his 'great metrical experiment', as Bridges calls it; and how the latter was shocked by such 'presumptious [*sic*] jugglery', adding that he would not for any money read the poem again.[4] What must be stressed at the outset is Bridges's strong opposition to Hopkins's experiments, and his negative attitude towards his efforts at 'combining . . . opposite and, one wd. have thought, incompatible excellences, markedness of rhythm—that is rhythm's self—and naturalness of expression'.[5] Bridges could not encourage Hopkins's dramatic and oratorical style, his audacities of construction and his

[1] *GMH & RWD*, Letter XXIIA, January 28, 1882, p. 100.
[2] *Further Letters*, Letter CLXXVIB, January 28, 1884, p. 351.
[3] *GMH to RB*, Letter XXX, April 3, 1877, p. 40.
[4] Letter XXXVIII, August 21, 1878, p. 46.
[5] *Ibid.*

obscurities, and he always tried to bring him back to more sober diction. Hopkins had to maintain his own views against a fairly constant opposition. Time after time, he had to appeal to Bridges as to his only public ('You are my public and I hope to convert you'),[1] asking for words of encouragement: 'I must absolutely have encouragement as much as crops rain'.[2] At the beginning Bridges gave them both reluctantly and clumsily, which brought Hopkins's retort:

It gave me of course great comfort to read your words of praise. But however, praise or blame, never mingle with your criticisms monstrous and indecent spiritual compliments like something you have said there.[3]

Considering that the two poets had in fact no great sympathy with each other's conceptions of poetry, we may doubt whether Bridges was ever in a position to help Hopkins. In their friendly exchange of criticisms each poet was careful to preserve his own integrity. But the more reluctant of the two to accept critical remarks and to act upon them was certainly Hopkins. Believing as he did in his own powers and in the validity of his theories, he always had an answer for objections. 'Please read more than once, . . . You must not slovenly read it with the eyes but with the ears';[4] 'Take breath and read it with the ears, as I always wish to be read, and my verse becomes all right';[5] 'Some of my rhymes I regret, but they are past changing, grubs in amber: there are only a few of these; others are unassailable. Some others there are which *malignity may munch at* but the Muses love'.[6] It seems that Hopkins felt about his poetry what he felt—with questionable justification—about one of his musical compositions: 'If the whole world agreed to condemn it or see nothing in it I should only tell them to take a generation and come to me again.'[7] But as the years went by he paid greater heed to Bridges's remarks.

[1] *Ibid.*
[2] Letter CXXIX, May 17, 1885, p. 219.
[3] Letter XLI, May 30, 1878, p. 52.
[4] Letter XL, May 21, 1878, p. 51.
[5] Letter LIX, April 22, 1879, p. 79.
[6] Letter CII, May 11, 1883, p. 180.
[7] Letter CXXVII, April 1, 1885, p. 214.

After having invited 'minute criticism'[1]—which he took little notice of—he could still say half a dozen years later that he would be glad of his friend's comments,[2] and two years later again the first draft of a sonnet was accompanied with the following plea:

And please do not put it aside 'for further neglect' but answer smart . . . Call in the Canon [Dixon], have a consultation, sit, and send result by return—or soon.[3]

In this instance he obtained what he wanted within a week, and was able to write, 'I am obliged for your criticisms, "contents of which noted", indeed acted on.'[4] Unfortunately, we cannot know what emendations Hopkins made on the recommendation of his critic. It would have been fascinating to see what suggestions he accepted, and what he rejected. But on the whole, and taking into account his great independence of spirit, we think it fair to say that Hopkins for the most part followed his own advice. The letters of Bridges and the criticisms they contained acted on him as an incentive; they roused him to personal creation.

They also drew from him commentaries and line-by-line explanations of his more obscure sonnets or poems, and we must be thankful to Bridges for having forced Hopkins to write glosses of his difficult passages. Thus Bridges obliged him to 'aim at being intelligible'. It is true that Bridges, either because he did not apply his mind, or because to difficulties of style and language were added those of religion, seldom understood Hopkins's thought when it was far-fetched or complicated. Such was the case with the sonnets, 'In the Valley of the Elwy', 'The Sea and the Skylark', 'Henry Purcell', and with 'Tom's Garland'.[5] Of this last poem, Hopkins remarked with some melancholy,

I laughed outright and often, but very sardonically, to think you

---

[1] Letter LXII, August 14, 1879, p. 87.
[2] Letter CXXVI, March 24, 1885, p. 211.
[3] Letter CLXVII, October 3, 1888, p. 293.
[4] Letter CLXVIII, October 19, 1888, p. 296.
[5] *GMH to RB*, pp. 76, 164, 170, 273.

and the Canon could not construe my last sonnet; that he had to write to you for a crib. It is plain I must go no farther on this road; if you and he cannot understand me who will? Yet, declaimed, the strange constructions would be dramatic and effective. Must I interpret it? . . .[1]

A long page of explanations follows the query; it cannot have seemed too long to Bridges or the good Canon.

So seldom did Bridges express his agreement with the form or thought of a poem that Hopkins recorded the compliments he received, or frankly admitted he did not expect them. He was 'somewhat surprised' at his liking 'so much' the sonnet entitled 'The Handsome Heart'.[2] He received encouragement from what Bridges said of his fragment of an intended play on 'St. Winefred'.[3] His lovely lyric, 'Margaret, are you grieving?' brought him a 'very flattering and endearing' letter.[4] He was told that Gosse liked his pieces, and in 1881 he was urged to 'persuade Hall Caine' to put his 'Andromeda' into the selection of sonnets the latter was to edit.[5] When Hall Caine decided not to print any of Hopkins's sonnets, because the purpose of his book was to 'demonstrate the impossibility of improving upon the acknowledged structure whether as to rhyme-scheme or measure',[6] Bridges acted as a faithful friend. He wrote a letter expressing his discontent and refused to contribute any of his own sonnets—a gallant attitude, of which Hopkins disapproved. 'One sonnet was not worth quarrelling about'.[7] On another occasion, when an unsigned article in the *Saturday Review*, written in a humorous tone, had seemed to allude to Hopkins as an obscure poet, Bridges tried to appease his friend by saying it could only have been done out of spite.[8] But all these marks of kindness cannot hide the fact that Bridges's strong objection to Hopkins's poetry continued unchanged to the end. Hopkins's letters, on the whole, do not reveal it as

[1] Letter CLIX, February 10, 1888, p. 272.
[2] Letter LXII, August 14, 1879, p. 86.
[3] Letter CXXIX, May 17, 1885, p. 218.
[4] Letter LXXI, January 26, 1881, p. 121.
[5] Letter LXXV, June 16, 1881, p. 132.
[6] Letter LXXIII, May 1, 1881, p. 128.
[7] Letter LXXIV, May 14, 1881, p. 130.
[8] Letter XCI, October 21, 1882, p. 158.

much as Bridges's famous 'Preface to Notes'.[1] But we cannot doubt that the letters of his own that Bridges destroyed were full of the same harsh criticism. Does not Hopkins remark sardonically, after contemplating the possibility of reaching fame through the imprudent praise of men like Gosse, 'But I don't want it and beg you will not expose me to it; which you can easily forbear from doing now that you disapprove of my γένος as vicious, and surely you shd. not vitiate taste?'[2] We may indeed wonder how a man who differed so much in taste from Hopkins could keep his poems, and take infinite pains to copy them or to obtain the latest compositions. Logic, of course, is out of the question here. We can only affirm that Bridges was at once shocked and attracted. He hoped Hopkins would gradually get rid of his eccentricities and concentrate on the real qualities of his new rhythm—its flexibility and its natural vitality. For he was not wholly averse to 'sprung rhythm'.

IV. BRIDGES TRIES HIS HAND AT SPRUNG RHYTHM

After the first shock caused by Hopkins's violent syntax and poetic licence, Bridges expressed the wish to know more about the principles of rhythm that his friend had fixed for himself. He believed that they would prove a means of justifying any kind of licence, and within a fortnight of reading *The Wreck of the Deutschland* he sent a parody of it, which Hopkins did not take in bad part. (He merely observed, 'Your parody reassures me about your understanding the metre.')[3] But when Bridges was in possession of all the necessary explanations he was not long in trying his own hand at sprung rhythm. As early as February, 1879, that is, less than eighteen months after being acquainted with the new rhythm, he sent a number of poems that were supposed to follow the rules set down by Hopkins; and in his pamphlet of *Poems* in 1880 he wrote a note, explaining what he had set out to do.

It is an important statement, for it clearly shows (a) that Bridges considered the 'new prosody' as legitimate as the old;

---

[1] *GMH Poems*, 1948, pp. 202–209.
[2] Letter CLXVIII, October 19, 1888, p. 295.
[3] Letter XXXVII, August 21, 1877, p. 44.

(b) that he insisted on the possibility of four or five *unaccented* syllables following on each other rather than on the other possibility—which to Hopkins was even more important—of two or three *accented* syllables following on each other; and (c) that he gave full credit to Hopkins (though he did not name him) for this new principle of scansion. The note is dated Christmas, 1879.

The poems in the smaller type, like those similarly distinguished in the author's last series, are written by the rules of a new prosody, which may well exist by the side of the old. It is left to the judgment of the reader: but the author hopes that these verses will be read with attention to the natural quantity and accent of the syllables—for these are the interpretation of the rhythm —and not with the notion that all accents in poetry are alternate with unaccented syllables, nor with the almost universal prejudice that when two or more unaccented syllables intervene between two accented syllables the former must suffer and be slurred over: a prejudice which probably arises from the common misuse of unaccented for short syllables.

The use of feet which correspond to paeons, and the frequent inversions of feet in these new rhythms, render it possible for four or five unaccented syllables to follow on each other.

The author disavows any claim to originality for the novelty: this is almost entirely due to a friend, whose poems remain, he regrets to say, in manuscript.[1]

In the pamphlet of *Poems*, 1879, four pieces were printed in smaller type as being in what Hopkins called 'a mitigated sprung rhythm'—'The Passer-by', 'The Downs', and two sonnets beginning, 'I would be a bird' and, 'So hot the moon' (the latter of which was cancelled from later editions).[2] In the pamphlet of *Poems*, 1880, three more pieces were offered 'to the judgment of the reader': 'London Snow', 'The Voice of Nature', and 'On a Dead Child'. In the *Academy* of April 5, 1879, an anonymous reviewer remarked on 'The Passer-By' as 'an

---

[1] *Poems, Third Series*, 1880, Note, p. 4.

[2] In a letter to Dixon (*GMH & RWD*, Letter V, February 27, 1879, p. 21) Hopkins mentions only three of the four poems, omitting 'I would be a bird'. This may have been an oversight, or he may have doubted whether the sonnet was intended to be in sprung rhythm.

attempt at a choric rhythm which we take to be choriambic in base'. But in the *Academy* of May 14, 1881, the anonymous reviewer—Hopkins thought it was Saintsbury—while professing admiration for the poet's work, wrote:

For the author's experiments in a new prosody we do not care much, though they contain at least the elements of some fine poetry. When the new prosody is worth much, it seems to us to be reducible with advantage to the old.[1]

There was a certain diffidence in Bridges's note which showed that he had not dared to follow Hopkins in all his audacities. Hopkins was quick to see the contrast between his own genuine manner and Bridges's imitation of it. He was not satisfied and said so.

The pieces in sprung rhythm—do not quite satisfy me. They do read tentative, experimental. . . . *The Downs* is the best. . . . *The Passer-By* in particular reads not so much like sprung rhythm as that logaoedic dignified-doggerel one Tennyson has employed in *Maud* and since.[2]

London Snow is a most beautiful and successful piece. It is charmingly fresh, I do not know what is like it. The rhythm, as I told you, is not quite perfect. That of the child-piece is worse and that piece is worse, indeed *it is* Browningese, if you like; as for instance, 'To a world, do we think, that heals the disaster of this?' or something like that. You are certainly less at your ease in sprung rhythm.[3]

From such severe criticism one would gather that Hopkins was unwilling to let others use his new prosody. Indeed it is difficult to absolve him entirely from this charge. Superficially there is much in Hopkins that is Browningese; why should it be a fault in Bridges, when it is not in him? Can sprung rhythm be resorted to for other purposes than those chosen by its creator? There lies the crux of the matter. Sprung rhythm lends itself essentially 'to expressing passion'; it is meant to translate 'the instress of feeling'. It is dramatic rhythm: stress is the life of it.[4] Bridges 'treats it in theory and practice as something in-

---

[1] Quoted by Abbott, *GMH to RB*, Letter LXXIV, p. 129, note.
[2] Letter LIV, February 22, 1879, p. 71.
[3] Letter LXX, October 26, 1880, p. 111.
[4] Letter XL, May 21, 1878, p. 52.

formal and variable without any limit but ear and taste', and this is not how Hopkins looks at it. Bridges introduces a notion of quantity which is alien to it; he is ready to use paeons, that is, three unstressed and one stressed syllables for one foot, but ignores the central rule of sprung rhythm,

> that the stress alone is essential to a foot and that therefore even one stressed syllable may make a foot and consequently two or more stresses may come running, which in common rhythm can, regularly speaking, never happen.[1]

Bridges will seldom use monosyllabic feet; he is less intent on concentration and abrupt beats than Hopkins. In fact the advantage of the new prosody lies for him in its flexibility, rather than in its passionate rush.[2] Finally the difference between the two poets is, in the very use of sprung rhythm, one of mood and theme. The poet of storms and wrecks and harrowing spiritual conflicts could never describe the stately majesty of a splendid ship passing by, nor the lazy floating down of the snow,

> Hiding difference making unevenness even.
> ('London Snow', 8.)

Symbolically these last words are most revealing. Bridges is the poet of 'stealthy' motion, of soft things 'loosely lying'; Hopkins could never make unevenness even. But we are not obliged to choose between the smoothness of the one and the rough-hewn forms of the other, since both possess intrinsic beauty.

Bridges's poems in sprung rhythm, which in their own style represent a positive criticism of Hopkins's manner, are better than experimental verses. They have an unmistakable quality of their own and the supple movement of the lines is in perfect accord with the delicate logaoedic rhythm of the stresses. No better example of his art, after he had turned to his own profit some of the prosodic principles of his friend, can be found than the opening stanza of 'The Downs'.

---

[1] *GMH & RWD*, Letter XII, December 22, 1880, p. 39.

[2] There is a passage in *GMH to RB*, Letter LXXI, p. 122, which clearly shows the opposite tendencies of the two poets. Hopkins makes suggestions about the rhythm of 'London Snow' which 'would make it perfect'. He would like Bridges to omit articles, conjunctions and prepositions, so as to give more tautness to the lines. In fact his suggestions would spoil the quiet flow of words.

O bold majestic downs, smooth, fair and lonely;
O still solitude, only matched in the skies:
    Perilous in steep places,
    Soft in the level races,
Where sweeping in phantom silence the cloudland flies;
With lovely undulation of fall and rise;
    Entrenched with thickets thorned,
By delicate miniature dainty flowers adorned!

Indeed the lines seem to rise and fall with the very undulation of the hills. The stresses fall without effort on the words that must be set in relief. The contrast between trimeters and penta-meters is deftly drawn by the three different stress-patterns of the shorter lines and the variety in the length of unstressed syllables. The sibilant sounds and the unostentatious allitera-tions, the pauses in the first four lines, and the unhurried sweep of the second part of the stanza all combine to bring out the peacefulness of the mood. And in the two instances where stress follows stress (stíll sólitude—stéep pláces) there is no bold sur-prise, but the necessary underlining of a true feeling and a real fact. The poet's mastery can be seen in the vocabulary, the images, the movement and the soft sounds.

It is strange that Hopkins should have considered that the rhythm of 'On a Dead Child' was worse than that of 'London Snow'. For in that poignant poem two stanzas are highly sug-gestive of his own manner, while they remain in keeping with the sad theme of the piece. The exclamations, the interroga-tions, the parentheses, the differences in the length of the lines are such as we find in *The Wreck of the Deutschland* or *The Loss of the Eurydice*. They are proof of a definite influence.

Thy mother's treasure wert thou;—alas! no longer
    To visit her heart with wondrous joy; to be
        Thy father's pride;—ah, he
Must gather his faith together, and his strength make
    stronger.

So quiet! doth the change content thee?—Death, whither
    hath he taken thee?
    To a world, do I think, that rights the disaster of this?
        The vision of which I miss,

Who weep for the body, and wish but to wárm thĕe aňd
ăwáken thee.

(Stanzas 2 & 6)

The double feminine endings—táken thee, awáken thee—can
be compared to similar endings in *The Wreck*—knéw in them,
astréw in them (Stanza 21). The triplet feet of the last line
with a first paeon for the penultimate foot may remind us of a
line in *The Wreck*:

> To flash from the flame to the flame then, tówĕr frŏm thĕ
> grace to the grace.

(Stanza 3)

And we must not forget that pity for an innocent young child,
as well as the searching question about a world that should
'right' this disaster, are not far removed from the pity and
spiritual anguish expressed by Hopkins in *The Loss of the Eurydice* about the 'redeeming' of the 'boldboys' of 'lovely manly
mould' drowned in the 'rivelling snowstorm'.

The influence of Hopkins was never denied by Bridges. Indeed he was the first to point to possible echoes of his friend's
poems in his own lyrics. He even seems to have taken some
pleasure in underlining those that Hopkins had not detected
himself. But although Hopkins often warned his friend against
echoes, he did not object to echoes of his own poems; he made
allowance for the strong poetical bonds that linked them. 'I do
not think it desirable that I shd. be wholly uninfluenced by
you or you by me; one ought to be independent but not unim-
pressionable; that wd. be to refuse education'.[1] The echoes he
objected to were those from classical authors that would be
familiar to cultivated readers; since his own poems stood little
chance of being published, echoes from them had little importance.

'Hail is hurling' did remind me of myself but I do not well know
why: I have something about hail and elsewhere several things
about hurling, but that does not amount to hail hurling. 'Father
fond' wd. never have occurred to me, at all events it never had.[2]

---

[1] *GMH to RB*, Letter LIX, April 22, 1879, p. 80.
[2] *Ibid.*

Bridges had written in 'The Passer-By',

> When skies are cold and misty, and hail is hurling.

and in 'Morning Hymn', which praises the Sun,

> and near
> As father fond art found.

In the first instance, Hopkins is correct; there is no hurling of hail in his poems, although he describes 'the sharp and sided hail' in 'Heaven-Haven', and the 'Deutschland' 'hurling the haven behind' her in *The Wreck*. Here Bridges is rather imitating Hopkins's alliterative and consonantal style. In the second instance Hopkins should have remembered the last line of his sonnet, 'In the Valley of the Elwy',

> Being mighty a master, being a father and fond.

Bridges's borrowing of the words and his transfer of the thought from God to Sun are self-evident.

Bridges liked to borrow or imitate. Thinking of poetry as an art in which he desired to perfect himself, he did not believe that his own expressions had any special virtue and was ready to admit into his own poems expressions he admired for their intensity or their nobility. At the same time it is remarkable to see him directly influenced by *The Wreck of the Deutschland*, the poem he had so strongly objected to. Its novelty and boldness, which had struck him as affectation in 1878,[1] had won him over in less than two years. Besides its humorous tone, there is an unmistakable ironical triumph in the conclusion of Hopkins's remarks on the echoes he detected in the *Poems* of 1880.

Truth compels, and modesty does not forbid, me here to say that this volume has at least three real echos (or echoes) of me. I do not wish them away, but they are there. The 'snow-mossed wonder' line recalls 'For though he is under' in the Deutschland. 'O look at the trees' the first line of the Starlight sonnet, and 'throned behind' again comes from the Deutschland. I fancy there is another I cannot now recall. O yes, it is in The Voice of Nature. 'Precipitate all o'er-

[1] Letter XLI, May 30, 1878, pp. 53-54.

rides and swerves nor abides' (is it?) : this is in the Deutschland too. I cannot quote it but it ends with 'abides'. It is easy to see why this is : that is the longest piece extant in sprung rhythm and could not help haunting your memory. I do not want them altered, and 'throned behind' having found its way into the midst of a lovely image would not like to be parted from its company.[1]

V. BRIDGES SUGGESTS THE INFLUENCE OF WHITMAN

But if Hopkins condescendingly acquiesced in such echoes—no doubt because they did not sound unpleasantly to his ear—he was not ready to admit certain comparisons or parallels that Bridges drew when criticizing the image of a sonnet or the free-verse prosody of the *Leaden and Golden Echoes*. Hopkins keenly resented any remark that seemed to throw doubt on his complete originality. He did not like this sort of argument: You use the same image as you objected to in my poem, or, You imitate Walt Whitman. He immediately protested and offered a full load of reasons to vindicate his personal claims.

In an early draft of a sonnet[2] in *The Growth of Love*, 1889, Bridges used the words 'golden foil', and he reminded Hopkins, when the latter objected to the expression, that he himself had written in 'God's Grandeur',

> The world is charged with the grandeur of God.
> It will flame out, like shining from shook foil.

Hopkins wrote back,

You were, you say, driven to it: I protest, and with indignation, at

[1] Letter LXX, October 26, 1880, p. 112. The relevant passages are:
(a) *R.B.*   . . . from under the white-mossed wonder. (London Snow).
    G.M.H.   . . . he is under the world's splendour and wonder. (The Wreck, Stanza 6).
(b) *R.B.*   O look at the trees, they cried, O look at the trees! (London Snow).
    G.M.H.   Look at the stars! look, look up at the skies! (Starlight Night).
(c) *R.B.*   who once were throned behind /All beauty. (Disillusion).
    G.M.H.   Grasp God, throned behind /Death. (The Wreck, Stanza 32).
(d) *R.B.*   Precipitate all o'errides, and turns nor abides. (The Voice of Nature).
    G.M.H.   a sovereignty that heeds but hides, bodes but abides. (The Wreck, Stanza 32).
[2] Sonnet LXII, 'Sweet sleep, dear unadornèd bride of toil'. Discarded in the final edition, 1898.

your saying that I was driven to the same image. With more truth might it be said that my sonnet might have been written expressly for the image's sake. But the image is not the same as yours and I do not mean by foil set-off at all; I mean foil in its sense of leaf or tinsel, and no other word whatever will give the effect I want. . . . Moreover as it is the first rhyme, presumably it engendered the others and not they it.[1]

Hopkins was quick to see the difference in the sense of the word under discussion. He scored his point neatly, and in the printed version of 1889 Bridges dropped the 'golden foil' image and rhymed on the words 'turmoil' and 'despoil' as suggested by Hopkins in the same letter.

About the 'fancied resemblance' between *The Leaden Echo and The Golden Echo* and the poems in *The Leaves of Grass*, Hopkins pleaded Not Guilty. We need only record here his main arguments. He had not read more than half a dozen pieces of Whitman's at most; but he 'knew in his heart' that Whitman's mind was more like his own than any other man's living. He was aware 'that there was to the eye something in my long lines like his', that both were in irregular rhythms and that the one would remind people of the other; but there the likeness ended. He considered that Whitman's poems were mostly in an irregular rhythmic prose, whereas his own were in an elaborate stressed rhythm and everything in his long, highly-wrought lines was weighed and timed. He did not finally deny all resemblance, but he emphasized the contrast between his own carefully thought-out irregularity and Whitman's haphazard 'savage' style. Neither in matter nor style, he averred, could he be said to owe anything to Whitman.[2]

Nevertheless there is in the two *Echoes* much that is suggestive of Whitman's free, irregular and rhapsodic style.[3] Although Hopkins's reasoning is weighty, there were in his temperament, in his sensuous apprehension of reality, in his deep probing of the 'self', in his offering of all things 'counter, original, spare, strange' and in his love of 'the weeds and the wilderness', more than passing similarities with Whitman. Both were original

---

[1] Letter XCVII, January 4, 1883, pp. 168–9.
[2] Letter XC, October 18, 1882, pp. 154–8.
[3] See W. H. Gardner, *Gerard Manley Hopkins*, Vol. II, pp. 105–108.

poets and meant to keep their originality at all costs. But there was an essential difference between them: one was a pagan who rejoiced in all the physical joys of the earth, while the other, as a Christian ascetic, offered them to God or renounced them. It is difficult to say more than Hopkins, who admits, up to a point, a certain influence. We agree with the American critic, Mr. Templeman, who writes,

Though it is not yet certain exactly how much of Whitman's poetry Hopkins was closely aware of, he clearly had read some of Whitman, and that with seriousness, careful analysis and subsequent frank avowal of possible influence.[1]

What must be stressed here is Bridges's indirect influence in preventing Hopkins from yielding to Whitman's powerful attraction. Dr. Gardner says that 'in his essential sanity Hopkins was closer to Whitman [than to Baudelaire], whose impetuous rhythms, dynamic style, and pervasive nature-mysticism are often so like his own.'[2] And in many passages of his long study Dr. Gardner insists on the similarities between the two poets; only in a brief note, which might easily be overlooked, does he express the opinion that Hopkins deliberately avoided the 'insidious attraction' of Whitman.[3] The letter of October, 1882, to which he refers the reader does not justify such a conclusion. In fact Hopkins denies imitation, and the sprung rhythm of the *Echoes* is quite different from the free rhythm of the *Leaves of Grass*. But the truth of the matter is that Bridges was responsible for having drawn Hopkins's attention to a dangerous attraction, and for having prevented any further unconscious imitation. The danger lay in the poetical kinship and temperamental analogies which could lead the Jesuit poet, almost unawares, into the unbridled, enthusiastic world of Whitman. As soon as a possible resemblance was hinted at, Hopkins saw to it that no such reproach could ever again be levelled against him.

[1] W. D. Templeman, 'Hopkins and Whitman, Evidence of Influence and Echoes,' *Philological Quarterly*, January, 1954, pp. 48–65.

[2] *Op. cit.*, Vol. II, p. 376.

[3] *Ibid.*, p. 195, note 1.

VI. MUTUAL GAINS

The Whitman incident offers one of the best instances of the assistance which Bridges's literary friendship brought to Hopkins. There was a real influence in his classical and somewhat sedate criticism. He knew he could not change Hopkins's idiosyncrasies, nor did he wish them to be utterly changed. But in the disparity of their personalities and in the frank give-and-take of their judgments on each other's poems, there was profit for both, and a greater balance in their artistic tendencies. Just as Hopkins tried to divert Bridges from too much preciosity and smoothness, and led him towards an independent use of sprung rhythm, so Bridges tried to lead Hopkins to a gradual rejection of wildness and eccentricities. As death ended their friendship just when it might have produced more positive results, we can record few gains. Bridges owed Hopkins more subtlety in his rhythms, a more exacting use of words, and more finish in his composition. As for Hopkins, although other influences contributed to his mastery of a more masculine and less profuse diction, it is fair to say that Bridges had a share in this evolution. When in his 'Preface to Notes' Bridges wrote,

It is lamentable that Gerard Hopkins died when, judged by his latest work, he was beginning to concentrate the force of all his luxuriant experiments in rhythm and diction, and castigate his art into a more reserved style,[1]

he was expressing far more than a friend's grief. His was the sorrow of a man of letters who knew that his 'long jobations'[2] about his correspondent's literary eccentricities and singularities had borne fruit. His criticism was no doubt discouraging at times but we agree with Mr. Pick when he says that 'it had the effect of making Hopkins consider with double care the effects he was trying to produce'.[3]

[1] *GMH Poems*, 1948, p. 209.
[2] *GMH to RB*, Letter LXXIII. April 27, 1881, p. 126: 'You give me a long jobation about eccentricities. Alas, I have heard so much about and suffered so much for and in fact been so completely ruined for life by my alleged singularities that they are a sore subject'.
[3] *Op. cit.*, p. 201.

All the facts recorded in the last two chapters, the frank, abrupt or diffident interchange of comments, suggestions, corrections, agreements and disagreements, tend to illustrate the need of an audience for any poet. Bridges and Hopkins, more than most poets, required a small band of trustful friends on whom they could try out their verse. Instinctively they liked to work in solitude, they drew apart and fought shy of any public recognition or fame. In Hopkins's case, this attitude accords with the humble sacrifice of a religious; with Bridges, a particular aloofness and a violent distrust of the mob and the *communis criticorum* explain his policy of publishing his earlier works either anonymously or in small editions printed at the private press of his friend Henry Daniel.[1] Daniel's black-letter editions, printed on handmade laid paper, with uncut edges, were a pleasure to the eye of the learned collector of rare books; they were rather awe-inspiring to the public at large. At first Hopkins seemed to share, but with some reluctance, his friend's feelings about the unintelligent or unfeeling common reader. He wrote in 1881, 'What you say about the run of people not liking nor knowing what to make of your writing and this giving you satisfaction opens out a wide vein of to me saddening thoughts which I shall not now enter on'.[2] But later he was to take no sentimental view of the matter and kept urging Bridges to 'come before the public in the usual manner'.[3] He tried to laugh him out of a course of conduct that was prejudicial to his future renown.

For consider: you aim at oblivion; for that you descend into Daniel's den; for that you print 24 copies (so that the College of Apostles on parting could have taken two copies only for the needs of all Scythia, suppose, all Parthia, all India, and so on). Now, as some philosopher Cicero quotes said, *undique tantundem viae ad inferos est* (Anaxagoras, by George); that is you can be forgotten 'as hard' at Dublin

---

[1] The Reverend C. H. O. Daniel (1845–1919), Fellow and later Provost of Worcester College, Oxford, set up a private press at Oxford in 1874 to interest his friends by presenting old and new literature of a high order as elegant in form as it was various in kind. He was a chief precursor of the Kelmscott Press of William Morris. See *Memorials of C. H. O. Daniel*, Oxford, 1921.

[2] *GMH to RB*, Letter LXXI, January 26, 1881, p. 123.

[3] Letter CXIII, April 16, 1884, p. 192.

as anywhere else, at Lampsacus as at Clazomenae: what do you want more?[1]

Hopkins was keenly aware that an audience was necessary for a poet. Being afraid lest his refusal to have his own poems printed might influence his poet-correspondents Patmore, Dixon and Bridges, to do the same, he insisted on the duty that was theirs to become known.

By the bye, I say it deliberately and before God, I would have you and Canon Dixon and all true poets[2] remember that fame, the being known, though in itself one of the most dangerous things to man, is nevertheless the true and appointed air, element, and setting of genius and its works. What are works of art for? to educate, to be standards. . . . To produce then is of little use unless what we produce is known, if known widely known, the wider known the better, for it is by being known it works, it influences, it does its duty, it does good. We must then try to be known, aim at it, take means to it.[3]

This, in its way, was a long jobation. But the insistence, the emphasis put upon fame, 'the being known', must be seen as a deliberate effort to shake Bridges out of his indifference, of which Hopkins strongly disapproved—all the more so, since Patmore had told him of his own disapproval. 'Bridges,' wrote Patmore, 'professes to feel a profound indifference as to whether people read his poems or not. I cannot understand this.'[4] The small circle of friends that Bridges knew and met at Yattendon or Oxford, men like Wooldridge, Daniel, Gosse, Lang and Dobson,[5] no doubt gave him the impression that these 'happy few' were the best audience he could wish for. In some ways they were, and this may explain why Bridges never made any strong bid for popular recognition. (That came to him late in life, by a happy combination of circumstances.) But Hopkins's

[1] Letter CLXX, March 20, 1889, p. 302.
[2] Congratulating Patmore on a new edition of his works Hopkins wrote: 'Your poems are a good deed done for the Catholic Church and another for England, for the British Empire.' *Further Letters*, Letter CLXXXI, June 4, 1886, p. 366.
[3] *GMH to RB*, Letter CXXXVI, October 13, 1886, p. 231.
[4] *Further Letters*, Letter CLXXVIIA, April 7, 1885, p. 361.
[5] The names of these literary friends of Bridges are often mentioned in Hopkins's letters.

repeated warning that a poet depended on an audience and that only those who wrote for an audience finally reached it was certainly profitable.[1] It is just as certain that Bridges, Dixon and, to a lesser degree, Patmore were enough of a friendly audience for Hopkins to go on writing poems, since they could oppose, although by fits and starts, his own self-searching and even crippling scruples.

[1] From 1890 onwards, Bridges had his poetry published by commercial firms, George Bell, J. & E. Bumpus, Smith Elder, Heinemann, and the Oxford University Press.

V

The Varied Interests of Two Cultured Minds

I. PROSODY AND MILTON

The surprising thing about the correspondence between Hopkins and Bridges is that it never stayed in the narrow channel of reciprocal criticism of their poetical works. If we infer from Hopkins's practice that little space was devoted in their letters to the merely anecdotal, and if we consider that Hopkins, as a priest living a rather secluded life, could discuss few subjects with Bridges with complete freedom, the importance and variety of the observations found in the letters are remarkable. In fact we see the two friends ever ready to enter upon an examination of some literary or artistic problem. Although Hopkins once wrote, 'I have the passion for explanation and you have not',[1] the two friends shared that passion and tried through their letters to profit by the information, the expositions and the commentaries that they could lavish on each other. It is just possible that Hopkins may have urged Bridges to write on Milton's prosody, to study with the greatest care the difficult art of chanting psalms, and to revise his views on the modern novel or on such poets as Keats and Dryden. His letters tend to give that impression, and at times, as we shall see in the case of Milton, Bridges seems to have been the writer and publisher of studies which they had pursued jointly.

But another interpretation is also possible. Bridges, who knew the quality of Hopkins's searching intellect, may have deliberately sought his advice on the various questions he himself was studying; he may also, simply by mentioning his preoccupations, have started a course of reflection and personal effort

[1] *GMH to RB*, Letter CLXI, May 25, 1883, p. 275.

which were for Hopkins a means of keeping in touch with the intellectual world at large, and of fighting against his fits of melancholy. In fairness to both poets, it is impossible to choose between these interpretations: too much evidence is missing. Although we may admit that Hopkins possessed the greater speculative power of the two, the results that Bridges achieved by hard and conscientious work show that he was endowed with a mind virile enough to think his own way into whatever matter he studied. The simplest conclusion, which is likely to be the truest, is that there was a constant reciprocal influence. On prosody, on music, on literary criticism, each of them had something to say, and their independence is obvious. But they deliberately chose to share their reflections, and since Hopkins had decided to play the mute and obscure part in this collaboration, the duty remained with Bridges to acknowledge that part whenever it was necessary. This he did not fail to do.

Prosody was a problem which attracted their attention all their lives. The preceding chapter has already shown this. Both poets were consciously in revolt against the aesthetic movement which had begun with Pater, Rossetti and Swinburne. Their own aesthetic philosophy, their worship of beauty and pursuit of an art that would combine the functions of poetry and music, owed much to these three men; but they were not satisfied with the Symbolist Movement, and each in his own way was trying to discover a new style in which Beauty and Truth would be praised through quiet dignity or through passionate intensity. The explanation of their avoidance of the main poetical current of the day may be found in a common study of Milton's prosody. At the beginning it was conducted in strict isolation, and in the end it led them to different conclusions; but the effect each achieved had the same virtue of keeping the genuine rhythms of speech.

In the very first letter in which Hopkins criticized his friend's poems there are direct allusions to Milton, to his rhythm, and to the choruses of *Samson Agonistes*. There is also proof that Bridges had already told Hopkins that he was trying to use some of Milton's irregular rhythms in his sonnets.[1] At the same

[1] Letter XXX, April 3, 1877, pp. 32–40.

time, and before Bridges had written to him on the matter, Hopkins, who had 'paid much attention to Milton's rhythm', had 'composed two sonnets with rhythmical experiments of the sort'. He could well add, 'How our wits jump!' One might almost speak of telepathy. In fact what Bridges was trying to do in a tentative manner was to take advantage of Milton's subtle inversion of stresses to justify his own irregularity. Hopkins, however, in 1877 had already gone further 'in the way of irregularity', and had invented his own sprung rhythm; but he had come to this after reflecting on Milton's 'counterpointed pentameters'.[1] He could give instances to Bridges:

> These are the lines, I suppose, which these folk think will not scan:
>
> By the waters of life, where'er they sat—   (*P.L.* XI. 79)
>
> Light from above, from the fountain of light— (*P.R.* IV. 289)
>
> But to vanquish by wisdom hellish wiles—   (*P.R.* I. 175)
>
> Home to his mother's house private returned— (*P.R.* IV. 639)
>
> etc. The choruses of Samson Agonistes are still more remarkable: I think I have mastered them and may some day write on the subject.[2]

This looked promising, and was so much in accordance with Bridges's own inquiry that he immediately asked Hopkins to send him his notes. There was the promise of a letter 'laden to her gunwales with judicious remarks';[3] but no letter was sent. Bridges pleaded to be 'put out of his agony',[4] but Hopkins's next letters are short and do not deal with the subject. Since the friends met in London in the summer holidays, we may assume that they discussed the matter orally, and it is almost certain that Hopkins showed Bridges the notes he had written for his pupils at Stonyhurst in 1873. Nevertheless he never wrote the essay he had spoken of, and it was left to Bridges to

---

[1] *GMH Journals*, 'Lecture Notes: Rhetoric, Rhythm and Other Structural Parts', p. 280.

[2] *GMH to RB*, Letter XXX, April 3, 1877, p. 38.

[3] Postcard XXXI, April 6, 1877, p. 40.

[4] Letter XXXII, June 13, 1877, p. 41.

write it. It seems that the latter entertained the hope that Hopkins would do the task, for in the introduction to his little book on *Milton's Prosody* he says, with unfeigned humility, 'Indeed, it was not until after I despaired of persuading others more competent than myself to execute the work, that I undertook what I have done.'[1] In spite of the plural, I doubt whether any other person, more competent than Hopkins and Bridges, could have made the accurate analysis of Milton's blank verse. It is true that J. A Symonds had published an article on the subject as early as December, 1874;[2] but because their own views on prosody were involved, Bridges and Hopkins probed deeper. In his letters to Dixon and Patmore, Hopkins gives many instances of his careful reading of Milton's poems. His study of Milton's counterpointed lines, and cadences, and mastery of phrase, his endeavour to achieve a Miltonic 'plainness and severity' in his own sonnets,[3] 'hoping in time to have a more balanced and Miltonic style',[4] the fact that he had 'collected' Milton's 'later rhythms',[5]—all this must have been personal knowledge that he passed on to Bridges. But the two experts understood Milton's practice differently. Whereas Milton's counterpointed or mounted rhythm led Hopkins to invent his own sprung rhythm, the somewhat loose or supple structure of Milton's verse strictly tabulated by Bridges led him to invent his own neo-Miltonic and loose Alexandrines.

Hopkins would have liked Bridges to explain what Milton was aiming at. He believed that the majority of Milton's irregularities were groping their way towards the principle of metrical equivalence, which was essential to prosody but had only been understood and admitted by the poets of the nineteenth century. Bridges did not feel so certain about it. He deliberately 'refrained from attempting to give any explanation of the laws of English prosody' and 'avoided as far as possible entering even upon the borderland between prosody and poetry'.[6] For

---

[1] *Milton's Prosody*, 1893, p. 5.
[2] 'The Blank Verse of Milton', *Fortnightly Review*, December, 1874; reprinted in *Blank Verse* (1895).
[3] *GMH to RB*, Letter LXII, August 14, 1879, p. 87.
[4] *Ibid.*, Letter LIII, February 15, 1879, p. 66.
[5] *GMH & RWD*, Letter III, October 5, 1878, p. 14.
[6] *Milton's Prosody*, p. 5.

this non-committal attitude Hopkins upbraided him. He obtained from Bridges a note on metrical equivalence which was finally expanded into an appendix.[1] The latter must be quoted at some length, for it shows how Bridges acknowledged his friend's theories, paid tribute to his scholarship, and accepted or rejected his opinions with independent frankness.

My friend, the late Father Gerard Hopkins, to whom I sent the MS. of my tract for criticism, blamed my omission of any statement of what he considered the truth on [metrical equivalence]. He wrote thus to me:

'I cannot but hope that in your metrical paper you will somewhere distinctly state the principle of equivalence, and that it was quite unrecognized in Milton's and still more in Shakespeare's time. All, but especially young students, need to be made clearly to understand what metrical equivalence is, that it is in use in English now, and that it was not then,—and that it was Milton's artifices, as you explain them, that helped to introduce it'.

In quoting this I consider that I have done my duty by the theory. I suppose that the statement represents fairly what some metrists hold, for it is the opinion of one who was learned and acute on all such questions. I go with it so far that I am ready to grant that in English two short syllables may sometimes be equivalent to one long one; but it seems to me wrong to imagine that English rhythms can ever be explained or governed by such a fiction as this is, when it is made a general law.[2]

In the remarks that follow, Bridges seeks to establish that in the English tradition the syllabic and stress systems are mixed; Shakespeare came to determine his rhythm by stresses as he threw off the syllabic trammels of his early style,

and Milton did just the same in *Samson Agonistes*, though he learnedly disguised his liberty by various artifices. . . . If once the

---

[1] To H. C. Beeching's edition of *Paradise Lost*, Book I, Clarendon Press, 1887, Bridges contributed a paper entitled, 'On the Elements of Milton's Blank Verse in *P.L.*' As a supplement to this he published in 1889 a pamphlet 'On the Prosody of *Paradise Regained* and *Samson Agonistes*'. The two 'tracts', as Bridges called them, were partly rewritten, appendices were added, and the whole was published under the title *Milton's Prosody* by the Clarendon Press in a limited edition in 1893 and in a regular issue in 1894. Revised and enlarged editions appeared in 1901 and 1921.

[2] *Milton's Prosody*, Appendix F, pp. 67–68; cf. *GMH to RB*, Letter CLI, August 25, 1887, p. 259.

notion be got rid of that you must have so many syllables in a line to make a verse, or must account for the supernumerary ones in some such manner as the Greeks or Latins would have done, then the stress will declare its supremacy; which, as may be seen in Shakespeare and Milton, it is burning to do.[1]

To Hopkins the principle of metrical equivalence was merely a satisfactory explanation of the rhythmical structure of a line, which according to the syllabic system could not have been scanned.[2] But as a principle it involved more complex equivalences than 'one long = two short'; it opened the way to sprung rhythm in which one stressed syllable may be equivalent to a varied number of unstressed syllables. In Hopkins's sprung rhythm the stress declares its supremacy, the syllabic system is discarded, but the presence or absence of unstressed syllables must be accounted for; there is no free use of them and a system of marks compels the reader to follow the intentions of the poet. Although it is no longer a case of having so many syllables in a line to make a verse, the structure of the line, the stresses and their respective impact depend on the quality and number of the syllables. Hopkins allowed outrides or hurried feet, *i.e.*, supernumerary syllables in verses strictly governed by natural speech-stress.

Bridges does not go so far, or rather he draws a firm line between the syllabic and the stress systems. Whereas Hopkins merges one system into the other, Bridges considers that the stressed rhythm can do away with scanning. This is where he parts company with Hopkins. He writes:

If the number of stresses in each line be fixed (and such a fixation would be the metre), and if the stresses be determined only by the language and its sense, and if the syllables which they have to carry do not overburden them, then every line may have a different rhythm; though so much variety is not of necessity . . . [Milton] wrote in the choruses of *Samson* a rhythmical stressed verse, and

---

[1] *Op. cit.*, pp. 68–69.

[2] Here are a few examples given by Bridges:

> Of rainbows and starry eyes, the waters thus.—(*P.L.* VII, 446.)
> And all the flourishing works of peace destroy.—*P.R.* III, 80.)
> With touch ethereal of Heaven's fiery rod.—(*S.A.* 549.)

scanned it by means of fictions. *He need not have troubled himself about the scansion at all. If the stressed rhythm is the beauty of the verse, it is a sufficient account of it.* But this seems too simple to be understood.[1]

The two sentences that Bridges took the trouble to italicize express a revolutionary opinion. But is scansion so easily waved aside? Is it as simple to understand as he wants us to believe? Is he not giving speech-stressed verse too much liberty? His arguments tend to destroy each other when he says for instance that English poets, writing pure speech-stressed verse,

will discover the laws for themselves, and will find open to them an infinite field of rhythm as yet untouched. There is nothing which may not be done in it, and it is perhaps not the least of its advantages that it is most difficult to do well.[2]

Laws discovered for themselves, and an infinite field of rhythm, do not seem to lead to great difficulties. Stricter laws and a narrower field would entail a more painful task for the poet; beauty hard-won is more impressive than effortless grace.

The above quotations help us to understand what Hopkins meant when he wrote, 'With all my licences, or rather laws, I am stricter than you and I might say than anybody I know'.[3] Bridges in his appendix pleads for a more supple prosody, as if he were still arguing with his friend and advocating greater freedom. It is of great importance to notice that, although he seems to grant that the future of English verse lies in the realm of stress prosody—being still in 1893 under the influence of Hopkins—Bridges finally followed the opposite course in his own practice. He invented a system that was to have all the advantages of sprung rhythm without its violent and rough stress pattern. For this purpose he went back to the twelve-syllable verse and devised a line with no 'accentual bumping' and no 'decided enforced accent';[4] such a line, he was to term

---

[1] *Op. cit.*, p. 71.

[2] *Op. cit.*, p. 72.

[3] *GMH to RB*, Letter XXXVII, August 21, 1877, p. 44.

[4] R. Bridges, *Collected Essays*, Vol. II, 1933, pp. 87–91, '*New Verse*: Explanation of the Prosody of my Late Syllabic "Free Verse" '. 'In all this work from earliest to latest [Milton] delighted in the Alexandrine without its hemistichs, and here was a promising field of freedom which it was most exciting to explore. I had no

'neo-Miltonic' or 'loose Alexandrine'. In the poem in which he
first used it he explains humorously—and to a parrot at that!
—his new experimental metre.

> I am writing verses to you and grieve that you sh'd be
> *absolument incapable de les comprendre,*
> *tu, Polle, nescis ista nec potes scire*:—
> Alas! Iambic, scazon and alexandrine,
> spondee or choriamb, all is alike to you—
> my well-continued fanciful experiment
> wherein so many strange verses amalgamate
> on the secure bedrock of Milton's prosody.[1]

The last line gives the clue to the whole scheme, which Bridges
took seriously enough, since the same 'loose Alexandrines'
were to be used for the long philosophical poem, *The Testament of Beauty*. Milton's prosody had led Bridges to explore the
possibilities of the alexandrine in order to avoid the five-foot
line and the accentual pattern—the dot-and-go-one bumping—
of blank verse.

If we agree that there are as many metrical theories as there
are metrists, and consider with Bridges that 'no art can flourish
that is not alive and growing, and [that] it can only grow by
invention of new methods or by discovery of new material',[2]
we may admire the creator of the 'loose Alexandrines' for the
skill with which he produced a new verse diametrically the
opposite of Hopkins's sprung rhythm, although 'the secure
bedrock of Milton's prosody' was common to both. The two
poets had great technical acuteness and a very sensitive ear; but
while Hopkins was trying to set up a 'permanent principle of
scansion'[3] for his prosody, Bridges failed to find 'any definite

notion how the thing would hold together when thus apparently freed from all
rule. It was plainly the freest of free verse, there being no speech-rhythm which it
would not admit. . . . Because one of the main limitations of English verse is that
its accentual (dot and go one) bumping is apt to make ordinary words ridiculous;
and since, on theory at least, there would be no decided enforced accent in any
place in this new metre, it seemed that it might possibly afford escape from the limitations spoken of'.

[1] *Poet. Works*, p. 510, 'Poor Poll'.
[2] *Collected Essays*, Vol I, 1930, Essay II, 'Humdrum and Harum-Scarum', p. 54.
[3] *GMH to RB*, Letter XXXVII, August 21, 1877, p. 45.

prosodial principle'[1] for either the syllabic or the stress systems, and thus gave himself much elbow-room for his new experiments.

In a careful study of the metre of *The Testament of Beauty*[2] Mrs. Elizabeth Cox Wright has shown how Bridges invented his new metrical prosody and justified it theoretically. She quotes extensively from the various essays on poetry and prosody which he wrote between 1909 and 1923.[3] She does not fail to see that Bridges's remarks are sometimes rather confusing, and that 'it is dangerous business to say what a writer probably meant when, so careful in analysis and practised in composition, he leaves an idea apparently at loose ends'.[4] She proves that Bridges discards the principle implied by 'feet' by following Milton's free speech rhythms, and accepts Patmore's suggestion that the important thing is the temporal line length.[5] He

---

[1] *Collected Essays*, Vol. II, Essay XV, 'Letter on English Prosody', pp. 67 and 74.

[2] E. C. Wright, *Metaphor, Sound and Meaning in Bridges's 'The Testament of Beauty'*, University of Pennsylvania Press, 1951.

[3] *Op. cit.*, p. 34. Cf. *Collected Essays* Nos. II and XV, and the notes to *Poems in Classical Prosody*, 1912, and *October & Other Poems*, 1920.

[4] *Op. cit.*, Ch. III, 'The Theoretical Justification of the New Metre', p. 42.

[5] Derek Patmore, in 'Three Poets discuss New Verse Forms' (*The Month*, August, 1951, pp. 69–78), gives long extracts from letters of Coventry Patmore, Hopkins and Bridges concerning their respective innovations. He quotes extensively from letters, hitherto unpublished, of Bridges to Patmore. Hopkins had introduced Bridges and his poems to Patmore; in return, Bridges had introduced the older poet to Hopkins's poems. Both friends had read and discussed Patmore's *Study on English Metrical Law* (first published 1857, reprinted as an introduction to *Amelia*, 1878). Bridges no doubt expressed their common opinion when he wrote on August 29, 1883: 'As far as I can see we agree in what we arrive at; but I should be impatient of your path'. The most revealing passage is to be found in a letter dated September 28, 1883, in which Bridges tries to induce Patmore to give his learned opinion on the new prosody of stressed speech-rhythms he and Hopkins were using. 'The interest which you take in the grammar of English verse has led me to hope that you would not be disinclined to give an account in print of what Hopkins and I call the new prosody. We both regard it—without prejudice to the conventional prosody, which you will have seen I use independently of it—as the true solution of English verse. Perhaps we write it rather differently; I should say Hopkins most correctly, I more popular or practically—but I think that we both want an outsider to say something. Your learned essay gives you a standpoint, and anything which you say must have a definite meaning; and your judgment would be at once unprejudiced and weighty. Then I think that—supposing the new prosody to be worth your attention—the completeness of what you have hitherto written rather demands that you should treat this theory . . .

'I shall never write on prosody myself. I think it likely that Hopkins might do so,

liberates the speech-rhythms under the discipline of isochronous lines, marked by a pause at the line-end, and builds his twelve-syllable verse on a framework of strict unaccented time.

By using other poetic devices, such as alliteration, assonance, rhyme, subtle phrasing and varied tempo, Bridges gives to his new metre the possibility of expressing all kinds of speech-rhythms. No doubt, as Mrs. Wright rightly concludes, 'Bridges's invention emerges as fitted almost exactly to his task';[1] but it is no less obvious that his invention has been worked out by taking Hopkins's theory and practice exactly *a contrario*. Hopkins liberated his speech-rhythms under the discipline of iso-chronous feet, strongly marked by the stresses, with no pause at the line-end, and built his verse on a framework of strict, accented time while the number of syllables could vary according to the pace of thought and feeling.

In the friendship of the two poets we have often found instances of their mutual help and of influences leading to independent decisions or achievements. No better example of the subtle links between the two metrists, and of the working of their minds along similar-dissimilar lines, can be found than the invention by Bridges, thirty years after Hopkins's death, of a type of verse which owed its existence to his conscious efforts

but I am very anxious that there should be something dogmatic written soon, as people are already beginning to copy the style without understanding it.'

In 1883, in his enthusiastic defence of the new prosody, Bridges believed that 'something dogmatic' could be written about it. Yet he felt shy about writing anything himself. Later, as we have shown, he was to see the whole problem in a different light. He returned to a syllabic unaccented prosody. Hopkins had pointed out to him that in Milton there were *blank stresses* instead of the full number of stresses expected; this was one of his cues. Patmore's time-unit of the line was another cue; he also went to Italian and classical precedents. (See G. A. Kellog, 'Bridges's Milton's Prosody and Renaissance Metrical Theory', *P.M.L.A.*, March, 1953, pp. 268–85.)

It seems from a passing remark of Hopkins in a letter of January 12, 1888, that Bridges discussed the new prosody with Patmore as late as that year, and failed to bring Patmore either to accept his views or to criticize them in a paper. Bridges was disappointed, and said so to Hopkins, adding that he had forgotten that people believed in their own theories. It was 'a cynical remark' that did 'not please' Hopkins. Bridges had contemplated mentioning Patmore's doctrines in his essay on Milton's prosody; Hopkins thought he had no need to: 'They are mostly of wider scope and would be introduced best into a paper on English versi-fication as a whole or on versification simply.' Bridges followed this advice, and Patmore is not mentioned in his essay. (See *GMH to RB*, Letter CLVII, p. 269.)

[1] *Op. cit.*, Ch. IV, 'The End-Pause', p. 74.

at reaching freer speech-rhythms[1] through means that Hopkins would have totally disavowed. That both friends claimed Milton as the model and inspirer of their opposite prosodies is an irony of literature that they would certainly have enjoyed together had Hopkins lived long enough.

II. A COMMON HOBBY: MUSIC

If poetry and prosody were quite naturally the subject-matter of most of their letters and conversations, music, literature and religion were other important topics for discussion between Bridges and Hopkins. Religion and literature are not unexpected, but music would be so, if we did not bear in mind that in 1866, at Rochdale, Bridges had disclosed to his friend that he was composing 'airs'. Hopkins was impressed and attracted. Almost immediately he began to learn the violin at Edgbaston Oratory—it was Newman's pastime to play trios and quartets with his friends—and a few years later, at Roehampton, he tried to learn the piano—'self-taught alas! not for execution's sake but to be independent of others and learn something about music.'[2] Wanting to learn something about music meant for him the possibility of discussing musical composition with Bridges and trying to enter into friendly competition with one who wrote melodies as easily, if not as often, as he wrote verses. Hopkins must have envied the ability of his friend who could turn with no embarrassment from one art to another. He admired him, and had so much confidence in his powers that he could write in 1879, 'I feel sure you have a genius in music—on the strength of the only piece I know "O earlier": it is an inspiration of melody, but somewhat "sicklied o'er", as indeed the words are.'[3] Now this piece, written for

---

[1] The two poets had the same end in view: a fresher diction and a broader freedom were the needs of modern poetry. To Sir Henry Newbolt, Bridges, on giving him *Milton's Prosody*, had said: 'We must get out of the old ruts; the English poets have been on the right road, but they have worn it into ruts. We must follow the road but there is no reason why we should keep to the ruts.' (H. Newbolt, *op. cit.*, p. 194.) Hopkins had expressed the same idea in his well-known remark: 'The effect of studying masterpieces is to make me admire and do otherwise.'

[2] *GMH to RB*, Letter XXVII, January 22, 1874, p. 30.

[3] Letter LXII, August 14, 1879, p. 85.

a song from *Ionica* (1858) by William Johnson Cory,[1] a master
at Eton and a respected minor poet, had also roused the interest of Grace Hopkins, one of the poet's sisters, who had
'become musical beyond the common' and wanted to write an
accompaniment to Bridges's melody, as she was to do for her
brother's music for Bridges's *Spring Odes*; she was even to set
music to one of Bridges's *Shorter Poems*, 'Sometimes when my
lady sits by me'.[2] Clearly it was a case of strong emulation.
Brother and sister were eager to enter the realm of music and
hoped to make good use of their talents, feeling certain that
they could rely on Bridges's help and advice.[3] But help and
advice by letter could amount to little, and from the evidence
we possess Bridges does not seem to have had much confidence
in the efforts of his friends, who were too patently amateurs.
The story of Hopkins's systematic endeavours to learn the art
of counterpoint, canon and harmony is one of a sustained fight
against great odds, and the results are very poor. Apart from
the melody written for Dixon's delightful poem 'Fallen Rain',
which is according to a musical critic 'a tune of real distinction', none of his melodies for various poems, and no exercises of
his, are of any real value.[4] Hopkins himself could report, with a
feeling of sadness, the ironical remark of a pianist who had
played one of his tunes: 'Your music dates from a time before
the piano was invented'.[5] Bridges was as ruthless in a comment
on Grace's accompaniment. He wrote, 'If your sister has learnt
harmony I can't understand what the moderns mean'; and
her brother could only offer as an excuse, 'Grace did learn

---

[1] Cory (1823–92) took the Greek anthologists for his models and some of his
verses have a classical perfection. He is said to have influenced A. E. Housman.

[2] Letter LXXXI, April 3, 1882, p. 144.

[3] Grace is mentioned in her brother's letters a good many times. Reading between the lines one gathers the impression that Hopkins may have played with the
idea of a possible match between Bridges and his sister. He was 'overjoyed' to
hear of his friend's visits to Oak Hill. But when Grace and Robert discussed music,
she felt 'embarrassed' by his learning and he seems to have found her 'odd'. (See
Letter LXIV, October 22, 1879, p. 98.)

[4] For Hopkins as musician see *GMH Journals*, Appendix II (by John Stevens),
pp. 457–97; *GMH & RWD*, Appendix III, pp. 168–70; and Gardner, *op. cit.*,
Vol. II, Appendix A, pp. 379–92.

[5] Hopkins mentions the remark to Bridges (Letter CXXXV, October 6, 1886,
p. 229) and to Patmore (*Further Letters*, Letter CLXXXII, same date, p. 371.)

harmony, but girls are apt not to study things thoroughly and perhaps she has not kept it up as she should.'[1]

It is strange to see Hopkins devoting his little spare time between 1879 and 1889 to the technicalities of musical composition, while Bridges, who certainly was more learned in the art and could at any time turn to musical friends like Wooldridge and Hubert Parry[2] for competent criticism, abandoned musical composition altogether. Whatever tunes he may have written he must have destroyed, according to Mrs. Bridges who failed to find any among his papers.[3] Hopkins, who found the writing of poetry 'slow and laborious', contrasted it with musical composition, which came 'so easily, for I can make tunes almost at all times and places and could harmonize them as easily if only I could play or read music at sight.'[4] Considering the bad state of his health, this may sufficiently explain his dismal assertion in April, 1881, 'Every impulse and spring of art seems to have died in me, except for music.'[5] Music was not for him an escape from poetry; it merely seemed not so laborious a task. Besides, his lack of technical knowledge gave him the impression that he could invent rules of his own, derived from the Greek modes which, as a Greek scholar, he knew well. John F. Waterhouse says that he might have been led to write pure melodies and 'become a composer of the little-tried art of the unaccompanied solo song'.[6]

This may sound a generous appreciation of the poet's musical

---

[1] *GMH to RB*, Letter CLV, November 6, 1887, p. 264.

[2] Sir Hubert Parry, 1848–1918, wrote the music for four of Bridges's odes; and to him Bridges dedicated in 1891 his dramatic oratorio *Eden*. Educated at Eton and Oxford, Parry was a man of means and leisure. He wrote some fine cantatas. He had a keen understanding of English prosody, and knew how to handle it in composition.

[3] *GMH to RB*, p. 14, footnote.

[4] Letter LXXVII, September 16, 1881, p. 136.

[5] Letter LXXII, April 3, 1881, p. 124.

[6] J. F. Waterhouse, 'Gerard Manley Hopkins and Music' (*Music and Letters*, July, 1937, pp. 227–35). In the course of this article, the critic puts forward Miss Phare's opinion that Hopkins turned to music because he shrank from his agonizing vision of a world torn between right and wrong; music seemed to escape the blight of original sin. As a philosopher he could consider a melody morally neutral, but we know enough about him to be certain that he did not write music for that reason. He was interested in music because it was new to him and because he thought that 'theoretically he had real lights upon it', as well as on counterpoint. (Letter CXLV, p. 249.)

gifts. It is safer to consider Hopkins's exercises as so many experiments in a field that lay close to the poetical one. In fact when Hopkins and Bridges were studying music they were, each in his own way, pursuing the same object, *i.e.*, testing their new conceptions of rhythm and training their ears to the nicest subtleties of pitch, tone and quantity. Hopkins writes, 'I wish I could pursue music; for I have invented a new style, something standing to ordinary music as sprung rhythm to common rhythm: it employs quarter tones';[1] and his efforts at breaking new ground are set in relief when he says to Bridges, 'I have the key to the history of modern music in what my inquiry points to, viz. that modern harmony could not arise till the old system and its tuning was got rid of.'[2] Bridges had less revolutionary views, for, if he believed that music in England was in a sorry plight, he held that a return to Elizabethan and Restoration principles was necessary and that a truer sense of melody and more satisfactory relations between poetry and its musical setting could be reached by a closer study of their respective properties. Both poets were agreed about the golden rule expressed by Bridges in his essay, 'A Practical Discourse on some Principles of Hymn-singing':

There is no escape from art; art is only the best that man can do, and his second, third, fourth or fifth best are only worse efforts in the same direction, and in proportion as they fall short of the best the more plainly betray their artificiality.[3]

Once again we see the two poets working side by side quite independently, but each sustained in his individual, self-appointed task by the other's endeavours. It is possible that Bridges encouraged Hopkins to devote time to music because he felt, as a doctor, that it might relieve his unrest and gloom, and distract his mind from pondering over his state of physical weakness. But at the same time Bridges knew that he could benefit by his friend's remarks. For instance Hopkins's interest in the old modal system and in plain chant, his rejection of

---

[1] Letter LXVIII, June 18, 1880, p. 103.
[2] Letter CXLVII, March 29, 1887, p. 233.
[3] *Collected Essays*, Vol. II No. XXII, p. 64.

modulation, his admiration of Purcell and of the madrigalists[1] find many echoes in the essays that Bridges wrote on musical subjects from 1896 to 1912.[2]

In Hopkins's letters we find little information about Bridges's views. We know he admires Purcell but not exactly for the reasons given in Hopkins's sonnet on the musician. Explaining the image in the sestet, Hopkins said it meant that Purcell, 'seemingly intent only on the thought or feeling he is to express or call out, incidentally lets you remark the individualizing marks of his own genius.'[3] Bridges must have objected, for in his next letter Hopkins writes, 'By the by your remark on Purcell's music does not conflict with what my sonnet says, rather it supports it. My sonnet means "Purcell's music is none of your d——d subjective rot" (so to speak).'[4] Now if we set Hopkins's comments beside the following passage we shall understand Bridges's objection.

It is characteristic of all early art to be *impersonal*. As long as an art is growing, artists are engaged in rivalry to develop the new inventions in a scientific manner, and individual personality is not called out. With the exhaustion of the means in the attainment of perfection a new stage is reached, in which individual expression is prominent, and seems to take the place of the scientific impersonal interest which aimed at nothing but beauty; so that the chief distinction between early and late art is that the former is impersonal, the latter personal.[5]

This does not mean that Bridges did not care for the individual genius of such early composers as Palestrina and Purcell. But

[1] In a letter dated September 10, 1888, Hopkins informs Bridges about a series of articles on the English madrigalists by A. M. Wakefield in *Murray's*. He alludes to a collection of English motets, madrigals and part-songs made by Bridges and arranged according to 'schools'. (Letter CLXIV, p. 285, and note.)

[2] *Collected Essays*, No. XXI. The Musical Setting of Poetry (1896); No. XXII, Some Principles of Hymn-Singing (1899); No. XXIII, About Hymns (1911); No. XXIV, English Chanting (1911); No. XXV, Chanting (1912); and No. XXVI, Psalms noted in Speech-Rhythm (1912).

[3] *GMH to RB*, Letter LX, May 26, 1879, p. 83.

[4] Letter LXI, June 22, 1879, p. 84.

[5] *Collected Essays*, No. XXII, Some Principles of Hymn-Singing, pp. 58–59. From a long note on the same pages one gathers that Wooldridge, who was then Slade Professor at Oxford, had developed the same theme in his recent lectures on painting.

he liked their impersonal or 'pure music', because it seems 'not to interfere at all with, or add anything to, the sacred words . . . It seems rather as if the sacred words had suddenly become musical. Not so with Mozart or Beethoven'. He thus pleads for reserve and dignity, and no doubt such qualities belonged to the 'inscaping' of Purcell's genius by Hopkins. The latter wished to agree with Bridges about genius not being 'subjective'. But to this classical judgment, he added his own romantic stressing of the individual mark that genius sets on any artistic creation. The two notions are essential, and must be considered as complementary.

On another important matter—the revival of hymns and sacred melodies—to which Bridges was later to devote much time and care, there is little to be learnt from Hopkins's letters. But it may be assumed that he and Bridges discussed the problem, and that Hopkins shared the interest that led Bridges in the 'nineties to compile the *Yattendon Hymnal*. There exists one piece of indirect but tangible evidence of this.

Among Hopkins's poems are a number of English translations of Latin prayers and hymns, which can be considered as a pious exercise, natural for a priest.[1] One of these is a translation of 'Jesu dulcis memoria', a hymn in praise of the name of Jesus, written in the fourteenth century by a Benedictine abbess.[2] Hopkins's manuscript is undated; but in Bridges's play, *The Christian Captives*, written in 1886, the second act begins with the singing in Latin of this very hymn, the melody of which deeply moves the heroine of the tragedy, Almeh, daughter of the King of Fez. It cannot be a mere coincidence, nor is it a surprise to find another version of the same hymn in the *Yattendon Hymnal*. There is a great difference between the

[1] The four Latin hymns translated by Hopkins are 'Jesu dulcis memoria', 'Adoro te supplex', 'O Jesu vivens in Maria', 'O Deus, ego amo te'. (*GMH Poems*, Nos. 130–3, pp. 185–8.)

[2] In R. C. Trench's *Sacred Latin Poetry*, 1849, the hymn is attributed to St. Bernard, an attribution accepted by Bridges. The Latin version of the relevant stanza as given by Bridges reads:

> Jesu, dulcedo cordium,
> Fons veri, lumen mentium,
> Excedens omne gaudium
> Et omne desiderium.

translations by the two friends; Hopkins is nearer to the Latin, though he misses what Bridges holds to be 'a chief point' of the structure of the original—the four-fold rhyme.

Hopkins, Stanza 5]   Jesu, a springing well Thou art,
                      Daylight to head and treat to heart,
                      And matched with Thee there's nothing glad
                      That can be wished or can be had.

Bridges, Stanza 7]   Jesus doth all my heart require,
                      Truth's fount, and pure enlight'ning fire,
                      Transcending earthly joy, and higher
                      Than all the longing of desire.

In his hymnal Bridges also included an English rendering of the well-known prayer by St. Francis Xavier, 'O Deus ego amo te'. He chose the translation by E. Caswall in *Hymns Ancient and Modern*. We find that Hopkins tried his hand at a new translation of the prayer into English, and we may ask ourselves whether Bridges did not ask his friend to translate both hymn and prayer with a view to including them in his hymnal. The other hymn, 'Adoro te' by St. Thomas Aquinas, and the prayer 'O Jesus vivens' by the French Oratorian, Father Condren, translated by Hopkins at an earlier date in his religious life, may not have been intended for possible inclusion in the hymnal, but merely to provide Bridges with typical or remarkable prayers and sacred songs.

The *Yattendon Hymnal*, which Bridges and Wooldridge published in 1895–9, was a collection of a hundred hymns with tunes that the chief editor had chosen for his village choir. He intended it as a model for Anglican worshippers who found in their traditional hymn-books poor devotional verse and worse hymn-melodies. It is clear that, long before the new hymnal was published, Bridges had been thinking of the difficult relations of music and poetry. The problem was how to handle musical composition without damage either to the poetical declamation or to the musical phrase. He discussed the matter with his musical friends, Wooldridge, Parry, William Rockstro,[1]

---

[1] William Rockstro, 1823–95, was an authority on ancient music and an instigator of the study of modal music in England. He set an accompaniment to Hop-

and Frederick Gore Ouseley,[1] and also with Hopkins, to whom he did not fail to give his frank opinion when the latter sent him his melodies on his or Dixon's lyrics. The Rector of Yattendon was the Reverend H. C. Beeching,[2] who soon after his arrival in 1885 became a friend of the Bridges; he collaborated with the poet in his efforts to restore St. Augustine's principles for church singing:

The music must express the words or sense; it should not attract too much attention to itself: it should be dignified: and its reason and use is to heighten religious emotion.[3]

As both a poet and a competent student of music Bridges was capable of achieving his double aim: he wanted better hymns and better tunes. By choosing hymns with a truly poetical quality, and by studying the art of English chanting, he was following in the footsteps of the Tractarians[4] who had deliberately turned to the old Latin hymns of the Church, and to the musicologists who had pointed to the beauty of plain-song or to the purity of English music in the sixteenth and seventeenth centuries. Whatever agnostic philosophy may have been Bridges's, his deeply ingrained respect for Christianity and his love of dignified religious services made him a passionate advocate of reform. We understand the artist's 'horror' when he writes:

kins's tune for his patriotic song: 'What shall I do for the land?' (See Letter CLXV, p. 289.)

[1] Sir Frederick Gore Ouseley, 1825–89, was Professor of Music at Oxford from 1855 to his death. Hopkins had sent him his first attempt in harmony, but did not get any answer. This gave the poet an opportunity for a terrible pun: 'Sir Frederick may wallow and choke in his own Oozeley Gore'. (See Letter CXXIII, p. 202.)

[2] Canon H. C. Beeching, 1859–1919, edited *Paradise Lost*, Bk. I, in 1887, to which Bridges contributed the essay on Milton's blank verse that was to grow into *Milton's Prosody*. In 1890 he married Mary Plow, Bridges's niece. In 1895, he edited *A Book of Christmas Verse* and *Lyra Sacra*, anthologies in which poems of Hopkins were included.

[3] *Collected Essays*, No. XXII, p. 27.

[4] *E.g.*, John Mason Neale, 1818–66, a great hymnologist, who deliberately returned to medieval poets from Prudentius to Adam de St. Victor to revive English hymn-singing. In the original edition of *Hymns Ancient and Modern* (1861), one-eighth of the contents is by Neale, translated or original. Few people remember today that he is the author of the famous Christmas carol 'Good King Wenceslas'.

There is something very strange and surprising in . . . this contrast between the primitive Church with its few simple melodies that ravished the educated hearer, and our own full-blown institution with its hymn-book of some 600 tunes, which when it is opened fills the sensitive worshipper with dismay, so that there are persons who would rather not go inside a church than subject themselves to the trial.[1]

And beyond doubt Hopkins would have agreed with his friend, and praised both thought and style, if he could have read the conclusion of his essay :

And if we consider and ask ourselves what sort of music we should wish to hear on entering a church, we should surely, in describing our ideal, say first of all that it must be something different from what is heard elsewhere; that it should be a sacred music, devoted to its purpose, a music whose peace should still passion, whose dignity should strengthen our faith, whose unquestioned beauty should find a home in our hearts, to cheer us in life and death; a music worthy of the fair temples in which we meet and of the holy words of our liturgy; a music whose expression of the mystery of things unseen never allowed any trifling motive to ruffle the sanctity of its reserve.[2]

With such a lofty ideal in mind, Bridges selected for his hymnal forty hymns from *Hymns Ancient and Modern*, a few Methodist hymns by Charles Wesley and Isaac Watts, and himself translated or adapted thirty-four, chosen from among the most ancient Latin and Greek hymns, the Reformation hymns, and the Psalms; he also wrote nine original hymns.

The present Rector of Yattendon[3] has given me the following information about the *Yattendon Hymnal*.

The motive behind this work was undoubtedly to raise the standard of current hymnology. For a century or more, hymns had been rather a one-sided affair in the Liturgy of the Church, leaning towards the popular and sentimental. Hymns which clearly were

---

[1] *Collected Essays*, No. XXII, p. 26.
[2] *Ibid.*, p. 65.
[3] The Reverend Kenneth R. Johnson, whom I most heartily thank for his kindness.

written and sung for the purpose of stressing man's need for conversion, they were sung for man's comfort rather than for God's glory. Robert Bridges was therefore in the forefront of a move to redirect worship towards a more intellectual and spiritual level and to raise music from a merely 'sugary' level to a more essentially religious quality. This movement, which I believe had its origin in Dr. Bridges, gained much impetus when in 1906 the *English Hymnal* was published. No fewer than 13 hymns from the *Yattendon Hymnal* were included in the 'E. H.' This latter book is now widely used in preference to the *Ancient and Modern* hymn book, which had reigned supreme for a very long time, and still is used very extensively.

I would say that Dr. Bridges had no other norm in selecting hymns and tunes than his own innate sense of literary and musical beauty.

While he lived here, Dr. Bridges appointed himself 'Precentor' of the village church, and undoubtedly took a great deal of interest in the church music. My own belief is that it was not very popular. I feel that the music was altogether 'too refined' for country folk, though there is no doubt that the choir worked hard. The organ accompaniment was slight, it was the singing that mattered.[1]

Mr. Johnson here makes it quite clear that Bridges wished all congregations to give beauty and dignity to their worship. He may have aimed a little too high. But it is easy for us to recognize Hopkins's friend in his determination to bring his Church to praise God and sing His Glory with hymns from the common treasure of Christianity, set to good music.

There is one passage in Bridges's essay on hymn-singing which, when we recall the many years during which he and Hopkins exchanged letters and talk about music, will be tinged for us with the glow of a personal confession. Music for them was more than a common hobby, more than a joy fully shared; it was an immaterial bridge that spanned their spiritual separation, a comfort and a promise. For Bridges gravely said:

Music being the universal expression of the mysterious and supernatural, the best that man has ever attained to, is capable of uniting in common devotion minds that are only separated by creeds, and it comforts our hope with a brighter promise of unity than any logic offers.[2]

[1] Private letter from Yattendon Rectory, November 30, 1957.
[2] *Collected Essays*, No. XXII, p. 65.

Neither Bridges nor Hopkins could have been the great masters of prosody they were if they had not been deeply interested in the technique of music. Both, like Browning, could employ musical terms correctly. Both had a true sense of good music, and their admiration of Bach, Palestrina, Gibbons, Blow, Purcell, Handel, Corelli, Chopin and Weber was set in the right places. In the renascence of English music that began in the 'eighties each of them had his part, one altogether obscure and tentative, the other brilliant and positive.

III. LITERARY AND RELIGIOUS CRITICISM

Being utterly devoted to their work, one as doctor and professional poet, the other as parish priest, teacher and intermittent writer of sonnets, Bridges and Hopkins did not feel any strong interest in the work of their literary contemporaries. But they were not ignorant of them. Bridges had many literary friends both in London and at Oxford. Hopkins in his rather secluded life had a more bookish knowledge of the literary activities of his time. He read the *Athenaeum*, the *Academy* or the *Saturday Review* with particular care, obviously wishing to be informed, if somewhat cursorily, at least accurately. We have seen that it was 'an appreciative review of a Mr. Bridges' poems' in the *Academy* of January 17, 1874, that led Hopkins to renew his friendly correspondence with the poet.[1] An unsigned article in the *Saturday Review* of October 14, 1882, roused his suspicion: he was afraid Bridges might have betrayed him 'to suspects and dangerous people'.[2] The unkind allusion in the review may have been meant for him, or it may not; but it did not fail to catch his eye. Again when Bridges suggested that Whitman might have influenced him in the writing of his

---

[1] *GMH to RB*, Letter XXVII, January 22, 1874, p. 29.

[2] Letter LXXXIX, October 16, 1882, p. 153. 'Look at this. . . . "On some luckless day the bookseller sends out his catalogue, with such items as *Love Lies Bleeding*, by G. Hopkins. Pages unopened. Autograph poem and inscription by the author. Published at Five Shillings Fourpence'. Then these catalogues fall into the hands of Hopkins and his friends, and there is wailing and shrieking on Parnassus." It seems to be meant for me.' But since Hopkins had published no book of poems, how could it be a personal allusion to him? *Love Lies Bleeding* is the title of a sonnet by Christina Rossetti. Hopkins's friends, among whom Bridges stood foremost, may have been aimed at.

Echoes, out of a dozen pieces of Whitman that he admitted having read, two were in the *Academy* or the *Athenaeum* 'and short extracts in a review by Saintsbury' in the *Academy* again.[1]

But reading literary reviews is second-hand reading. We must admit that Hopkins, when he was a Jesuit, devoted little time to literary reading. All the great masters of English literature he has known from the time of his university studies; from Chaucer, Spenser and Shakespeare down to the Romantics and the Pre-Raphaelites, he is cognizant of their works. He read a few novels, and the novelists of his generation, whom he admired for their descriptive qualities, drew great praise from him;[2] but he is apt to place on the same level Blackmore, Hardy, Stevenson and Charles Reade.[3] Bridges felt that the scanty reading the Jesuit poet allowed himself to do was insufficient, and that his art suffered from it. He felt sure that more reading would have drawn him out of his singularities. Hopkins was not prepared to admit that more reading would have this effect. He felt 'how great the loss is of not reading'. He said: 'I *must* read something of Greek and Latin letters'. But as he considered that every original artist when studying masterpieces was bound to 'do otherwise', he suggested, no doubt ironically, that 'more reading would only *refine my singularity*, which is not what you want'. He could even find an excellent argument against Bridges, whose judgment he considered less liberal than his own.

Wide reading does two things—it extends knowledge and it adjusts the judgment. Now it is mostly found that a learned judgment is less singular than an unlearned one and oftener agrees with the common and popular judgment, with which it coincides as a fine balance or other measure does with the rule of thumb. But, so far as I see, where we differ in judgment, my judgments are less singular than yours; I agree more than you do with the mob and with the *communis criticorum*. Presumably I shd. agree with these still more if I read more and so differ still more from you than now. Who for instance is singular about Dryden, you or I?[4]

---

[1] Letter XC, October 18, 1882, pp. 154–8, and Additional Note P, pp. 311–16
[2] Letters CXXXVIII, CXLVI, CLII, pp. 237, 251 and 262.
[3] Both Blackmore and Reade are likely to be remembered as 'men of one book', *Lorna Doone* (1869) for the former and *The Cloister and the Hearth* (1861) for the latter.
[4] Letter CLXVI, September 25, 1888, p. 291.

Although Hopkins ends with a shrewd Parthian shot, his reasoning is markedly specious. His judgment could not be deemed an unlearned one, and reading has little to do with agreeing or not with the mob.

What Bridges meant by more reading was more reading of the great writers of Greece and Rome, of Italy and Spain. He was far less interested in such writers as Hardy and Stevenson than in Homer, Menander, Terence, Dante, Michelangelo, Cervantes, Lope de Vega and Calderon.[1] As a writer of poems and plays, Bridges deliberately sought his inspiration in a close contact with the literature of classicism. From the poets and playwrights he read and studied he learnt the art of splendid execution. Borrowing ideas, thoughts and feelings did not matter to him as long as he could refine on them and try to say in his own tongue 'what oft was thought but ne'er so well expressed'. Hopkins certainly cared for beautiful form and faultless craftsmanship; but he gave more importance to self-expression, and he did not feel the need to turn continually to the great masters for an inspiration which, if it were so derived, could not be genuine. The great writers of the past could not light in his heart 'sweet fire the sire of muse' or give him 'the fine delight that fathers thought'.[2] Inspiration must spring out of himself or be, as he said, 'nowhere none'.[3] On this subject, as on many others, the two poets were at loggerheads. Hopkins's passionate, romantic nature was less attached to the strict rules of art than was the quiet and composed temper of Bridges. For the latter 'decadence' was a real danger. No doubt his cult of beauty, his neo-platonic idealism, made him aware of the pitfalls of aesthetics. Being at the same time a staunch defender of the great literary traditions and an experimentalist, he felt that to devote too much attention to 'the last fine shade'[4] or to the extraordinary in thought and style would lead his contemporaries to artificiality. He believed that Hop-

---

[1] Bridges's plays and many sonnets of *The Growth of Love* testify to the direct influences of these masters.

[2] Words from Hopkins's last sonnet, 'To R.B.', *Poems*, No. 75.

[3] 'For good . . . is nowhere none'. *Ibid.*, No. 110, 'On a Piece of Music'.

[4] In *The Decadent Movement in Literature*, 1893, Arthur Symons said: 'To fix the last fine shade, the quintessence of things, is the ideal of the Decadence'. Quoted by W. Y. Tindall in *Forces in Modern British Literature*, p. 18.

kins was advancing apace along that perilous road. That is why
he wrote to him: 'The first touch of decadence destroys all
merit whatever'.

Hopkins was not afraid of the word. He fully realized that a
literary tradition, having exhausted its driving power, must be
changed, and that new, complex or strange expressions were a
means to launch a new tradition. A decadent work could be
good or bad, better or worse than non-decadent works. No
moral value was implied by the word; it was a normal phenomenon in an age of transition. In his answer to Bridges he chose
examples from the history of painting, but his views on literature are similar to those he expresses on the age of Raphael.

'The first touch of decadence destroys all merit whatever': this is
a hard saying. What, all technical merit—as chiaroscuro, anatomical
knowledge, expression, feeling, colouring, drama? It is plainly not
true. And, come to that, the age of Raphael and Michelangelo
was in a decadence and its excellence is technical. Everything after
Giotto is decadent in form, though advancing in execution. Go to.[1]

It was to be expected that Hopkins should stand by the Pre-
Raphaelites; but if we read him well, the decadence he admits
is a relative one, and he refuses to condemn technical excellence
and perfect execution which in themselves represent an important advance.

The passage quoted is typical of what I shall call Hopkins's
homely common sense. As a literary critic he had a balanced
judgment. He could say to Bridges, 'Make [Lang] understand
that those snags that are in my style are not in my heart and
temper'.[2] If he could praise his friends Dixon and Patmore a
little more or far more than they deserved, he could praise or
blame with fairness and an independent mind.[3] He could be
fair to Matthew Arnold and rebuke Bridges who called him
'Mr. Kidglove Cocksure'.[4] He could express the most sensitive

---

[1] Letter CLXIX, February 23, 1889, p. 300.

[2] Letter XCI. October 21, 1882, p. 159.

[3] Gardner, *op. cit.*, Vol. II, Ch. IV, 'Hopkins as a reader and critic', deals fully
with the matter.

[4] Letter XCVIII, January 28, 1883, p. 172. Hopkins adds, 'I have more reason
than you for disagreeing with him and thinking him very wrong, but nevertheless I
am sure he is a rare genius and a great critic'.

understanding of Wordsworth's *Ode on Immortality* and yet be alive to the 'odious goodiness and neckcloth' in his sonnets, 'which half throttles their beauty'.[1] What he says about Browning reveals at once a sound opinion and a deep insight into Bridges's true feelings about his own poems:

I always think that your mind towards my verse is like mine towards Browning's: I greatly admire the touches and the details, but the general effect, the whole, offends me, I think it repulsive.[2]

Few men could write, even to their best friend, with such uninhibited candour, which in this particular instance works both ways.

One letter of his deserves special attention, since it gives us the rare opportunity of setting Bridges's answers side by side with Hopkins's critical remarks. The two men had been discussing William Barnes and Robert Louis Stevenson. Hopkins had expressed his admiration for them, and Bridges had disagreed. Elaborating his case with zest and with a wealth of arguments, Hopkins wrote back a letter which Bridges felt he could not leave without vindicating his own views. He wrote a note at the end of Hopkins's letter and made interlinear comments which tend to minimize his own opposition. The note implies that Bridges was quite aware that Hopkins had been scoring hands down against him.

Wishing to keep this letter[3] I have made a few notes in justification of my criticisms, which were no doubt ill expressed—to give rise to such misrepresentation. The letter gives a true picture of G.M.H.'s views of English literature, and his judgment of modern writers.

About Louis Stevenson I may add that my chief 'objection' to his works is merely a want of sympathy. I admire his art much, but he is constantly offending my feelings.[4]

---

[1] Letter XXX, April 3, 1877, p. 38.
[2] Letter LXXVII, September 16, 1881, p. 137.
[3] A strange remark on the part of Bridges. We may infer from it that Bridges did destroy a few letters he did not wish to keep. We know that two of Hopkins's letters written between March 20 and April 29, 1889, were destroyed by Bridges. He may have destroyed more.
[4] Letter CXXXVIII, October 28, 1886, pp. 235–7, note.

About Barnes, Hopkins merely said that he excelled in 'local colour' and that everyone agreed about it. He objected to his friend's narrow-minded remark about 'the supposed emotions of peasants'. Bridges made no comment. Then Hopkins devoted two long pages to Stevenson; although he had not read *Treasure Island*, he dealt with two of Bridges's criticisms of the novel and dismissed them as trifling. In his interlinear comments Bridges pointed out that his objections concerned the art of the novelist.[1] It is plain that Hopkins failed to convince him that he was wrong. Being unbiassed, we may say that Bridges was applying far too strict rules to a work of pure romance. About *Dr. Jekyll and Mr. Hyde*, Bridges spoke of 'the gross absurdity' of the interchange. In fact he submitted the story to the critical eye of a physician who cannot accept the means employed by Stevenson; in his note he says that the means should have been magical, and not physical, but it is important that they should appear as scientific means. He objects to the trampling scene; but it is true to the human monster Stevenson sought to depict. It is obvious that Bridges fails to appreciate either the romantic world of *Treasure Island* or the grim moral lesson of *Dr. Jekyll and Mr. Hyde*. He is entitled to his own judgment, but we must surely agree with Hopkins, who writes, 'This sour severity blinds you to [Stevenson's] great genius'. Hopkins had a more child-like love of the art of story-telling, and for the sake of a good tale or a gripping dramatic adventure, he could skip over little blemishes which Bridges damned as 'bad art'.

Hopkins's more catholic taste, revealed in his enthusiastic praise of novelists as widely different as Stevenson, Hardy, Blackmore and Mrs. Gaskell,[2] certainly shocked Bridges, who never felt attracted by novelists, and who sought to protect his

---

[1] Bridges objected to the narration being made by the boy Jim 'sometimes in a vein untrue to his character as required by his actions, the two being incompatible and bad as art'. To 'a fault of plot' Hopkins had answered, 'One blot is no great matter.' Bridges's ruthless marginal comment is, 'There are others in plenty.'

[2] About Mrs. Gaskell, Hopkins wrote, 'Now come on Mrs. Gaskell. What ails poor Mrs. Gaskell? One book of hers I have read through, *Wives and Daughters*; if that is not a good book I do not know what a good book is'. Letter CXLVI, February 17, 1887, p. 251.

own artistic and literary taste by systematically ignoring a
genre that was unprofitable to his poetical genius. Besides, the
more he cared for perfect expression, the more fastidious and
hard to please he became. His aristocratic temper also prevented him from giving easy praise. Hopkins was far more
generous, but he was aware of his own excesses and of his
friend's reserve. Having admired Dixon's *Lyrical Poems*, which
the 'good Canon' had dedicated to him, and feeling that not a
few blemishes might have been veiled for him by love, he was
delighted to hear Bridges give unrestrained praise to the book.
'Till you spoke,' he wrote, 'I had almost despaired of my judgment and quite of publishing it'.[1] At other times, he could rebuke Bridges for his lack of liberality. About Hardy and
Stevenson, whom he considered as 'men of pure and direct
genius',[2] he wanted his friend to share his judgment:

> No, I do not ask 'enthusiastic praise'. But is it not the case that the
> day when you could give enthusiastic praise to anything is passing
> or past?[3]

The simple answer to the question is that the two poets differed
in taste. But one feels at times that they enjoyed their differences. It gave more zest to their letters. Hopkins could refuse to
admire Doughty's *Arabia Deserta*[4] just because Bridges liked it.
And Bridges could refuse to admire Dryden just because Hopkins thought he was 'the most masculine of our poets'. And
although the Jesuit poet had qualified his judgment by adding,

> his style and his rhythms lay the strongest stress of all our literature
> on the naked thew and sinew of the English language, the praise
> that with certain qualifications one would give in Greek to Demos-
> thenes, to be the greatest master of bare Greek,[5]

[1] *Ibid.*, p. 250.
[2] *Ibid.*, p. 251. 'Perhaps you are so barbarous as not to admire Thomas Hardy—
as you do not Stevenson; both, I must maintain, men of pure and direct genius'.
[3] Letter CLV, November 6, 1887, postscript, p. 267.
[4] Letter CLXIII, September 7, 1888, pp. 283–4. *Travels in Arabia Deserta* (1888)
was praised by William Morris and a few other writers, but remained unknown to
the general public for many years. Both subject and style should have won the
admiration of Hopkins. It is a picturesque description of Arabian life; allegorically
it is the spiritual journey of a solitary man; and it is told in vigorous, uncommon
style.
[5] Letter CLV, postscript, pp. 267–8.

Bridges never wavered in his poor opinion of the great Restoration poet. In 1903, in a short article entitled, 'Dryden on Milton',[1] in spite of the guarded remark that he had not written 'in order to run down a poet with whose works I am by choice unfamiliar', he was as brutal in attack as he must have been when answering Hopkins:

But my chief puzzle about Dryden has been to understand how, when he substituted 'epigram' and wit in poetry for romance and imagination, he did not see how monstrously *dull* he was. He sinks to dullness of metre, dullness of rhythm, dullness of rhyme (of which he was most proud), dullness of matter; a dullness gross as his ruinous self-conceit; nor is it a point of disputable or changing taste and fashion, as some critics would believe; it is broadly demonstrable.[2]

No disagreement could be more complete. It turns into another 'Battle of the Books', a struggle between the two critics to obtain a crushing victory over the opposing side. But literary criticism today would certainly not endorse Bridges's unfair arraignment of the author of *Absalom and Achitophel*.[3]

Fortunately, there is one poet who won the joint praise of the two friends. That independently each should be loud in praise of Keats, the poet of Beauty, is no surprise. Any discordance about Keats would have revealed a flaw in their literary friendship far deeper than the few cracks we noticed in the course of our survey. Hopkins and Bridges could disagree about Dryden, about the use of archaic language, about the 'unreality' of the Greek gods in plays.[4] But Keats was for both of them a master and a model. If they chose to write on Keats, one knew in advance that their judgments would concur, and would be most illuminating. Hopkins's remarks lie scattered in his letters. To

---

[1] *Collected Essays*, No. X, 'Dryden on Milton', pp. 271–82. First printed as 'The Causerie of the Week' in the *Speaker*, October 24, 1903.

[2] *Ibid.*, pp. 273–4.

[3] In a recent pamphlet on Dryden (Writers and their Works, No. 7, Longmans, 1956, p. 26) Bonamy Dobrée writes: 'Whatever words he uses, his is still the language that might be spoken by men to men. It is never, pejorativel y speaking "poetic". This is one of his great triumphs.'

[4] Letter CXXIX, May 17, 1885, pp. 217–18.

Bridges and to Dixon he made brief allusions to Keats's rich colouring, to his deep feeling for concrete beauty, wild or natural. In two letters to Patmore, who had classed Keats with the feminine geniuses among men, he pleaded strongly for the 'distinctively masculine powers' that his mind had 'in abundance'. He admitted that 'he lived in mythology and fairyland the life of a dreamer. Nevertheless I feel and see in him the beginnings of something opposite to this, of an interest in higher things and of powerful and active thought'.[1]

For Keats died very young and we have only the work of his first youth. Now if we compare that with Shakspere's early work, written at an age considerably more than Keats's, was it not? such as *Venus and Adonis* and *Lucrece*, it is, as far as the work of two very original minds ever can be, greatly like in its virtues and its vices; more like, I do think, than that of any writer you could quote after the Elizabethan age. . . . He was young; his genius intense in its quality; his feeling for beauty, for perfection intense; he had found his way right in his Odes; he would find his way right at last to the true functions of his mind. . . .[2]

Reason, thought, what he did not want to live by, would have asserted itself presently and perhaps have been as much more powerful than that of his contemporaries as his sensibility or impressionableness, by which he did want to live, was keener and richer than theirs.[3]

The whole passage shows Hopkins at his best as a sensitive literary critic. Modern criticism has endorsed these views.[4] Bridges agreed with them, since in spite of many guarded remarks on the poet's immaturities, his 'Critical Introduction to Keats' begins thus:

If one English poet might be recalled today from the dead to continue the work which he left unfinished on earth, it is probable that the crown of his country's desire would be set on the head of John Keats, for he was smitten down in his youth, in the very maturing of

---

[1] *Further Letters*, Letter CLXXXVII, May 6, 1888, p. 386.
[2] *Ibid.*, Letter CLXXXVI, October 20, 1887, pp. 381–2.
[3] *Ibid.* Letter CLXXXVII, p. 386.
[4] F. R. Leavis in *Revaluation*, 1936, p. 272, writes, 'The induction to the revised *Hyperion*, then, justifies the high estimate of Keats's potentialities.'

powers, which, having already produced work of almost unrivalled beauty, held a promise of incredible things.[1]

Again when Bridges, towards the end of his long and careful study, comes to the description of the 'main qualities' of Keats's poetry, he writes:

There is one, as yet unmentioned, which claims the first place in a general description, and that is the very seal of his poetic birthright, the highest gift of all in poetry, that which sets poetry above the other arts; I mean the power of concentrating all the far-reaching resources of language on one point, so that a single and apparently effortless expression rejoices the aesthetic imagination at the moment when it is most expectant and exacting, and at the same time astonishes the intellect with a new aspect of truth. This is only found in the greatest poets, and is rare in them; and it is no doubt for the possession of this power that Keats has been often likened to Shakespeare, and very justly, for Shakespeare is of all poets the greatest master of it; the difference between them here is that Keats's intellect does not supply the second factor in the proportion or degree that Shakespeare does; indeed, it is chiefly when he is dealing with material and sensuous subjects that his poems afford illustrations; but these are, as far as they go, not only like Shakespeare, but often as good as Shakespeare when he happens to be confining himself to the same limited field.[2]

The passage develops persuasively the same argument as Hopkins had put forward in his letters to Patmore.

The last paragraph of the essay is worth considering in relation to the severe criticism of Hopkins's mannerisms in Bridges's 'Preface to Notes'. He justifies his censure of Keats's faults in terms that he would certainly have used for Hopkins, had he felt called upon to apologize for what the great majority of critics have deemed far too adverse strictures.

If my criticism should seem sometimes harsh, that is, I believe, due to its being given in plain terms, a manner which I prefer, because by obliging the writer to say definitely what he means, it makes his mistakes easy to point out, and in this way the true busi-

---

[1] *Collected Essays*, No. IV, 'A Critical Introduction to Keats', p. 77. The essay was written for the Muses Library edition of Keats's *Poems*, 1896.

[2] *Ibid.*, pp. 158–9.

ness of criticism may be advanced; nor do I know that, in work of this sort, criticism has any better function than to discriminate between the faults and merits of the best art: for it commonly happens, when any great artist comes to be generally admired, that his faults, being graced by his excellences, are confounded with them in the popular judgment, and being easy of imitation, are the points of his work which are most liable to be copied. Keats has had some such imitators, and would, I imagine, have been glad to be justified from them.[1]

Bridges is quite aware of his 'plain' outspokenness, but he feels it is advantageous both to the writer and to the reader. Even in the case of a poet of genius, he must sort out the good from the bad, the more so because the poet of genius is sure to have imitators who will copy the bad as much as the good and will endanger the poet's greatness. Bridges, who lived to read a few servile imitations of Hopkins's sprung rhythm,[2] felt fully justified in having pointed out Hopkins's singularities and given his criticism 'in plain terms'.

By a kind of tacit agreement, as we have seen, the two friends had decided to leave religion and religious controversy out of their talks and letters. They knew they differed in religion; both meant, as Hopkins once put it, 'to open up no further question'.[3] But Bridges, as the years went by, came to realize that his friend was both a saintly man and a priest, whose theological studies gave weight to his comments on the Scriptures. He could refuse to listen to sermonizing and moral lessons, in order to keep his own freedom to think and act as he chose. Nor did he wish to be told to pray or to give alms.[4] He could be interested, however, in Hopkins's interpretation of a difficult passage in St. Paul, and could even ask him to write a prayer for a book Mrs. Waterhouse was compiling in 1883.[5]

[1] *Ibid.*, pp. 170–1.

[2] In an unpublished letter to Kate Hopkins, dated March 26, 1916, he tells her as a proof that Gerard's poems in *The Spirit of Man* had been well-received, 'I had some MS. poems sent me the other day for inspection which showed strong traces of his influence!' (Bodleian Library.)

[3] *GMH to RB*, Letter XCIII, November 26, 1882, p. 163.

[4] See Letters LI, p. 60; LII, pp. 62–63; and LXXI, p. 118.

[5] Letter CVI, July 26, 1883, p. 183, note; and Letter CX, October 24, 1883, pp. 186 ff.

Asking Hopkins for a Christian prayer was an act of confidence and kindness. But what was Bridges hoping to obtain? Did he expect from his Jesuit friend something that would appeal to all Christian denominations and gloss over the doctrinal differences which, to him and Mrs. Waterhouse, were so prejudicial to spiritual union? If such was his expectation, it was frustrated. Hopkins sent a very moving prayer, but it was the prayer of a devout Roman Catholic, humbly acknowledging the One True God in Three Persons, and closing with the traditional doxology. As Mrs. Waterhouse intended to edit an undoctrinal prayer-book, the prayer was not included, but Bridges pasted it into his own copy of Hopkins's poems with the title of 'A Prayer written for Protestants'. The title is misleading, for there is no allusion in the text to any Church and no passage can be considered as answering the description. The main theme insists on man's sins, his frailty, and his breaking of his promises, and on God's grace and everlasting mercy. The meditation is stern,[1] but Hopkins reminds us that God desires not the sinner's death. God deserves to be loved and has commanded us to love Him. The Ignatian spirit inspires him when he writes, 'With sorrow we own against ourselves that whereas we should have glorified thy majesty we have grievously come short of thy glory'.[2] Although it is obvious that Hopkins had tried to bring into his prayer the essential doctrine of the Church, there is a tone of personal humility, obedience, repentance and love for which any reader can feel reverence and admiration.[3]

Humility was a central virtue with Hopkins. Hence the importance he attached to the verses of the Epistle to the Philippians in which St. Paul explains how Christ, Who was in the form of God and equal to God, exhausted Himself of His godhead in order to behave only as God's slave by taking the form of man and humbling Himself to death.[4] To Hopkins this was an

---

[1] When Hopkins writes, 'We wither at thy rebuke, we faint at thy frown, we tremble at thy power and threatened punishments', he insists on the terrible justice of God in the true Augustinian spirit.

[2] The opening sentence of the *Spiritual Exercises* is 'Man was created to praise God'.

[3] The prayer is printed in full in *GMH & RWD*, Appendix I, pp. 159–60.

[4] Philippians, ii. 5–11.

insight that St. Paul gives of Christ's life and character 'which is very secret and seems to me more touching and constraining than everything else is'.[1] I have shown elsewhere[2] that this text was of real importance for the Jesuit poet, who held that it not only revealed some of the mystery of Christ's Incarnation, but showed that, by this very act of annihilating Himself and thinking it 'no snatching-matter for him to be equal with God', Christ attained even greater glory and loveliness. But if we consider the occasion of Hopkins's quoting this passage to Bridges, we find that he used it to illustrate a long moral disquisition on the qualities of the 'gentleman'. He had agreed with Bridges that the greatest artist or thinker was 'essentially lower than a gentleman that was no artist or thinker'. But the gentleman—'if there is such a thing on earth'—although he is 'in the position to despise the poet, were he Dante or Shakespeare, and the painter, were he Angelo or Apelles, . . . if he is a gentleman perhaps this is what he will not do.'

> The quality of a gentleman is so very fine a thing, that it seems to me one should not be at all hasty in concluding that one possesses it. People assume that they have it, take it quite for granted, and claim the acknowledgment from others: now I should say that this also is 'no snatching-matter'. And the more a man feels what it means and is—and to feel this is certainly some part of it—the more backward he will be to think he can have realized in himself anything so perfect.[3]

Hopkins is trying to prove that the highest ideal of the gentleman precludes any self-conscious feeling and any pride in the person who is aware that he may possess this fine quality. He must 'hold himself back', just as Christ did; by not 'snatching at' the truest and highest good, he will hold it all the more steadfastly. Was the argument, which tends to refine upon the current notion of the gentleman and lift it to the moral plane of a great virtue, an indirect lesson to Bridges, who certainly prided himself on being a gentleman?[4] Or, more simply and

---

[1] Letter XCIX. February 3, 1883, p. 175.
[2] See *Etudes Anglaises*, Paris, IXe Année, No. I, Janvier-Mars, 1956, 'The Windhover de G. M. Hopkins', p. 18.
[3] Letter XCIX, February 3, 1883, p. 175.
[4] In his *Idea of a University*, 1852, Newman had given a fine portrait of the 'gentle-

without the intention of acting the friendly moralist, was Hopkins emphasizing a passing comment made by Bridges on poets and gentlemen, and endeavouring to give a sound Christian and moral basis to his judgment? The end of the letter seems to favour the second interpretation, although it will be noted that Hopkins chooses Canon Dixon and no other when he gives an instance of gentlemanliness.

As a fact poets and men of art are, I am sorry to say, by no means necessarily or commonly gentlemen. For gentlemen do not pander to lust or other basenesses nor, as you say, give themselves airs and affectations nor do other things to be found in modern works. And this adds a charm to everything Canon Dixon writes, that you feel he is a gentleman and thinks like one.[1]

Bridges did not fail to see that his friend had *not* said he was a gentleman. Either taking the omission seriously, or with deliberate misunderstanding, he accused Hopkins of having written to tell him he was 'no gentleman'. But the latter assured him that he was not 'aiming at him', except that when making remarks of universal application he could not, for instance, say 'all must die' and politely except his hearer and himself. Taking up an argument which he had often put forward in his letters he added,

If I had wanted a conspicuous instance of a blackguard I should have taken myself. . . . but [I] refrained because I thought it might look as if I wanted to draw a faint protest from you and because humility is such a very sensitive thing the least touch smutches it.[2]

Clearly a discussion on the gentleman and the blackguard could not lead the two correspondents very far, when one of them was ever ready, with a will intent on following his Master, to belittle himself and destroy the least speck of self-conceit he could detect in himself. Bridges, as we know, was not a little

man', whom he saw as the perfect master of all the human virtues, his religion, when he is not a Christian, being 'the embodiment of those ideas of the sublime, majestic and beautiful, without which there can be no large philosophy'. Hopkins is portraying the gentleman who seeks to lead a true Christian life.

[1] Letter XCIX, p. 176.
[2] Letter C, March 26, 1883, pp. 176–7.

given to self-conceit, and no doubt he thought Hopkins's remarks far too scrupulous for the common man. Such remarks amounted to hair-splitting. He knew Hopkins was no blackguard, and it would have drawn a strong, not a faint, protest from him if Hopkins had really believed that he was one. He might not be a perfect gentleman, but he certainly wished to be considered as one. His whole attitude in life, his dignity, his grave love of Beauty, his artistry, his intolerance of 'fools', his impatience with singularity, his unwavering conviction that nothing was worth doing unless it was done supremely well—everything in him pointed to one ideal: that of the gentleman. His world was one of law and order and simple discipline.

Hopkins's world was also a world of order and discipline. But it was at the same time a world of love. There was in the Jesuit poet a Pauline passion for sanctity that raised him far above the world of common morals and good manners. His whole life, his poems, his sermons and meditations testify to it. It is most revealing to find him explaining[1] a passage in the Epistle to the Galatians which Bridges had found 'hard', no doubt because St. Paul paradoxically considers the old Law as keeping in bondage, while Christians who have been called unto liberty need no law. The Law of Moses was a burden; the Law of Christ is one of love and liberty, the liberty to serve one another by love, to live in the Spirit and walk in the Spirit. In the course of his argument St. Paul says that they that are Christ's must not 'be desirous of vain glory, provoking one another, envying one another' (v. 26); he reminds them that 'if a man think himself to be something when he is nothing, he deceiveth himself' (vi. 3). Hopkins, it will be remembered, had said something quite similar about the gentleman. In the two chapters of the epistle, St. Paul is explaining to his disciples in Galatia that the old Jewish rites have no value whatever in the new religion of Christ. But, taken symbolically, his strong contrast between law and liberty illustrates the hidden spiritual difference between Bridges and Hopkins. Although it is difficult

---

[1] Letter CLXIV, September 10, 1888, pp. 286–9. Hopkins gives an explanation of Galatians, v. 22–vi. 10, verse by verse. He does not go into the difficulties of the text, but tries to give the logical sequence of St. Paul's thought.

to prove such things, one feels that Hopkins had reached in his own life a spiritual level far above the strict code of good morals that Bridges adhered to.

The passage from Galatians vi, taken at its face value, seems to set side by side two contradictory demands. How could St. Paul write, 'Let every man prove his own work, and then shall he have rejoicing in himself alone and not in another' (vi. 3), and 'As therefore we have opportunity, let us do all good unto all men' (vi. 10)? Bridges gave his own interpretation of these verses, but all that comes down to us in Hopkins's short postscript is that the two interpretations partly agreed and partly disagreed. We shall never know where the disagreement was, or how important it was. Again, we may well imagine that the solitary artist in Bridges, the writer who lived within his own world and kept himself to himself, was anxious to know what his religious friend had to say about this difficult text, and how he made the two contrary injunctions appear intelligibly reconcilable. If there was a man who could explain to him how each one of us has to bear his own burden and yet how 'in another way exchange, intercourse, commerce of good with good' was a service that the spiritual had humbly to impart to the unspiritual,[1] Hopkins was that man. When one remembers the influential part Bridges took in many activities outside his own poetical world from the 'nineties onward, one may feel that Hopkins's earnestness, his deep love of all men in need, and his fine Christian spirit, may have provided Bridges, however unobtrusively, with a great incentive. As a poet of Beauty, Bridges might have remained an aesthete; he might have remained the poet of delicate lyrics and perfect craftsmanship. He became the compiler of the *Yattendon Hymnal*; the editor of *The Spirit of Man* (an anthology of English and French verse and prose which, during the tragic First World War, bore testimony to the noblest thoughts and feelings of Man); and the author of *The Testament of Beauty*, in which the scholar, the humanist, the worshipper of Beauty, and the liberal Christian tell us the best they know and try to convince as well as to move us.

[1] *Ibid.*, p. 288.

Conclusion

I. TRUE FRIENDS

As we come now to reflect upon the course of the strange friendship between the doctor-poet and the Jesuit-poet, we cannot help once more regretting Bridges's unhappy decision to destroy his side of their correspondence. Whenever possible we have tried to deduce the content of his letters from Hopkins's answers. Once or twice, but only too rarely, we were in a position to know what he had actually said, and what his reactions or objections had been. At other times we could fortunately turn to his poems or essays for an indirect but trustworthy echo of the thoughts or feelings he must have expressed in his letters. Almost always we came to the conclusion that, whether he agreed with Hopkins or not, he gave to what Hopkins had said the most thoughtful consideration. Even so, much remains obscure. There are disagreements of which we shall never know the cause; and the help they gave each other in their writing or their passing moods—despondency, 'griggishness', or solitary aloofness—can never be fully recorded. The silence to which Bridges wilfully condemned himself is prejudicial to the just appreciation of his influence. It gives an importance to Hopkins's letters which is appropriate when we consider them in relation to his other writings, but which destroys the proper balance of a correspondence that never was a one-sided affair. As one American critic puts it, 'It is something like Beethoven's violin concerto without the violin'.[1]

This is true. We miss the violin. Moreover a few bars of the concerto have been destroyed or obliterated by Bridges. Two complete letters are missing and part of one has been scratched out.[2] When he felt that our knowledge of all the facts was not

---

[1] Ned O'Gorman, 'The Poet revealed to his Friends', *The Commonweal*, Vol. LXII, No. 16, July 22, 1955, pp. 403–404.

[2] The two letters before the last, dated April 29, 1889, were destroyed. Part of Letter LXXII is missing; four lines of Letter C have been erased; names of friends are scratched out. We agree with Abbott who says in his preface to the Letters (p. v)

required, Bridges struck out the useless passages which in his eye were too private or intimate. Had he left more marginal notes, like those on the letter about Stevenson, how helpful they would have proved!

Modern criticism, which is eager to base its judgments on careful study of all available facts—including the most intimate, since it believes that these are the most revealing—may regret the delicacy of feeling that led Bridges to act in this way. Yet it is a splendid proof of Bridges's love for Hopkins. He never meant to give us a false image of his friend: he merely refused to give details that might have diverted our interest from the poet for the poor benefit of knowing all about the man, his weaknesses or his harrowing pains. As long as he could feel that he had not been unfair to Hopkins's complex personality and singular genius he was at peace with himself. And his own silence—if one admits, as we have tried to show, that much of his own side of the friendship went into his essays and his later poems—may have been for him a way of restoring the true balance between his own work, which had been published in full, and the work of a great friend who had remained in humble obscurity.[1]

Critics have been puzzled by the friendship of two men who had apparently so little in common. In fact they had much in common, they appreciated their own differences, and neither of them had a better friend on earth. They had in common their Oxford, Rochdale and London memories, their love of poetry and music, their interest in the technicalities of prosody, their passion for new experiments. The Jesuit ascetic and the Anglican agnostic[2] had little patience with each other's reli-

that it is difficult to say whether the series is otherwise complete, but the evidence seems to show that little is lost.

[1] In an unpublished letter to Mrs. Hopkins on March 28, 1909, Bridges shows that he is fully aware of the human and artistic interest of Gerard's letters. 'When the time comes, if ever that time come, I should wish a selection of Gerard's letters to accompany his poems in a limited edition; with R.C. patronage such a book would be sufficiently well received and it would, I think, be valuable and take its place among "dappled things". I should like to know your wishes.' (Bodleian Library.)

[2] The words Anglican and agnostic sound contradictory, but it is a fact that Bridges remained a member of his national Church whatever his philosophical opinions may have been.

gious tenets, but their mutual confidence was not shaken;[1] Bridges knew that Hopkins was in dead earnest, and Hopkins, who repeatedly told his friend that he was wrong,[2] either hoped eventually to convert him or at least to prevent him from indulging his cynical vein.

It is also obvious that neither Canon Dixon nor Coventry Patmore could have enjoyed the same kind of intimacy with either poet. They belonged to an older generation, and their own literary and poetical interests were widely different from those of Bridges and Hopkins. They could be courteous; they could praise or fail to understand. They could admire Hopkins's holiness of mind or Bridges's poetical genius. But if Dixon could feel the 'terrible pathos' of Hopkins's sonnets, he was as incapable as Patmore of understanding how his intricate modes of composition could be 'the spontaneous expression of [his] poetical feeling'.[3] And the relations between Dixon, Patmore and Bridges, however friendly, remained on the formal level of dignified and gentlemanly intercourse.

The relationship between Bridges and Hopkins was one of ease, simplicity, frankness and informality. One feels that they both enjoyed their freedom from pretence or mawkishness. Bridges did not always like the 'griggish mood'[4] of Hopkins, who for his part liked to tease Bridges about his somewhat severe sense of propriety. They discussed 'the strictly funny'[5] and Bridges objected to his friend's comic poems.[6] A remarkable fact about their correspondence is that Hopkins, though he frequently complained of languishment of body and mind, and fits of sadness, could write to Bridges in the most pleasant mood; he joked and played on words, and indulged in humorous twists and turns of style that bear witness to a deep inward

---

[1] In a letter to Hopkins, Coventry Patmore, speaking of Bridges, wrote: 'I confess that I feel much more at home with such a man than I do with many a very orthodox and exemplary member of the "visible" Church, who believes all and perceives nothing.' Hopkins certainly agreed with him. *Further Letters*. Letter CLXXVIG, August 18, 1884, p. 357.

[2] Letter LII, January 29, 1879, p. 64, and Letter XCIII, November 26, 1882, p. 163.

[3] *Further Letters*, Letter CLXXVI E, April 5, 1884, p. 355.

[4] *GMH to RB*, Letter XCVI, December 20, 1882, p. 167.

[5] Letter LXXVI, June 28, 1881, p. 133.

[6] Letter LXXIV, May 14, 1881, p. 129.

happiness whenever he answered his friend's letters. To Bridges as musician he once began a letter, 'The magic nib has to my surprise minuetted and gavotted into the syllables of your name. The first movement shall be something of a stately saraband.'[1] In answer to the announcement of Bridges's engagement, he wrote, 'The secret out: I too am engaged [*here the page turns*] on examination papers and must therefore be very brief.'[2] When Bridges had been too long in answering, he would write in mock-anger—'Kindly also be damned to you for not writing and believe me affectionately yours.'[3]—or in words that conjure up a whole Parliament of Fowls: 'Bridges, have at you. Not a low, not a crow, not a bark, not a bray from either of us has crossed the Channel this long while.'[4] It was to Bridges that he disclosed the poor state of his health and the melancholy of his mind. No other confidant was told with bitter humour, 'I am recovering from the effects of my Welsh holiday and returning to helplessness.'[5] And who but the most trustworthy friend could have received the confession of a man so painfully aware of his shortcomings?

It kills me to be time's eunuch and never to beget. . . .[6]

All my work is scaffolding. . . .[7]

Why do I complain, when I have seen such lovely things and met such good people, unless that I always complain?[8]

Is not this last remark the frank avowal of his major defect? There was in Hopkins a rich vein of gaiety, a spirit of fun, but melancholy, restlessness and self-pity often triumphed over his liveliness. No one can doubt that, beside the spiritual aid of his Church and his religious Order, the true friendship Bridges gave him helped him to fight against his fits of nervous prostration, and to keep them under control to the end.

[1] Letter LXXIII, April 27, 1881, p. 125.
[2] Letter CXIV, April 30, 1884, p. 192.
[3] Letter CXII, March 25, 1884, p. 191.
[4] Letter CLXI, May 25, 1888, p. 274.
[5] Letter CXLI, November 26, 1886, p. 245.
[6] Letter CXXX, September 1, 1885, p. 222.
[7] Letter CXXXIV, October 2, 1886, p. 229.
[8] *Ibid.*, p. 228.

It has been more difficult to throw light on the unassuming influence of Hopkins's friendship on Bridges. Outwardly Bridges seems to need no help. Physically and morally he stands secure in the conviction of his own strength. But our study has revealed that his self-assurance may have been at times a mask.[1] As he was launching out into a literary career, he wanted to be encouraged. Hopkins gave him the necessary confidence in his own poetical powers. His interest in prosody, in the creation of a personal rhythm and a new style in verse, and in almost continuous experiments, was roused and sustained by Hopkins, who goaded him into action as much by condemnations as by compliments. All his essays—on Milton's prosody, on poetry and metre, on music, on Keats—were written with the consciousness that he was speaking not only for himself but also for the friend who had discussed these matters with him but had lacked the time or the physical strength to write his own essays about them.

The close co-operation of the two poets is clearly revealed in a letter Bridges wrote to Mrs. Manley Hopkins[2] in 1890 when he was contemplating the publication of his friend's poems.

I should myself prefer the postponement of the poems till the memoir is written, *or* till I have got my own method of prosody recognized separately from Gerard's. They are the same, and he has the greater claim than I to the origination of it, but he has used it so as to discredit it: and it would be a bad start in favour for the practice we both advocated and wished to be used.

However impatient of Hopkins's practice Bridges may have been—and it was late in life when he overcame his violent disapproval of it—he pays his debt to his friend and admits he owes him the very method of prosody he himself is using: a fact to which we have already given due consideration. In 1890

---

[1] Bridges, whose farouche self-consciousness proceeded from a certain social maladjustment between his 'wild desires' and his conditions of life, needed to be *mothered* by Hopkins, just as Hopkins needed to be *judged* on the purely human level by a sensibility very different from his own.

[2] Unpublished letter, August 4, 1890 (Bodleian Library). Parts of it are quoted in S. Nowell-Smith's article, 'Bridges, Hopkins and Dr. Daniel', *T.L.S.*, December 13, 1957. All the letters from Bridges to Mrs. Hopkins and her daughter Kate, quoted in this section and the next, are in the Bodleian, and are hitherto unpublished.

Bridges was still following some of the rules of sprung rhythm; he needed a little time in order to create his own free speech-rhythm and feel more independent of Hopkins. This he was to achieve by the end of the century, when he published in 1899 his *New Poems*.

We are fortunate in finding in Laurence Binyon, a minor poet of the 'nineties, a good witness to the poetical partnership which Bridges alludes to in the above letter. In 1890 Binyon met Bridges, who introduced him to Hopkins's poetry but carefully avoided shewing him 'examples of Hopkins's more difficult manner'. Binyon was interested: 'It seemed to promise scope for fresh effects and for admitting a fresh kind of matter into verse'. He ventured on experiments in it, but followed Bridges's manner rather than Hopkins's.[1] In 1937, in the course of a review of W. B. Yeats's preface to *The Oxford Book of Modern Verse, 1892–1935*, Binyon, wishing to be faithful to his own past, expressed disagreement with Yeats's assertion that 'the publication of Hopkins's work in 1918 made "sprung rhythm" the fashion'.

This is not quite a complete account of the matter. . . . Bridges took the idea from Hopkins and wrote many poems in this stress-metre before 1890. His example spread, and the result was a great broadening of the conception of rhythm in verse, so that critics of the 'nineties would have been outraged by what had become common form in 1918. Then Hopkins's poems appeared, and by their extreme originality carried many writers away, who do not, however, seem to have bound themselves by any such strict rules as Hopkins himself observed. Bridges in the end preferred a syllabic metre, founded on the *Samson* choruses, and, like them, so free in rhythm that the effect, though a little different from that of stress-metre, had the same virtue of keeping the rhythms of speech. All this movement has been in the main liberating and fruitful. England is far richer in poets at the end than at the beginning of the period.[2]

Binyon's protest pays tribute to Bridges's new prosody, which he rightly considers as different from Hopkins's sprung rhythm.

[1] L. Binyon, 'Gerard Hopkins and his Influence', *University of Toronto Quarterly*, April, 1939, quoted by Nowell C. Smith in 'Thoughts on Laurence Binyon's Poetry', *English*, Vol. IV, No. 23, 1943, p. 144.
[2] *English*, Vol. I, No. 4, 1937, p. 340.

He is accurate in his estimate of Bridges's influence, but Hopkins's manner did come as a shock to poets and critics of the 'twenties because it was really new to them. It cannot be denied that Bridges's purpose had been to withhold his friend's more difficult poems—those written in his most unaccommodating style—from the general public as long as he could. He believed that people would not understand his strange audacities— 'those snags that were in his style', as Hopkins had admitted. To Mrs. Hopkins he had given this very argument. 'Readers would not see that the peculiarities of his versification were not part of his metrical system, but a freakishness corresponding to his odd choice of words.'[1] But before we examine how Bridges understood his duty as the legatee of Hopkins's poems, we must consider how Hopkins's spiritual life, his integrity, his earnestness, the beauty of his character, and his sanctity influenced his friend.

Bridges's silence on this matter is perhaps more revealing than any remark he might have made. He paid tribute to Dolben's great charm, to Dixon's patience, tenderness and sympathy, and to Bradley's simplicity and purity of mind;[2] but he never openly acknowledged any particular feeling of reverence or admiration for Hopkins. To Gerard's parents, when he wrote some time after his death, he spoke of his 'strange life' and of the 'spiritual consolation it is possible to have from the consideration of his single-hearted devotion'.[3] Unless his own grief was too deep for words he had much more to say, and we should have liked him to express feelings similar to those his mother demonstrated when she wrote to Mrs. Hopkins, 'I looked upon him always as a Holy spiritual, more than an Earthly being, and I loved to know and feel he was Robert's real friend. I shall never forget his tenderness during Robert's illness.'[4] Reading his letters, Bridges must have been well aware of Hopkins's deep concern for his spiritual welfare. He may have felt irritated by the moral severity which made Hopkins speak of Whitman as 'a great scoundrel', of Milton as 'a

---

[1] Letter to Mrs. Hopkins, August 4, 1890.
[2] *Three Friends*, pp. 104, 146–7, 229.
[3] Letter to Mrs. Hopkins, June 19, 1889.
[4] Mrs. Molesworth to Mrs. Hopkins, July, 1889. (Bodleian Library).

very bad man', of Swinburne and Hugo as 'those plagues of
mankind'.[1] But when he read, 'As I am criticizing you, so does
Christ, only more correctly and more affectionately, both as a
poet and as a man; and he is a judge qui potest et animam et
corpus perdere in gehennam,'[2] he must have understood how
intense Hopkins's faith was and how completely unified were
his spiritual and literary interests. When Hopkins explained
to him what a mystery was for a Catholic, and how the 'dogma'
of the Trinity was not an equation, 'the dull algebra of school-
men', but 'news of their dearest friend or friends',[3] Bridges's
own views may not have been changed in the least,[4] but he
must have been deeply moved. However strange his friend's
life, he knew that it was a dedicated life, and that it deserved
his reverence. We cannot help thinking that the poet who,
when he compiled *The Spirit of Man*, did not insert any original
poetry of his own, while he chose six excerpts from Hopkins's
poems,[5] was paying homage to one he set above himself. In
the preface to the book he made it quite clear that the essential
implication was 'that spirituality is the basis and foundation of
human life' and 'must underlie everything'.[6]

---

[1] These condemnations may be read in *GMH to RB*, p. 39 (Milton, Swinburne,
Hugo), p. 155 (Whitman). To Dixon, Hopkins spoke of 'crazy Blake' and said that
Goethe and Burns 'spoke out of the real human rakishness of their hearts'. *GMH
& RWD*, pp. 148 and 25.

[2] *GMH to RB*, Letter LIV, February 22, 1879, p. 73.

[3] Letter CX, October 24, 1883, p. 187.

[4] Mrs. Waterhouse sent Hopkins her *Book of Simple Prayers* in May, 1886. In the
letter accompanying it she expressed views that were almost certainly shared by
her son-in-law. 'You will think it sadly undogmatic and perhaps when I was
gathering it together I was a little too much afraid of dogma—as life goes on every
year leads one to be more sure that one need be afraid of nothing through which the
pure in heart have at any time seen their Lord—unless it has come to be in any
way a cloud between them and him—it also leads one to believe that any words
of ours are so infinitely far from saying anything about Him as he is, that the difference between one set of words and another is but little—and that what is spoken
in silence between Him and the Soul is the closest approach we can make to an
utterance—and that in that language there is the *answer* too, which is the highest
joy.' (*Further Letters*, Appendix III, Letter H1, May 10, 1866, p. 426).

[5] Letter to Mrs. Hopkins, January 27, 1916: 'When I was doing the book it
gave me great pleasure to think of the happiness that it might give you to see some
of dear Gerard's work in really worthy company—where his queernesses appear as
the personal sincerity which they were.'

[6] *The Spirit of Man*, 1916, Preface, first page. (The pages of the book are not
numbered.)

Hopkins's noble though obscure example lay deep in Bridges's heart. As life went on with its joys and successes and the fame of the Laureateship, how often Bridges must have reflected on his friend's fate and his own! We know what his thoughts were. In *The Testament of Beauty*, there are lines which to the uninformed may read impersonally; but to us, who can apply them to the two poets, they are a very personal confession and a glowing testimony of love and admiration for the saintly man who was Bridges's 'real friend'.

> Now in spiritual combat, altho' I must deem
> them the most virtuous who with least effort excell,
> yet, virtue being a conflict, moralizers hold
> that where conflict is hardest virtue must be at best;
> and in the rub of life and physical hindrance
> a man who has striven heroically and done great deeds,
> in spite of frailty or bodily disease or pain,
> may win more admiration and praise in the end than he
> who with comfort to himself, indolently as it wer,
> hath done as well; nay, for the very impediments
> may ev'n be envied, as old navigators wer
> in the glory they had got to hav outridden their storms.[1]
>
> (Ethick. 732–43)

II. THE LEGATEE OF HOPKINS'S POEMS

When Bridges was copying or pasting Hopkins's strange but very fine poems into his book, he firmly intended to publish them when opportunity presented itself. So long as Hopkins was alive, his scruples as a Jesuit, and his determination to sacrifice any possible literary fame, prevented Bridges from taking the means necessary to make him known. A recent writer has revealed that once before Hopkins's death Bridges planned 'to print some at least of his poems'.[2] This is important news. No allusion to it is to be found in any letter from Hopkins or Dixon, or in the memoir of Dixon; yet Bridges claims to have obtained the permission of both his friends. We may infer that

---

[1] *RB Poet. Works*, p. 678.
[2] S. Nowell-Smith, *op. cit.*

permission was given orally.[1] Fortunately his letters to the proposed printer of the book, the Reverend Henry Daniel, have been preserved, and through them we learn what the project was.

It appears that Bridges, having met Daniel early in 1880, wrote to him on August 11 of that year to suggest that, instead of a book of his own, 'a very nice little book . . . might be got up by putting together the verses of one or two of my friends'. There would be in fact five authors. With one exception, Nowell-Smith deduces from the letter the names of four of them: Bridges himself, Dolben, Dixon and Hopkins. Considering that Bridges's brother had published a book of poems anonymously[2] some months before, it is just possible that he may have been the fifth unknown author. Daniel, who was still a novice at printing, 'expressed some modest doubt of his skill'. Bridges did not wish to urge him 'to engage in what you might regret afterwards', and the project was dropped. Nowell-Smith reminds us that on February 15, 1879,[3] Hopkins had told Bridges that he did not mean to publish. I think it is likely that, apart from Daniel's reluctance to print this small anthology, Hopkins renewed his opposition on second thoughts; if so, the withdrawal of permission was fatal to Bridges's plan.

When Hopkins died, Bridges asked Father Wheeler to return to him any of his letters to Gerard. In his reply Father Wheeler said that Gerard had given instructions about his papers, and although no proper inventory was made at the time, Hopkins's papers, writings and note-books eventually came into the possession of his family or of Bridges. Almost immediately the latter, who knew that he was in possession of the complete poetical works of his friend, contemplated writing a memorial which would be printed privately. As early as August 12, 1889, Coventry Patmore wrote to Bridges to approve of his intention:

I am very glad to know that you are to write a memorial of him.

---

[1] As the plan took shape, in August, 1880, Bridges may well have discussed the matter with Hopkins, who was then in London. He had paid a visit to Dixon some time before. (*GMH & RWD*, Letter XII, December 22, 1880, p. 37. 'Bridges of course told me about his visit to you when I saw him in town this summer'.)

[2] *Wet Days*, By a Farmer, London, Kegan Paul, 1879. See *GMH to RB*, Letter LXVII, p. 100, note 2.

[3] Letter LIII, p. 66.

It is quite right that it should be privately printed. I, as one of his friends, should protest against any attempt to share him with the public, to whom little of what was most truly characteristic in him could be communicated.[1]

Patmore's opinion was shared by those who had read Hopkins's poems, and by his family. They felt that Hopkins was not a poet for the general public. This partly explains Bridges's slowness, once the principle of printing the memorial and poems had been accepted by Daniel. By October 11 Bridges had outlined his book in all its material details: 48 pages for the memoir, 12 for the early poems, 50 for the main corpus of poetry, 5 for Hopkins's note on his poems.[2] There would be two portraits, a facsimile of the poet's handwriting, and 'reproductions of studies'. And yet, in spite of such careful preparation, there was no privately printed edition of Hopkins's poems and of Bridges's memoir. On November 19, he feels that the poems '*must* be printed', but the memoir 'will be a disagreeable difficulty'. He hoped to manage it by Easter, 1890. He never managed it.

We may wonder why. It seems that Bridges was divided between his love and truth as he saw it, which was sad and cruel. He shrank from the task of telling even his private readers of the unhappiness and failure of Hopkins as a man, and his strangeness and oddity as a poet. Much as he loved his friend, we know that Bridges strongly disapproved of his 'eccentricities'. The shock of his death, coming at a time when Hopkins felt that the Irish policy was wrong and 'partly unlawful', and when he compared himself to 'prisoners made to serve the enemies' gunners',[3] strengthened Bridges's opinion that his friend's unhappy religious life had been years of waste and error. In the winter of 1889–90 Bridges no doubt thought it his duty to bring these facts to light, or else not to write the memoir. In fairness to his friend, and because he knew that to

[1] Quoted by Nowell-Smith from the *Fortnightly*, March, 1948, p. 201.

[2] The bibliographical description, in Nowell-Smith's article, reads: 'His memoir, in italic type, will fill pp. i–xlviii, followed on pp. xlix–lx by Hopkins's early poems in the same italic; the main corpus of poetry, with its separate title-page, will be printed in "common type" on pp. 1–50, followed by "a long note by G. H. on his own poems", pp. 51–55.'

[3] *Further Letters*, Note J, p. 447.

himself Catholicism was a sealed secret, he had meant to see as
many of Gerard's Roman Catholic friends as he could. But
Gerard's Roman Catholic friends in England were few;[1] most
of them had not seen him for a considerable time; they had
practically nothing to say to Bridges, unless it was to speak of
'the authority of his goodness',[2] or of 'his beautifully gentle and
generous nature'.[3] S. Nowell-Smith suggests that 'it is possible
that the "disagreeable difficulty" of November arose out of
some failure of communicativeness on the part of Gerard's
Roman Catholic friends', but he adds that there is no firm
evidence. I am inclined to think that there was no other difficulty than Bridges's own hesitations and misgivings.[4]

In May, 1890, he writes to Mrs. Hopkins: 'I have come round
to more my old state of feeling with regard to his memory',
which implies that he had felt differently for some length of
time. Obviously he knew that he could not view his friend in
the proper perspective if he wrote in a turmoil of emotion. But
the opinion he came to form within the next three years—
which he expressed in the short notice of Hopkins prefixed to
a selection of his poems in A. H. Miles's *Poets and Poetry of the
Century*[5]—was a severe one. To Gerard's mother he had
written, 'Gerard's failure and melancholy seem to me essentials';[6] and these two facts are duly recorded in the notice.[7]
The original draft ended with the statement that the poems
'miss some of those first essentials of beauty, which are attain-

[1] Alexander Wood was the only Oxford convert Bridges could have met. William
Addis had left the Roman Church in 1888 and Alfred Garrett was in Tasmania.
There were the Paravicinis at Oxford, the von Hügels, Coventry Patmore and, in
Dublin, Sir Robert Stewart. Mrs. Hopkins had received letters of condolence from
them.

[2] Letter of Coventry Patmore to Robert Bridges (August 12, 1889), *Further
Letters* (1956), p. 391, note.

[3] Mrs. Frances de Paravicini to Mrs. Hopkins, June 14, 1889 (Bodleian Library).

[4] The Jesuits in London were certainly not prepared to help Bridges in his difficult task.

[5] Vol. VIII, 1893, with volume-subtitle, 'Robert Bridges and Contemporary
Poets'. There is a four-page notice of Hopkins's life and work by Bridges (pp.161–4),
and six pages (pp. 165–70) are devoted to the poems.

[6] Letter to Mrs. Hopkins, February 24, 1893.

[7] 'He was not considered publicly successful in his profession' (p. 162). 'He
seems to have entirely satisfied the Society as classical examiner at Dublin. That
drudgery, however, and the political dishonesty which he was there forced to witness, so tortured his sensitive spirit that he fell into a melancholy state.'' (p. 163).

able by all poets alike'. Could a critic say anything worse? Canon Dixon regretted that the notice should end with such decided fault-finding. Bridges tried to explain to Mrs. Hopkins why he had passed so rigorous a sentence:

> It would be of course very easy to soften this: and *I shd. be extremely glad to have Mr. Hopkins's opinion, and yours, on the matter.* I would much rather have it SAID that I was unkindly severe, than that I allowed my judgment to be led astray by my personal feelings, and I do not wish to leave anything but good for the critics to say. The only damaging thing that they can say is that the poems are not good enough to justify Gerard's place among the 'poets'. Tho' this is absurd (if you look at some of the others) yet it is possible that the pedants might say it: and I think it is well to make it quite clear that those who hold the contrary opinion have their eyes fully open to the defects which the pedants might point to.[1]

One feels that Bridges is in fact 'led astray by his personal feelings', and that, in his efforts to protect Hopkins against the pedants, he is becoming one of them himself. However he 'altered the sentence but not the sense of the concluding paragraph': in a more subdued tone, he remarks that the poems 'very often, among verses of the rarest beauty, show a neglect of those canons of taste which seem common to all poetry'.[2] Twenty-five years will pass before Bridges admits to Mrs. Hopkins that 'the more one knows the poems the better one thinks of them'.[3]

That was written while Bridges was at work on the first edition of Hopkins's *Poems*, in January, 1918. In 1909 the Jesuits had tried, through Father Keating, to obtain from Hopkins's family the right to publish his poems. Bridges's extreme antipathy towards, and distrust of, Jesuits led him to urge Mrs. Hopkins not to tell them she had a copy of all the poems[4]. A few months earlier Edmund Gosse, who had been

[1] Letter to Mrs. Hopkins, May 2, 1893.

[2] Letter to Mrs. Hopkins, May 5, 1893. He submits the text that was finally printed in a postscript.

[3] Letter to Mrs. Hopkins, January 20, 1918. He also says: 'I feel sure that the book will be not only quite unique, but of convincing merit.' Such words allay the harshness of his critical notes.

[4] Letter to Mrs. Hopkins, May 7, 1909. 'If [Father Keating] finds out that you have a copy of all the poems he may bother you. . . . I do not think that Gerard

asked by the publisher Elkin Mathews to edit Gerard's poems for him, consented, and then withdrew. Bridges, informing the poet's mother, commented in his best contemptuous manner that Gosse had 'been up to his accustomed presumption'.[1] Clearly he had no intention of letting anybody do the task for which he felt responsible. His strong anti-Catholic bias made him imagine that there was a 'scheme of "booming" Roman Catholic pretensions to artistic eminence, just as they pull all the strings to glorify Francis Thompson',[2] and that the Jesuits at Farm Street 'had nothing much to do, and suffered from a weak form of literary ambition, so that the notion of editing Gerard's poems was attractive to them'.[3] The best way to explain Bridges's outbursts of temper, and his shocking unfairness, is to see them as the outward signs of a jealous love. He felt that outside himself and the poet's family no one had any right to Hopkins's literary production. His absolute confidence in his own views, and his determination to be the first editor of Hopkins's poems, rested on the years of deep friendship during which he had been Hopkins's best and almost only confidant. The Society's complete lack of interest in the poet's poems, notes and papers in 1889, and before, and for many years after, was to Bridges sufficient evidence that it had lost every moral right to claim them twenty years later.

The incidents with Gosse[4] and Father Keating[5] must have given Bridges the impression that he could not postpone editing

wd. have wished his poems to be edited by a committee of those fellows [*sic*]. In any case you will no doubt write me before taking any steps. I have not mentioned your name to Rev. K.'

[1] Letter to Mrs. Hopkins, April 2, 1909.

[2] Letter to Mrs. Hopkins, March 28, 1909.

[3] Letter to Mrs. Hopkins, October 11, 1909.

[4] Infuriated by Gosse's 'negotiations', Bridges's memory played him false. To Mrs. Hopkins he wrote on March 28, 1909: 'When he was visiting the Waterhouses at Yattendon in the 'seventies, I tried to get him to recognize the merits of Gerard's verse. He exhibited extreme antipathy'. But in 1879 Hopkins had written to Bridges: 'I do warm to that good Mr. Gosse for liking and, you say, "taking" my pieces: I may then have contributed fuel to his Habitual Joy." (Letter LIX, April 22, 1879, p. 79.)

[5] Father Keating contributed three long articles on G. M. Hopkins to the July, August and September numbers of *The Month* in 1909, the year he failed to obtain the poems for publication. His articles made Hopkins known to a fairly wide Roman Catholic circle.

the poems much longer.[1] When he became Poet Laureate in 1913, he must have felt all the more bound to take the necessary steps. The War broke out. He inserted a number of Hopkins's poems in *The Spirit of Man* in 1916. In September, 1917, he wrote to Mrs. Hopkins:

I have had lately some very authoritative appeals for the publication of all Gerard's poetical remains. The 'Spirit of Man' has had a wide sale, and his poems in it have commanded a good deal of attention. The other day Sir Walter Raleigh, whose judgment is very highly esteemed, said to me that Gerard's poems in the Sp. of Man were the only ones among the comparatively unknown writers whom I had introduced, which stood up alongside of the greater writers. . . .

I think that the time has come to publish all the poems. So I am writing to you to ask whether you have any objection to this being done. The Oxford Univ. Press will probably take the bk. if it is offered to them . . . I shall be glad if you will tell me what your wishes are.[2]

To Miss Kate Hopkins, who had answered him on behalf of her mother, he wrote a week later,

I am glad to hear that your Mother is agreeable to the notion of getting Gerard's poems published. Certainly the Wreck of the Deutschland will be printed. Indeed the idea is that every scrap that he wrote should be published. There is a strong feeling that any thing by him would be interesting . . .[3]

In January, 1918, he wrote to Mrs. Hopkins (who was in her ninety-seventh year), 'I am indeed glad that your life has been so prolonged, and hope that you will have the pleasure of

[1] The legal problem—who was Hopkins's literary executor?—was a difficult one. Certainly Bridges did not help towards an understanding between the family and the Society. The copyright remained the property of the family till the death of the poet's brother, Lionel, in 1952; it is now the property of the Society of Jesus. By a will dated July 11, 1878, registered in the High Court of Justice, Dublin, on July 13, 1889, Father Gerard Hopkins had left all his possessions to the English Jesuits. Normally Father Wheeler should have sent Hopkins's papers and poems to the Father Provincial in London. Quite unawares, by sending them to Bridges he gave precedence and eminence to the friendship of the two poets.

[2] Letter to Mrs. Hopkins, September 7, 1917.

[3] Letter to Kate Hopkins, September 13, 1917.

handling Gerard's book.'[1] On February 18 he sent Kate Hopkins his dedicatory sonnet for her and her mother's consideration. He was, he said,

rather afraid that you may think it too sad. Of course one is not quite responsible for the result of one's work—and if this does not please you, I must try again. You will remember that the poems will disclose the fact that Gerard suffered dreadfully from a sort of melancholy—and I do not think there wd. be any advantage in not recognizing this—besides I shd. judge it a good thing to tell the truth about, and show that medievalizing does not always produce complete ease of mind. But, pray, in criticizing the sonnet say what you and your Mother both think. I am not at all tender or sensitive in such matters.[2]

He obtained the necessary permission and the book was printed and published on December 19, 1918.[3] There was an inscription in Latin to 'Catharine' Hopkins, stating that the gift of that book of poems by her son was made 'in her 98th year'.[4] Mrs. Hopkins died on September 30, 1920, and Bridges in his letter of condolence to Miss Hopkins was able to say, 'I shall always I hope be very happy about the issue of that book, and the pleasure that it gave to your mother.'[5]

In his own way, at the time he had thought best, without renouncing his prejudices, but feeling certain that he had paid a fitting tribute to the 'ill-broker'd talent' of his Jesuit friend, Bridges had at last given to the English-speaking nations the 'lov'd legacy' of Gerard's poems. He was to live long enough to see their fame slowly but steadily spread.

[1] Letter to Mrs. Hopkins, January 20, 1918.

[2] Letter to Kate Hopkins, February 18, 1918.

[3] Bridges wrote an introduction and important notes to the poems, but there was no memoir. One feels that by 1918 he had come to realize that he could not be fair at once to the Anglican and the Roman Catholic periods of his friend's life.

[4] The Latin text is written in the best classical tradition: CATHARINAE/HVNC LIBRVM/QVI FILII EIVS CARISSIMI/POETAE DEBITAM INGENIO LAVDEM EXPECTANTIS/ SERVM TAMEN MONVMENTVM ESSET/ANNVM AETATIS XCVIII AGENTI/ VETERIS AMI-CITIAE PIGNVS/D D D/R B. This may have been composed by A. E. Housman, to whom Bridges had written a letter on May 25, 1918 (photostat in Bodleian Library) asking him to supply a dedication in Latin. See letter by S. Nowell-Smith in *T.L.S.*, November 6, 1959.

[5] Letter to Kate Hopkins, (postmark) October 7, 1920.

As the man who 'balanced his faculties' and as the friend of one who went 'to the extremes of emphasis', Bridges could never be wholly at ease with Hopkins's art. 'It would have been quite uncharacteristic of him to face what seemed to him plain imperfections other than sturdily'.[1] But we maintain that it is because their temperaments were as unlike as their physiques that there persisted between them a steadfast affection and a rare love.

In Hopkins's private papers (which Bridges knew 'ought never to have been sent—it was an oversight of the priests') he had read 'a very interesting and touching passage about his prayers that his poems might be protected from abuse':[2]

Also in some med[itations] today I earnestly asked our Lord to watch over my compositions, not to preserve them from being lost or coming to nothing, for that I am very willing they should, but [that] they might not do me harm through the enmity, or imprudence of any man or my own; that he wd. have them as his own and employ or not employ them as he shd. see fit. And this I believe is heard.[3]

Bridges may well have thought that he had been instrumental in God's purpose, and may have rested content, whatever the critics might say against his long delay and his narrow-minded criticism of Hopkins's mannerisms. In 1921 he could read in *Poetry* Edward Sapir's exclamation, 'From our best friends, deliver us, O Lord!'[4] Possibly it reminded him of his discussions with Hopkins about 'the strictly funny', and he may have felt outraged. But 'the feeling of innocence, the sense of integrity, the consciousness of rectitude' may have returned to him, as they did to his staggered correspondent years before.[5] After all, his very strictures had brought and would bring more friends to Hopkins than bland eulogies would have done.

For he *was* Hopkins's best friend, and in spite of his own shortcomings, of his ineradicable prejudices, of the differences

[1] 'Robert Bridges', front-page article, *T.L.S.*, June 26, 1953.
[2] Letters to Kate Hopkins, October 14 and November 28, 1918.
[3] *Further Letters*, Note J, p. 446.
[4] E. Sapir, 'G. M. Hopkins, a study,' September, 1921.
[5] *GMH to RB*, Letter LXXVI, June 28, 1881, p. 133.

and disagreements between them, he must have known, just as much as Hopkins knew in the depth of his heart, that their friendship belonged to history and literature and would keep their names together as closely as the love they had felt for each other.

CHRONOLOGY OF THE LIFE OF
ROBERT BRIDGES

1844   October 23: birth at Walmer, Kent, of Robert Seymour Bridges, eighth child (fourth son) of John Thomas Bridges and Harriett Elizabeth, third daughter of the Rev. Sir Robert Affleck, Bart.

1853   May 10: death of R.B.'s father.

1854   September: goes to Eton.

      October 31: R.B.'s mother marries the Rev. J. E. N. Molesworth, D.D.; the family move to Rochdale, Lancs.

1863   Michaelmas: goes up to Corpus Christi College, Oxford. [G.M.H. had entered Balliol in summer term.]

1866   February: death of R.B.'s younger brother Edward. [September: G.M.H. visits Rochdale.]

1867   Declines to stroke Oxford boat. May: strokes Corpus boat. [June: G.M.H. takes first in Greats.]

      July: in Paris. December: takes second in Greats.

1868   January to May: travels in Egypt and Syria with L. Muirhead; later visits Germany with W. Sanday.

      [July: G.M.H. in Switzerland. September: G.M.H. enters novitiate at Roehampton.]

1869   April: death of R.B.'s sister Harriett Louisa (Mrs. Plow).

      November 6: is entered as student at St. Bartholomew's Hospital, lodging at 35 Great Ormond Street.

1871   [August 2: G.M.H.'s "red letter".]

1873   November: *Poems*.

1874   [January: G.M.H. reads A. Lang's review of *Poems* in the *Academy*.]

      Graduates M.B. (Oxon.); lodging at 50 Maddox Street with H. E. Wooldridge; tours Italy.

1875–6 House physician to Dr. Patrick Black at Bart's.

1876   *The Growth of Love* (24 sonnets).

1877   Casualty physician at Bart's.

      April 21: death of Dr. Molesworth; R.B. and his mother move to 52 Bedford Square.

1878   Assistant physician, Hospital for Sick Children, Great Ormond Street, and physician, Great Northern Hospital, Holloway.

[August: G.M.H. preaches at Farm Street.]

1879   [January: G.M.H. introduces R. W. Dixon to R.B.]

February: *Poems by the author of "The Growth of Love"* (second series).

1880   April: is introduced to Dr. C. H. O. Daniel.

August: *Poems by the author of "The Growth of Love"*, third series.

1881   June: serious illness.

December–March (1882): in Italy with Muirhead; retires from medical practice.

1882   June: visits G.M.H. at Roehampton.

September: moves, with his mother, to Yattendon, Berks.

1883   July: *Prometheus the Firegiver* (Daniel Press).

1884   [February: G.M.H. becomes Professor of Greek at University College, Dublin.]

September 3: marries Mary Monica, elder daughter of Alfred Waterhouse, R.A.

December: *Poems* (Daniel Press).

1885   March: *Nero, Part I.* [H. C. Beeching becomes rector of Yattendon.]

December: *Eros and Psyche.*

1886   May 6: is visited by G.M.H. August: visits South Wales.

1887   August: is visited by G.M.H.

December 6: birth of daughter Elizabeth (Mrs. Daryush).

December: *On the Elements of Milton's Blank Verse* (in Beeching's *Paradise Lost*, Book I).

1889   May: *The Growth of Love* (79 sonnets, Daniel Press.)

[June 8: death of G.M.H. in Dublin.]

November: *The Feast of Bacchus* (Daniel Press).

1890   *Palicio*; *The Return of Ulysses*; *The Christian Captives*; *Achilles in Scyros.*

October: *Shorter Poems*, Books I–IV.

1892   August 4: birth of son Edward Ettingdene (Lord Bridges).

1893   May: *Milton's Prosody.*

December: *Shorter Poems*, Book V; *The Humours of the Court.*

Notice of G.M.H. in A. H. Miles, *Poets and Poetry of the Century*, Vol. VIII.

1894   June: *Nero, Part II.*

1895   *John Keats, a critical essay.*

June: withdraws candidature as Professor of Poetry at Oxford.

November: *Yattendon Hymnal*, Part I (Part II, 1897; Parts III–IV, 1899).

[Poems by G.M.H. in Beeching's *Lyra Sacra* and *A Book of Christmas Verse*.]

1898   *Poetical Works*, Vol. I (Vol. II, 1899; Vol. III, 1901; Vols. IV–V, 1902; Vol. VI, 1905).
1901   Starts experimenting in Will Stone's classical prosody.
1905   Spends winter in Switzerland.
1907   Builds Chilswell House, Boar's Hill, Oxford, and lives there.
1909   Edits *Poems by R. W. Dixon* with memoir.
1911   Edits *Poems of D. M. Dolben* with memoir.
1912   *Poetical Works* (1 vol.).
1913   May: founds Society for Pure English.
        July: appointed Poet Laureate by Mr. Asquith.
1916   *The Spirit of Man, an anthology* (including 6 poems by G.M.H.).
1917   Chilswell House burnt down; lives in Oxford pending re-building.
1918   December 19: *Poems of Gerard Manley Hopkins*.
1920   March 18: *October and Other Poems*.
1924   Three months at University of Michigan, Ann Arbor, U.S.A.
1925   December: *New Verse, written in 1921*.
1926   *Henry Bradley, a memoir*.
        Death of daughter Margaret (Mrs. Joseph).
1927–9 *The Testament of Beauty* (private edition; published October 24, 1929).
1929   June: awarded Order of Merit.
1930   April 21: dies at Chilswell House.
1935   January: *The Letters of G.M.H. to R.B.*
1940   June: *Correspondence of R.B. and H. Bradley*.

SELECT BIBLIOGRAPHY OF ROBERT BRIDGES

A chronological bibliography of Bridges's writings need not be given here. George L. McKay and Simon Nowell-Smith have, between them, recorded all the editions printed between 1873 and 1936. My aim is to guide the reader to the existing bibliographies (Section A); to analyse the accessible collected and other editions, with indications of the original appearance of the works they contain (Section B); and to record all such critical and biographical writings about Bridges (Section C) as are relevant to my study of his relations with Hopkins.

A. BIBLIOGRAPHIES

Notes on the Bibliography of Robert Bridges, by Henry Daniel. *Oxford Magazine*, June 19, 1895, pp. 446–7.

Bibliographies of Modern Authors: No. 1, Robert Bridges, by I. A. Williams. Chaundy 1921.

Bibliography of the Daniel Press, by Falconer Madan. In *Memorials of C. H. O. Daniel*, 1921, pp. 37–184.

English First Editions: Robert (Seymour) Bridges, a bibliographical check-list, by H. S. Boutell. *Publisher's Weekly* (New York), May 24, 1930, pp. 2650–4.

A Bibliography of Robert Bridges, by G. L. McKay. Columbia University Press and O.U.P. 1933.

Check-list of the Works of Robert Bridges, by Simon Nowell-Smith. *Book-Collector's Quarterly*, No. XVI, Oct.-Dec., 1934, pp. 30–40.

Cambridge Bibliography of English Literature. Vol. III, 1940, pp. 323–5 (S. Nowell-Smith), and Vol. V, 1957, pp. 599–600 (William White).

B. BRIDGES'S WRITINGS

I. POETICAL WORKS

Poetical Works of Robert Bridges, uniform edition in 6 vols.

Smith, Elder 1898–1905

Poetical Works, excluding the Eight

Dramas, Oxford Standard Authors, 1 vol.	O.U.P. 1912
2nd ed., enlarged	O.U.P. 1936
Re-issue with *The Testament of Beauty*	O.U.P. 1953

The contents of the 1-vol. edition are listed below in the order chosen by R.B., with details of original publication:

Prometheus the Firegiver	Daniel Press 1883
2nd ed.	Bell 1884
Demeter, a mask	Clarendon Press 1905
Eros and Psyche	Bell 1885
The Growth of Love (24 sonnets, anon.)	Bumpus 1876
2nd ed. (79 sonnets, anon.)	Daniel Press 1889
In *Poetical Works*, Vol. I (69 sonnets)	Smith, Elder 1898
Shorter Poems, Books I–IV	Bell 1890

The contents of Books I–III were the author's final selection from *Poems*, Pickering 1873; *Poems by the author of The Growth of Love* (second series), Bumpus 1879; *Poems by the author of The Growth of Love, third series*, Bumpus 1880; *Poems, Daniel Press* 1884. Book IV was first published in 1890.

Shorter Poems, Books I–V	Daniel Press 1893–4
2nd ed.	Bell 1894
New Poems. In *Poetical Works*, Vol. II	Smith, Elder 1899
Later Poems and *Poems in Classical Prosody*. In *Poetical Works*	O.U.P. 1912
October and Other Poems	Heinemann 1920
New Verse, written in 1921	Clarendon Press 1925
Two Pieces written after the War	
(a) Verses written for Mrs. Daniel (1919)	Clarendon Press 1932
(b) The Widow. In *The Legion Book*	Cassell 1929
The Testament of Beauty, privately printed	O.U.P. 1927–9
1st published ed.	Clarendon Press 1929

Eight Plays, excluded from *Poetical Works*, 1912, but included in the uniform edition (*supra*) as follows:

Vol. III, 1901	
Nero, Part I	Bumpus 1890
Achilles in Scyros	Bumpus 1890
2nd ed.	Bell 1892
Vol. IV, 1902	
Palicio	Bumpus 1890
The Return of Ulysses	Bumpus 1890

Vol. V, 1902
> The Christian Captives   Bumpus 1890
> The Humours of the Court   Bell and Bumpus 1893

Vol. VI, 1905
> The Feast of Bacchus   Daniel Press 1889
> 2nd ed.   Bell and Bumpus 1894
> Nero, Part II   Bell and Bumpus 1894

II. PROSE WORKS

Collected Essays, Papers &c. of Robert Bridges, uniform edition
in 10 fascicles   O.U.P. 1927–36

Vol. I
I. The Influence of the Audience on Shakespeare's Drama
(*Shakespeare's Works*, Stratford edition, Vol. X, 1907)   1927
II–III. Humdrum and Harum-scarum, a lecture on free
verse (*London Mercury*, November 1922); Poetic Diction
in English (*Forum*, May, 1923)   1928
IV. A Critical Introduction to Keats (privately printed
1895; in Muses' Library *Keats*, 1896)   1929
V. George Darley (*T.L.S.*, March 6, 1908, and *Academy*,
August 4, 1906)   1930
VI–VII. The Poems of Mary Coleridge (*Cornhill*, November, 1907); Lord de Tabley's Poems (*Speaker*, December
12, 1903)   1931
VIII–X. Dante in English Literature (*T.L.S.*, June 24,
1909); The Poems of Emily Brontë (*T.L.S.*, January
12, 1911); Dryden on Milton (*Speaker*, October 24,
1903)   1932
Vol. II
XI–XV. Studies in Poetry (*T.L.S.*, November 21, 1907);
The Springs of Helicon (*T.L.S.*, April 1, 1909); Wordsworth and Kipling (*T.L.S.*, February 29, 1912); Word-
Books (*T.L.S.*, August 4, 1910); A Letter on English
Prosody (*Musical Antiquary*, October, 1909); note on
Neo-Miltonics (written December, 1923)   1933
XVI–XX. The Bible (first half in *T.L.S.*, March 23, 1911);
Bunyan's *Pilgrim's Progress* (*Speaker*, April 1 and 8, 1905);
Sir Thomas Browne (*Speaker*, May 14, 1904); George
Santayana (*London Mercury*, August 1920); The Glamour
of Grammar (*T.L.S.*, May 30, 1912)   1934
XXI–XXVI. The Musical Setting of Poetry (*The Shilling
Garland*, No. ii, Elkin Mathews, 1896); A Practical

Discourse on Some Principles of Hymn-singing (*Journal of Theological Studies*, October 1899); About Hymns (Church Music Society *Occasional Papers*, No. ii, 1911); English Chanting (*Musical Antiquary*, April, 1911); Chanting (*Prayer-book Dictionary*, 1912); Preface to Psalms noted in Speech-rhythm (written 1912)   1935
XXVII–XXX. An Address to the Swindon W.E.A. (Clarendon Press 1916); The Necessity of Poetry (Clarendon Press 1918); Poetry (*Listener*, March 6, 1929); An Account of the Casualty Department (*St. Bartholomew's Hospital Reports*, Vol. XIV, 1878)   1936

A Tract on the Present State of English Pronunciation
Clarendon Press 1913
Previously in *Essays and Studies of the English Association*, Vol. I, 1910.

Milton's Prosody, with a chapter on accentual verse, revised final edition   O.U.P. 1921
Previous editions:
On the Elements of Milton's Blank Verse in Paradise Lost (anon., in H. C. Beeching's edition of *Paradise Lost*, Book I)
Clarendon Press 1887
On the Prosody of Paradise Regained and Samson Agonistes (anon.)   Blackwell 1889
Milton's Prosody   Clarendon Press 1893
Milton's Prosody by R.B. and *Classical Metres in English Verse* by W. J. Stone   O.U.P. 1901
Three Friends, memoirs of D. M. Dolben, R. W. Dixon, H. Bradley   O.U.P. 1932
Reprinted from volumes noted in Section III below.

III. ANTHOLOGIES AND SELECTIONS

The Garland of Rachel, compiled by H. Daniel   Daniel Press 1881
Contains a poem not reprinted by R.B.
The Poets and the Poetry of the Century, edited by A. H. Miles, Vol. III   Hutchinson 1893
Contains an introductory note by R.B. to a selection of poems by Hopkins. A new edition (*The Poets and the Poetry of the Nineteenth Century*, Vol. VII, Routledge 1906) contains also an introductory note by R.B. to a selection of poems by H. Newbolt.
The Yattendon Hymnal, edited by R.B. and H. E. Wooldridge, with music, in 4 parts   O.U.P. 1895–9

The words of certain hymns were reprinted in:

Yattendon Hymns	O.U.P. 1897
Hymns from the Yattendon Hymnal, by R.B.	Daniel Press 1899
The Small Hymn-Book	Blackwell 1899
The Yattendon Psalter (Yattendon 4-part Chants)	Clarendon Press 1897

The Last Poems of R. W. Dixon, selected and edited by R.B.
O.U.P. 1905

Poems by the late Rev. R. W. Dixon, a selection with a memoir
by R.B. Smith, Elder 1909

The Poems of D. M. Dolben, edited with a memoir by R.B.
O.U.P. 1911

2nd ed. (Oxford Standard Authors) O.U.P. 1915

S.P.E. Tracts Clarendon Press 1913–29
(The Society for Pure English was founded, and its prospectus written, by R.B. in May, 1913. He wrote "entirely or principally" *Tracts* Nos. 1, 2, 5, 8, 14, 15, 18 and 21, and contributed to Nos. 3, 4, 6, 7, 9, 10, 11, 13, 16, 17, 19, 22, 23, 24, 26, 28, 30 and 32. Full details in McKay's bibliography.)

The Spirit of Man, an anthology in English and French, made
by the Poet Laureate Longmans 1916
Includes original poetry by R.B.

Poems of G. M. Hopkins, edited with notes by R.B. O.U.P. 1918
Includes dedicatory sonnet by R.B.

The Chilswell Book of English Poetry, compiled and annotated
for schools by R.B. Longmans 1924

A Selection from the Letters of Sir W. Raleigh, with an introduction by R.B. Methuen 1928

The Collected Papers of H. Bradley, with a memoir by R.B.
Clarendon Press 1928
The memoir had been privately issued in 1926.

IV. LETTERS TO AND FROM ROBERT BRIDGES

The Letters of G. M. Hopkins to R. Bridges, edited by C.C.
Abbott O.U.P. 1935

Correspondence of R. Bridges and H. Bradley, 1900–1923
Clarendon Press 1940

Coventry Patmore and R. Bridges, some letters, by Derek Patmore,
in *Fortnightly*, March 1948

Further Letters of G. M. Hopkins, edited by C. C. Abbott,
2nd ed. O.U.P. 1956
Includes one letter from R.B.

XXI Letters, a correspondence between R. Bridges and R. C.
Trevelyan   Mill House Press 1955
Letters of R.B. to Mrs. Manley Hopkins and Kate Hopkins.
  Bodleian Library, MS. Eng. Lett. d. 143 and MS. Eng. Misc. a. 8.
  There are also in the Bodleian letters from R.B. to H.
  Bradley, A. H. Bullen, E. K. Chambers, "Michael Field",
  A. E. Housman, John Lane, Sidney Lee, Stanley Morison,
  Lionel Muirhead, Michael Sadler, H. G. and Margaret
  Woods, and others.

C. BIOGRAPHY AND CRITICISM

I. BOOKS

Warren, T. H.—Robert Bridges, Poet Laureate (a lecture
  given on November 8, 1913)   Oxford 1913
Young, F. E. B.—Robert Bridges, a Critical Study   London 1914
Kelshall, T. M.—Robert Bridges, Poet Laureate   London 1924
Pearsall-Smith, L.—Robert Bridges, Recollections *in* S.P.E.
  Tract No. 35   Oxford 1931
Guérard, A.—Robert Bridges, a Study of Traditionalism in
  Poetry   Cambridge, Mass. 1942
Thompson, E.—Robert Bridges, 1844–1930   Oxford 1944
Gordon, G. S.—Robert Bridges (Rede Lecture) Cambridge 1946
Wright, E. C.—Metaphor, Sound and Meaning in Bridges'
  Testament of Beauty   Philadelphia 1951

II. ARTICLES IN PERIODICALS—CHAPTERS OR PARAGRAPHS IN BOOKS

Warren, T. H.—Notice and selection of poems of Robert
  Bridges *in* Poets and Poetry of the Century, Vol. VIII,
  Ed. A. H. Miles   London 1893
Rothenstein, W.—Oxford Characters   Oxford 1893
Omond, T. S.—English Hexameters   Oxford 1897
Stone, W. J.—On the Use of Classical Metre in English
                                                London 1899
Yeats, W. B.—Ideas of Good and Evil (pp. 312–19) London 1903
Symons, A.—Studies in Prose and Verse (pp. 207–223) London 1904
Squire, J. C.—Robert Bridges' Lyrical Poems. *London*
  Mercury, I. No. 6 (April)   1920
Omond, T. S.—Some Thoughts about Verse. *English Associa-*
  tion Pamphlets, No. 55   1923
Raleigh, Sir W.—Letters, 2 Vols., 1879–1922   London 1926

Grierson, H. J.—Lyrical Poetry from Blake to Hardy
(ch. VI) London 1928

Twitchett, E. G.—The Poetry of Robert Bridges. *London
Mercury*, XXI. No. 122 (December) 1929

MacCarthy, D.—Notes on the Poetry of Robert Bridges.
Life and Letters, IV. No. 25 (June) 1930

Roth, G.—Robert Bridges. *Larousse Mensuel*, No. 282 (pp.
466–7) Paris 1930

Williams, C.—Poetry at Present Oxford 1930

Garrod, H. W.—Poetry and the Criticism of Life Oxford 1931

Abercrombie, L.—The Music of Poetry Oxford 1932

Evans, I. B.—English Poetry in the Later XIXth Century
(ch. X) London 1932

Newbolt, Sir H.—My World as in my Time, Memoirs London 1932

Mackenzie, C.—Literature in my Time (ch. XV, The Oxford Point of View) London 1933

Bullough, C.—The Trend of Modern Poetry London 1934

Rothenstein, Sir W.—Men and Memories London 1934

de Selincourt, E.—Oxford Lectures on Poetry (chs. IX–X)
Oxford 1934

Tillyard, E. M. W.—Poetry Direct and Oblique London 1934

Gilkes, M.—A Key to Modern English Poetry (chs. I–II)
London 1935

Roberts, M.—The Letters of G. M. Hopkins to R. Bridges.
London Mercury, XXXI. No. 185 (March) 1935

Swinnerton, F.—The Georgian Literary Scene (pp. 268–71)
London 1935

Yeats, W. B.—Introduction to The Oxford Book of Modern
Verse London 1936

Bush, D.—Mythology and the Romantic Tradition in English
Poetry (pp. 433 sqq.) Harvard 1937

Cock, A. A.—Bridges and The Testament of Beauty, with
some references to G. M. Hopkins. *France-Grande Bretagne*
(Avril) Paris 1937

Smith, N. C.—Robert Bridges *in* Dictionary of National
Biography, 1922–30 (pp. 115–19) Oxford 1937

Heywood, T.—Hopkins and Bridges on Trees. *Poetry Review*,
XXIX (pp. 213–18) 1938

Leavis, F. R.—New Bearings in English Poetry London 1942

Price, F.—Hopkins on Bridges. *Notes and Queries* (January 15) 1944

Abbott, C. C.—R. Bridges and G. M. Hopkins. *British Book
News*, 1944 (pp. 17–22) 1945

Church, R.—The Chemistry of Time, a Return to the
  Poetry of Bridges. *Fortnightly Review*, CLVII   1945
Gordon, G. S.—Hopkins and Bridges *in* The Discipline of
  Letters   Oxford 1946
Digeon, A.—Histoire Illustrée de la Littérature Anglaise,
  'Robert Bridges' (pp. 87–88)   Paris 1947
Tindall, W. Y.—Forces in Modern British Literature.
  1885–1946 (ch. VI, pp. 213–14)   New York 1947
Routh, H. V.—English Literature and Ideas in the Twentieth
  Century (ch. VI, pp. 109–11)   London 1948
Hyman, S. E.—The Armed Vision   New York 1948
Patmore, D.—The Life and Times of Coventry Patmore
                                                  London 1949
Heath-Stubbs, J.—The Darkling Plain   London 1950
Cohen, J. M.—The Road not Taken, a Study in the Poetry
  of Robert Bridges. *Cambridge Journal*, IV   1951
Patmore, D.—Three Poets Discuss New Verse Forms.
  Month IV, (August)   1951
de Sola Pinto, V.—Crisis in English Poetry, 1880–1940,
  'Hopkins and Bridges' (ch. III, pp. 59–84)   London 1951
(Anon.)—Bridges, the Poet. *Times Lit. Supplement*, front-page
  article (June 26, No. 2,682, pp. 405–406)   1953
Connolly, C.—Robert Bridges, a Reconsideration. *Sunday
  Times* (January 11)   1953
Groom, B. (in association with M. C. Masters)—The Diction
  of Poetry from Spenser to Bridges   Toronto 1955
House, H.—All in Due Time, 'Part Two: Victorians' (pp.
  159–74)   London 1955
O'Gorman, N.—The Poet Revealed to His Friends. *Common-
  weal*, LXII. No. 16, July 22   New York 1955
Faverty, F. E. (ed.)—The Victorian Poets, a Guide to
  Research, 'Robert Bridges' (pp. 242–5)   Harvard 1956
Nowell-Smith, S.—Bridges, Hopkins and Dr. Daniel. *Times
  Lit. Supplement*, special article. (Dec. 13, No. 2,911, p. 764)   1957

INDEX

PRINTED IN GREAT BRITAIN
BY EBENEZER BAYLIS AND SON, LTD., THE
TRINITY PRESS, WORCESTER AND LONDON